Choice Readings

Choice Readings

Mark A. Clarke
University of Colorado at Denver

Barbara K. Dobson
University of Michigan

Sandra Silberstein
University of Washington

Ann Arbor
THE UNIVERSITY OF MICHIGAN PRESS

Copyright © by the University of Michigan 1996
All rights reserved
ISBN 0-472-08329-5
Library of Congress Catalog Card No. 96-60040
Published in the United States of America by
The University of Michigan Press
Manufactured in the United States of America

1999   1998   1997   4   3   2

Acknowledgments

The three of us began working together in the fall of 1973. As we near the millennium, we find we are still on speaking terms with each other, still listing our names alphabetically, and increasingly aware that the debt we owe colleagues, friends, family, and students has kept pace with inflation. We cannot possibly hope to repay all the people who have contributed to this work over the past four years, but civility demands that we acknowledge their efforts on our behalf. We want to thank the following individuals for continuing friendship, interest, critiques, and time.

We have benefited greatly from the classroom testing and detailed critiques provided by our colleagues: Hisako Kikuchi Travis, Seattle; Barbara Bell, Cindy Chang, Diane Clark, Ruth Jones, Barbara Lewis, Peter Messinger, Kimberly Newcomer, Jill Straight, and Tim Teigen at the University of Washington ESL Center, Seattle; Cynthia Nelson at Macquarie University, Sydney; Susan Borst and Janice Oldroyd at Spring International Language Center, Denver. Judy Bender, University of Colorado at Denver, tracked down potential readings. Special thanks to Sharon Tsutsui at the University of Washington for helping with this effort from the outset.

The UMP staff continues to exemplify professionalism, expertise, and goodwill. Thank you to Assistant Director Mary Erwin who calmly revises deadlines as fast as we miss them; to Managing Editor Christina L. Milton, whose editorial suggestions often verge on coauthorship; to Director Colin Day, whose leadership provides a healthy environment for creativity; to Pam Friedman, whose sleuthing and perseverance yielded many a missing citation.

And, of course, very sincere thanks and belated apologies to spouses and children, who undoubtedly wondered if we would ever get off the phone.

Ann Arbor, Denver, Seattle, January 1996

Contents

To Students: Read This First

Choice Readings is an intermediate-level reading textbook for students of English as a second or foreign language. The authors believe that reading is an active, problem-solving process. Effective readers must use a number of skills. To decide how to solve reading problems, readers must decide which skills or strategies to use.

Here is an example of active problem solving. Below are several sentences using the word *choice*. Next to them, is a list of dictionary definitions for *choice*. Take a few minutes to match the sentences with the correct definition.

___ 1. The authors of *Choice Readings* believe that reading is an active, problem-solving process.

    a. *adj.* of high quality, preferred

___ 2. In this textbook, you will have many *choices* in the types of reading you will do, the order in which you will read things, and the skills you will use to solve reading problems.

    b. *n.* the name of a wonderful ESL/ EFL textbook

___ 3. We have tried to choose the best reading passages we could find; we hope you enjoy these *choice* readings.

    c. *n.* options, decisions, selections

You probably did not have trouble finding the correct answers: 1-b, 2-c, 3-a. To do this task, you probably used several skills. You could use the context of each sentence and your knowledge of the world to get a general understanding of the word *choice*. The dictionary definitions gave you additional information.

Good readers decide why they are reading a particular selection before they read it, and they decide which strategies and skills they will use to reach their goals. They develop expectations about the kinds of information they will find, and they read to see if their expectations are correct. The exercises and readings in *Choice Readings* will help you become an independent, efficient reader.

When you look at the Contents page, you will notice that there are two kinds of units in *Choice Readings*. The odd-numbered units (1–7) contain skills exercises. These exercises give students focused practice in getting information from texts. The even-numbered units (2–8) give you the opportunity to interact with and form opinions about the ideas in longer texts.

Skills and strategies are introduced in early units and practiced throughout the book. The large number of exercises gives students repeated practice. Many teachers and students choose to move between skills and reading selection units; feel free to jump around in the book. You should not worry if you do not finish each exercise, if you do not understand everything in a reading selection, or if you have trouble answering a question. In fact, there may be more than one correct response to a question. The process of trying to answer a question is often as important as the answer itself. That process will help you improve your problem-solving skills and encourage you and your classmates to think about, talk about, and respond to our choice readings.

To the Teacher

It is impossible to outline one best way to use a textbook; there are as many ways to use *Choice Readings* as there are creative teachers. However, based on the experiences of teachers and students who have worked with *Choice Readings,* we provide the following suggestions to facilitate classroom use. First, we outline general guidelines for the teaching of reading; second, we provide hints for teaching specific exercises and readings in the book; and finally, we suggest a sample lesson plan.

General Guidelines

The ultimate goal of *Choice Readings* is to encourage independent readers who are able to determine their own goals for a reading task, then use the appropriate skills and strategies to reach those goals. For this reason, we believe the best learning environment is one in which all individuals—students and teachers—participate in the process of setting and achieving goals. A certain portion of class time is therefore profitably spent in discussing reading tasks before they are begun. If the topic is a new one for the students, teachers are encouraged to provide and/or help access background information for the students, adapting the activities under Before You Begin to specific teaching contexts. When confronted with a specific passage, students should become accustomed to the practice of skimming it quickly, taking note of titles and subheadings, pictures, graphs, etc., in an attempt to determine the most efficient approach to the task. In the process, they should develop expectations about the content of the passage and the amount of time and effort needed to accomplish their goals. In this type of setting, students are encouraged to offer their opinions and ask for advice, to teach each other and to learn from their errors.

 Choice Readings was written to encourage maximum flexibility in classroom use. Because of the large variety of exercises and reading selections, the teacher can plan several tasks for each class and hold in reserve a number of appropriate exercises to use as the situation demands. In addition, the exercises have been developed to create variety in classroom dynamics. The teacher can encourage independence in students by providing opportunities for work in small groups or pairs, or by individuals. We recommend small-group work in which students self-correct homework assignments.

 Exercises do not have to be done in the order in which they are presented. In fact, we suggest interspersing skills work with reading selections. One way to vary reading tasks is to plan lessons around pairs of units, alternating skills exercises with the reading selections. In the process, the teacher can show students how focused skills work transfers to the reading of longer passages. For example, Sentence Study exercises provide intensive practice in analyzing complex grammatical structures; this same skill should be used by students in working through reading selections. The teacher can pull problematic sentences from readings for intensive classroom analysis, thereby encouraging students to do the same on their own when difficult syntax impedes comprehension.

 It is important to *teach, then test.* Tasks should be thoroughly introduced, modeled, and practiced before students are expected to perform on their own. Although we advocate rapid-paced, demanding class sessions, we believe it is extremely important to provide students with a thorough introduction to each new exercise. At least for the first example of each type of exercise, some oral work is necessary. The teacher can demonstrate the skill using the example item and work through the first few items with the class as a whole. Students can then work individually or in small groups.

Specific Suggestions

Choice Readings has been organized so that specific skills can be practiced before students need those skills for full reading selections. Although exercises and readings are generally graded according to difficulty, it is not necessary to use the material in the order in which it is presented. Teachers are encouraged:

   a) to intersperse skills work with reading selections,
   b) to skip exercises that are too easy or irrelevant to students' interests,
   c) to do several exercises of a specific type at one time if students require intensive practice in that skill, and
   d) to jump from unit to unit, selecting reading passages that satisfy students' interests and needs.

Skills Exercises

Nonprose Reading

Throughout *Choice Readings* students are presented with nonprose selections (such as maps, tables, forms) so that they can practice using their skills to read material that is not arranged in sentences and paragraphs. For students who expect to read only prose material, teachers can point out that nonprose reading provides more than an enjoyable change of pace. These exercises provide legitimate reading practice. The same problem-solving skills can be used for both prose and nonprose material. Just as one can skim a textbook for general ideas, it is possible to skim a graphic for the kind of information presented and for the main ideas. Students may feel that they can't skim or scan; working with nonprose items shows them that they can.

Nonprose exercises are good for breaking the ice with new students, for beginning or ending class sessions, for role playing, or for those Monday blues and Friday blahs. Because they are short, rapid-paced activities, they can be kept in reserve to provide variety, or to fill a time gap at the end of class.

The maps, tables, and other graphics exercises present students with realistic language problems they might encounter in an English-speaking environment. The teacher can set up simulations to achieve a realistic atmosphere. The application exercise is intended to provide practice in filling out forms.

Word Study

Upon encountering an unfamiliar vocabulary item in a passage, there are several strategies readers can use to determine the message of the author. First, they can continue reading, realizing that often a single word will not prevent understanding of the general meaning of a selection. If further reading does not solve the problem, readers can use one or more of three basic skills to arrive at an understanding of the unfamiliar word. They can use context clues to see if surrounding words and grammatical structures provide information about the unknown word. They can use word analysis to see if understanding the parts of the word leads to an understanding of the word. Or, they can use a dictionary to find an appropriate definition. *Choice Readings* contains numerous exercises that provide practice in these three skills. These exercises can be profitably done in class either in rapid-paced group work or by alternating individual work with class discussion. Like nonprose work, Word Study exercises can be used to fill unexpected time gaps.

Guessing the meaning of an unfamiliar word from context clues involves using the following kinds of information:

   a) knowledge of the topic about which you are reading,
   b) knowledge of the meanings of the other words in the sentence (or paragraph) in which the word occurs, and

c) knowledge of the grammatical structure of the sentence in which the word occurs, and

d) knowledge of discourse-level clues that can aid comprehension.

Context Clues exercises appear frequently throughout the book, both in skills units and with reading selections. Students should learn to be content with a general meaning of a word and to recognize situations in which it is not necessary to know a word's meaning. In skills units, these exercises should be done in class to ensure that students do not look for exact definitions in the dictionary. When Vocabulary from Context exercises appear with reading selections, they are intended as tools for learning new vocabulary items and often for introducing ideas to be encountered in the reading. In this case they can be done at home as well as in class.

Stems and Affixes exercises appear in each skills unit and must be done in the order in which they are presented. The exercises are cumulative: each exercise makes use of word parts presented in previous units. All stems and affixes taught in *Choice Readings* are listed with their definitions in the Appendix. These exercises serve as an important foundation in vocabulary skills work for students whose native language does not contain a large number of words derived from Latin or Greek. Students should focus on improving their ability to analyze word parts as they work with the words presented in the exercises. During the introduction to each exercise, students should be encouraged to volunteer other examples of words containing the stems and affixes presented. Exercises 1 and 2 can be done as homework.

Sometimes the meaning of a single word is essential to an understanding of the total meaning of a selection. If context clues and word analysis do not provide enough information, it will be necessary to use a dictionary. We believe that intermediate students should use an English/English dictionary. The Word Study: Dictionary Use exercise in Unit 3 provides students with a review of the information available from dictionaries and practice in using a dictionary to obtain that information. Exercise 1 requires a substantial amount of class discussion to introduce information necessary for dictionary work. The Dictionary Study exercises that accompany some of the reading selections require students to use the context of an unfamiliar vocabulary item to find an appropriate definition of these items from the dictionary entries provided.

Sentence Study

Sometimes comprehension of an entire passage requires the understanding of a single sentence. Sentence Study exercises give students practice in analyzing the structure of sentences to determine the relationships of ideas within a sentence. Students are presented with a complicated sentence followed by tasks that require them to analyze the sentence for its meaning. Often the student is required to use the available information to draw inferences about the author's message. Students should not be overly concerned about unfamiliar vocabulary in these exercises; the focus is on grammatical clues. Student errors often indicate structures that they have trouble reading, thus providing the teacher with a diagnostic tool for grammar instruction.

Paragraph Reading

These exercises give students practice in understanding how the arrangement of ideas affects the overall meaning of a passage. Some of the paragraph exercises are designed to provide practice in discovering the general message. Students are required to determine the main idea of a passage. Other paragraph exercises provide practice in careful, detailed reading. Students are required not only to determine the main idea of a passage but also to guess meanings of words from context, to answer questions about specific details in the paragraph, and to draw conclusions based on their understanding of the passage.

If Main Idea paragraphs are read in class, they may be timed. If the exercises are done at home, students can be asked to come to class prepared to defend their answers in group discussion. One way to stimulate discussion is to ask students to identify incorrect responses as too broad, too narrow, or false.

Restatement and Inference and Reading for Full Understanding exercises are short enough to allow sentence-level analysis. These exercises provide intensive practice in syntax and vocabulary work as well as in drawing inferences. In the case of the latter, lines are numbered to facilitate discussion.

Discourse Focus

Effective reading requires the ability to select skills and strategies appropriate to a specific reading task. The reading process involves using information from the full text and one's own knowledge in order to interpret a passage. Readers use this information to make predictions about what they will find in a text and to decide how they will read. Sometimes one needs to read quickly to obtain only a general idea of a text; at other times one reads carefully, drawing inferences about the intent of the author. Discourse-level exercises introduce these various approaches to reading, which are then reinforced throughout the book.

Skimming is quick reading for the general idea(s) of a passage. This kind of rapid reading is appropriate when trying to decide if careful reading would be desirable or when there is not time to read something carefully.

Like skimming, *scanning* is also quick reading. However, in this case the search is more focused. To scan is to read quickly in order to locate specific information. When we read to find a particular date, name, or number, we are scanning.

Reading for thorough comprehension is careful reading in order to understand the total meaning of the passage. At this level of comprehension the reader has summarized the author's ideas but has not necessarily made a critical evaluation of those ideas.

Critical reading demands that readers make judgments about what they read. This kind of reading requires posing and answering questions such as *Does my own experience support that of the author? Do I share the author's point of view? Am I convinced by the author's arguments and evidence?*

Discourse Focus exercises provide practice in all of these approaches to reading. Skimming and scanning activities should be done quickly in order to demonstrate to students the utility of these approaches for some tasks. The short mysteries can be valuable for group work since students can use specific elements of the text to defend their inferences. Prediction activities are designed to have students focus on the discourse signals that allow them to predict and sample texts. During group work, the diversity of student responses that emerges can reinforce the notion that there is not a single correct answer, that all predictions are, by definition, only working hypotheses to be constantly revised.

Reading Selections

Teachers have found it valuable to introduce readings in terms of ideas, vocabulary, and syntax before students are asked to work on their own. The section Before You Begin introduces the concepts and issues encountered in reading selections. After an introduction to the passage, several types of classroom dynamics have been successful with reading selections.

1. In class—the teacher reads the entire selection orally; or the teacher reads part, the students finish the selection individually; or the students read the selection individually (perhaps under time constraint).
2. In class and at home—part of the selection is read in class, followed by discussion; the students finish reading at home.
3. At home—students read the entire selection at home.

Comprehension questions are usually discussed in class with the class as a whole, in small groups, or in pairs. The paragraphs in the selections are numbered to facilitate discussion.

The teacher can pull out difficult vocabulary and/or sentences for intensive analysis and discussion *when they impede comprehension.*

Readings represent a variety of topics and styles. The exercises have been written to focus on the most obvious characteristics of each reading.

a) Well-organized readings with many facts and figures are appropriate for scanning and skimming. This type of reading can also be used in composition work as a model of organizational techniques.

b) If the reading is an editorial, essay, or other form of personal opinion, students should read critically to determine if they agree with the author. Students are encouraged to identify excerpts that reveal the author's bias or that can be used to challenge the validity of the author's argument.

c) Fiction, poetry, and personal experience narratives lend themselves to an appreciation of language. Teachers often find it useful to read some of these aloud to heighten this appreciation.

d) Expository reading selections, such as popular science and social science articles, offer students the opportunity to focus on reading for thorough comprehension. Exercises that accompany these selections also encourage students to use their critical reading skills in evaluating and applying the detailed information presented in the text.

Answer Key

Because the exercises in *Choice Readings* are designed to provide students with the opportunity to practice and improve their reading skills, the processes involved in arriving at an answer are often more important than the answer itself. It is expected that students will not use the Answer Key until they have completed the exercises and are prepared to defend their answers. If a student's answer does not agree with the Key, it is important for the student to return to the exercise to discover the source of the disagreement. In a classroom setting, students should view the Answer Key as a last resort to be used only when they cannot agree on an answer. The Answer Key also makes it possible for students engaged in independent study to use *Choice Readings.*

Sample Lesson Plan

The following lesson plan is meant only as an example of how goals might be translated into practice. We do not imply that a particular presentation is the only one possible for a given reading activity nor that the activities presented here are the only activities possible for achieving our goals. The lesson plan demonstrates how skills work can be interspersed with reading selections. Notice also that we have tried to achieve a classroom atmosphere that encourages individual initiative and group interaction. By integrating focused skill work with reading selections and by using activities that encourage students to debate answers and defend their opinions, we hope to create an energetic, text-based conversation.

The lessons described here would be appropriate for a class that had worked together for several weeks. This is important for three reasons. First, we hope that a nonthreatening atmosphere has been established in which people feel free to volunteer opinions and make guesses. Second, we assume that the students have come to recognize the importance of a problem-solving approach to reading and that they are working to improve skills and strategies using a variety of readings and exercises. We also assume that the class uses workshop formats and small-group activities for reading and writing instruction.

Although these lessons are planned for 50-minute, daily classes, slight modification would make them appropriate for a number of other situations. Approximate times for each activity are indicated. The exercises and readings are taken from Units 5 and 6.

Monday
Nonprose Reading: College Application and Tuition Chart (20 minutes)

a) The teacher asks how many students have applied to schools and gets students to discuss the kinds of information they are usually required to provide.

b) The students skim the college application and answer the Getting Oriented questions.

c) Taking into account the responses to Getting Oriented question 2, the teacher tells the students to work on the application. The goal is to have students work on the application as if they were actually applying to Washtenaw Community College. Pair and group work is encouraged.

d) The teacher moves around the room as the students work, talking with students, answering questions, encouraging an informal, information-seeking atmosphere in the classroom.

e) When the majority of the students has finished, the teacher asks individuals to read items and give their answers. Discussion and differences of opinion are encouraged.

f) The class goes next to the Tuition Chart. The teacher reads the directions aloud as students follow along. The students are then given time to work on answers to the questions.

g) Students give their answers and discuss their opinions about Bellevue Community College tuition rates.

Reading Selection 1: Advice Column (30 minutes)

a) The teacher asks students if they are familiar with newspaper advice columnists and if they have ever read Ann Landers or Dear Abby. S/he then continues in a conversational tone with questions 1–3 in the Before You Begin section.

b) Vocabulary work: The students have three minutes to do Vocabulary from Context exercise 1.

c) After they have supplied answers to the items, students take turns reading the sentences aloud and discussing the meanings of the italicized words. The teacher helps students with their guesses but does not provide definitions; the goal of the activity is as much improvement of the students' guessing abilities as it is mastery of vocabulary.

d) The teacher then reads the letter to Ann Landers and leads a discussion about the problem: What is the problem? Whose problem is it? What answer would the students give to the letter writer?

e) The teacher asks for a volunteer to read Landers's response aloud as s/he and the other students follow along in their books.

f) Students then have approximately ten minutes to work on the Comprehension questions. As the students work, the teacher circulates among them giving encouragement, answering questions, monitoring progress.

g) When most of the students have finished, the teacher leads a discussion of the questions. Students read items aloud and give answers, and the teacher moderates differences of opinion.

h) The teacher then directs students' attention to Vocabulary from Context exercise 2. This exercise is conducted as a whole-class activity, with one student reading each item aloud and other students calling out the answers; students flip back and forth from the exercise to the letters as disagreements are negotiated and answers arrived at.

i) The teacher reads through the guidelines for the Composition: Letter Writing exercise.

Homework: Write a draft of a letter to Ann Landers to bring to class on Tuesday.

Tuesday

Writer's Workshop: Letter to Ann Landers (40 minutes)

a) The teacher puts the students in groups of three or four, having decided ahead of time which students would be together. The most important criteria for grouping students would be general language proficiency and writing ability; each group is characterized by a range of student abilities.

b) Students read drafts of each others' letters and help each other improve them. Principles of cooperative learning have been used as the basis for these activities before, but the teacher reminds students that they are to (1) point to things they like in the letters, (2) ask for clarification of ideas, and (3) indicate possible grammar and spelling errors. The teacher moves among the groups as they work, encouraging them in their efforts at helping each other, modeling peer feedback techniques, discussing the contents of the letters. The effort here is to create a "workshop" atmosphere in which everyone—teacher and students—collaborates on improving each other's writing.

  c) Author's Chair: The teacher asks if there are volunteers to read their letters. Desks are arranged in a semicircle facing the "author's chair." Volunteers come to the author's chair and read their piece, following a set routine: 1) The author briefly introduces the piece, asking for feedback on particular aspects of the letter. 2) The author reads the letter. 3) The author calls on students who have comments, questions, or suggestions, taking notes on what they say.

  d) There follows a brief discussion of the letters, and students debate whether they will send them to Ann Landers. The teacher collects the letters, promising to look at them before the next day's class.

Word Study: Stems and Affixes (10 minutes)

  a) The teacher works through the chart of stems and affixes, definitions, and examples by reading aloud, answering questions and eliciting additional examples from the students as s/he goes.

  b) Students are given the remaining time to work on the exercises.

Homework: Stems and Affixes exercises 1 and 2.

Wednesday

Word Study: Stems and Affixes (15 minutes)

  a) Students work in pairs and small groups to check answers to exercises 1 and 2. The teacher circulates to monitor conversations, check comprehension, moderate disagreements, etc.

  b) The teacher asks if there are questions remaining about any of the items; a brief discussion of selected items follows.

Sentence Study: Restatement and Inference and Writing Conferences: Letters to Ann Landers (35 minutes)

  a) The teacher reads the directions and example for the Sentence Study: Restatement and Inference exercise, then gives students time to select their answers for the example sentence.

  b) The class compares their answers and the teacher leads the discussion.

  c) Students are given time to work on the items individually.

  d) Writing conferences: Students are given time to work on the Sentence Study: Restatement and Inference exercise and on the letters they are writing; the teacher holds brief writing conferences with students at their seats. S/he briefly goes over their letters with them, focusing on the ideas they are attempting to convey and the questions they are asking Ann Landers; discussions of grammar and vocabulary are conducted insofar as they contribute to a better understanding of the message.

  e) Students will continue to work on the letter, to be submitted on Thursday and sent to Ann Landers if they desire.

  f) Sentence Study: Restatement and Inference: The teacher reconvenes the class. Students read the cue sentences and the ones they have chosen as restatements and inferences. Differences of opinion are moderated by the teacher; when students are not able to convince each other through reference to the cue sentence, the teacher asks one of the protagonists to check the Answer Key and explain the correct answer(s).

  g) After two or three items have been discussed, students discuss the remaining sentences in groups, and the teacher returns to conferences with students on their letters to Ann Landers.

  h) With 15 minutes remaining in the class, the teacher reconvenes the class to finish checking the Sentence Study: Restatement and Inference exercise.

Homework: Work on the Ann Landers letters; bring final letter to class on Thursday.

Thursday

Composition: The teacher collects the Ann Landers letters; s/he will check them and return them on Friday.

Paragraph Reading: Main Idea (40 minutes)

a) The teacher reads the directions and the Before You Begin fable ("The Child Who Cried Wolf"). S/he then leads the class in a discussion of the nature of fables and the moral of this fable. The teacher works to elicit guesses from the students, refraining from giving the answer.

b) Students are grouped by threes, the teacher having organized the groups to assure diversity of native language and/or English proficiency as much as possible. They are given time to talk about fables from their own cultures. The teacher circulates to monitor conversations and aid in the discussions.

c) Class discussion: Individuals tell fables and provide morals from their own cultures. The teacher encourages students to take notes and supports the person telling the fable by writing key words and phrases on the board.

d) Small group work: The groups of three work on fables 1 through 9 together. Students take turns reading the fables aloud, followed by discussion; when they agree, they write the moral of the fable in the space provided.

e) Class discussion: Each group gives its moral for each fable as the teacher writes the morals on the board. Discussion follows. After the merits of each moral are discussed, a student is asked to select one saying from Vocabulary Study: Idiomatic Expressions that fits the fable, if there is one.

Reading Selection (10 minutes)

a) The teacher briefly describes two selections—Newspaper Article and Children's Literature—and asks for a vote on which one they should read first. The students vote for "Bugs Make Skin Crawl in Midwest."

b) The teacher leads a prereading discussion as the students answer the two Skimming questions.

c) The teacher reads the selection aloud as students follow in their books.

Homework: Reread the story and answer the Comprehension questions.

Friday

Composition: The teacher returns the Ann Landers letters to the students; envelopes and the address are provided for those who want to send their letter to Ann Landers.

Reading Selection 2: Newspaper Article (25 minutes)

a) The students' and teacher's chairs are arranged in a circle. With books open, the teacher facilitates a conversation about the cicada invasion of the Midwest. As questions arise, students consult the text to support their impressions of the article.

b) Still in circle, the Comprehension questions are reviewed and final questions answered.

Discourse Focus: Careful Reading/Drawing Inferences (25 minutes)

a) The teacher reads each mystery aloud.

b) Students work in small groups to solve the mystery. If necessary, they answer the questions that follow to arrive at an answer. Class discussion follows.

Homework: None; have a nice weekend.

Several aspects of this lesson plan invite comment. You will have noticed a tendency toward informality and lightness in the way that the lessons were conducted. This reflects the temperament of the teacher and should not be construed as a necessary element of a successful reading lesson. We believe that each teacher has his or her own style, that techniques and activities must be selected and modified to accommodate that style, and that each class has its own personality.

The lesson plan represents an active, problem-solving approach to the teaching of ESL reading that emphasizes communicative activities and results in the integrated use of reading, writing, speaking, and listening. Students are required to do more than merely read passages and answer questions. In most of the activities, we focus on "extending comprehension" through conversation and writing rather than merely "checking comprehension" through exercises. We work to create a classroom atmosphere that promotes risk taking in the use of language and in expressing one's own opinions.

The task at hand determines, to a large extent, what students do and how the teacher participates in class activities. We plan for many activities so that each day contains variety in terms of lesson content and classroom dynamics. In each lesson, the tempo and tasks change several times. In the course of a week, virtually all language and reading skills are practiced in a variety of contexts and with a variety of materials. This has important implications for the nature of the class and for the role of students and teacher.

The classroom dynamics change to fit the task. The college application and the fables, for example, begin as class discussions then become small-group work. The Ann Landers lesson is conducted with individual, small-group, and whole-class work at appropriate times. Throughout the week, however, we have emphasized the importance of student initiative—although the students work together a great deal, we want individual students to take responsibility for their learning and to develop their own inner criteria for the answers to questions and contributions to class discussion. Note, for example, the way that comprehension exercises are conducted. Students are asked to select the answers that reflect their understanding of the passages and to use text to defend their choices. In the Stems and Affixes exercise on Tuesday and Wednesday, the teacher introduces the exercise, but the students do the exercises and check their answers. In this way, the teacher emphasizes the importance of students' responsibility for and control over their work.

In this approach to teaching, the teacher's role varies according to the activity. During the Stems and Affixes exercise just mentioned, the teacher functions as a facilitator, intervening only when necessary to keep the activity going, and as a teacher in clarifying linguistic points or giving examples. As the students work on their letters to Ann Landers, the teacher functions as facilitator, participant and teacher. As facilitator, s/he organizes the writing workshop and author's chair, providing guidelines and orchestrating the conversations among students. As personal problems and solutions are discussed, s/he functions as a participant, exploring interesting issues with the students, expressing opinions just as the rest of the class does. And, finally, as teacher, s/he helps with questions of grammar, punctuation, and correspondence style.

Another important feature of the lesson plan is the opportunity provided to encourage students to exercise some choice in what they do and how they do it. As the teacher coaches them through vocabulary exercises and skimming and scanning work, comprehension discussions, and writing tasks, s/he constantly reminds students of a variety of ways that a task can be approached. Students come to establish expectations about texts and to select productive strategies to accomplish their goals. Just as the teacher provided a preview of reading selections and asked for student opinion on which to read first, s/he might introduce a text and ask the students how they plan to read it. A newspaper article will probably invite different reading strategies than a piece of children's literature.

Throughout the term, students are encouraged to shift gears, to vary their approaches to language tasks. As they become more proficient users of the language, they take more responsibility for what they read and write and for the opinions they express in conversations.

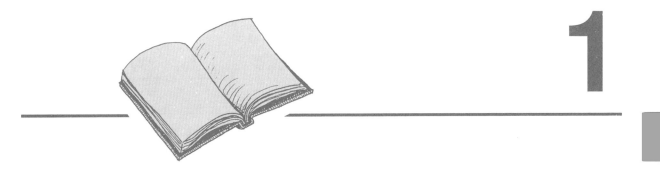

Discourse Focus

Reading for Different Goals

Good readers read differently depending on what they are reading and their purposes. There are four basic types of reading behaviors or skills: skimming, scanning, reading for thorough comprehension, and critical reading. Each is explained below, and exercises are provided to give you practice in each skill.

Skimming

Skimming is quick reading for general ideas. When you skim you move your eyes quickly to acquire a basic understanding of the text. You do not need to read everything, and you do not read carefully. You read, quickly, such things as the title and subtitles and topic sentences. You also look at pictures, charts, graphs, etc., for clues to what the text is about.

Use the page from the Friday edition of the *Denver Post* (p. 4) to answer the following questions. Move quickly from the questions to the page. Do not write out your answers completely; just make notes that will help you remember your answers. Your teacher may want to read the questions aloud as you skim to find the answers.

1. Why is this page called "Where to go? What to do?" _____

   How is the information organized? _____

   _____

2. What kind of information does it contain? _____

   _____

   Does anything here interest you? _____

   Are there other things that you might want to do on weekends that are not mentioned here? _____

   _____

3. Will this page contain information on renting an apartment? _____

4. Is there anything going on Sunday afternoon that you could do before going over to a friend's house for dinner?

_____

_____

Scanning

Scanning is also quick reading, but when you scan, you are looking for information about a question you want to answer. You are usually looking for a number or a word or the name of something. When you scan, you usually take the following steps.

1. Decide exactly what information you are looking for and what form it is likely to take. For example, if you want to know how much something costs, you would be looking for a number. If you want to know when something starts, you would be scanning for a date or a time. If you want to know who did something, you would be looking for a name.

2. Next, decide where you need to look to find the information. You would turn to the sports section of the newspaper to discover who won a baseball game, and you would scan the "C" section of the phone book for the phone number of Steven Cary.

3. Move your eyes quickly down the page until you find what you want. Read to get the information.

4. When you find what you need, you usually stop reading.

The following questions give you practice in scanning. Use the page from the *Denver Post* to answer the questions. Your teacher may want you to do this orally or by circling answers on the *Denver Post* page.

1. A friend is coming to town who likes jazz. Is there any jazz happening this weekend? Who? Where? When? How much does it cost?

_____

_____

2. You heard that there was going to be a car show in Denver this weekend. Is this true? _____

   If so, when? _____ Where? _____

   How much does it cost? _____

3. You like country music and notice that Merle Haggard will be performing. When will he perform?

   _____ Where? _____ At what time? _____

   How much will it cost? _____

Thorough Comprehension

When you read for thorough comprehension, you try to understand the total meaning of the reading. You want to know the details as well as the general meaning of the selection. When you have thoroughly comprehended a text you have done the following things.

1. You have understood the main ideas and the author's point of view.

2. You have understood the relationships of ideas in the text, including how they relate to the author's purpose.

3. You have noted that some ideas and points of view that were not mentioned were, however, implied by the author. This is called "drawing inferences."

4. You have understood most of the concepts in the passage as well as the vocabulary. This may require you to guess the meanings of unfamiliar words from context or to look up words in the dictionary.

The following questions give you practice in reading for thorough comprehension. Answer the questions according to your understanding of the page from the *Denver Post*. Your teacher may want you to work on these individually, in small groups, or in pairs. True/False items are indicated by a T / F before a statement. Some questions may have more than one correct answer. Others require an opinion. Choose the answer you like best; be prepared to defend your choices.

Look at the picture of the butterflies.

1. Where will "Ziegfeld: A Night at the Follies" be held? _____

2. T / F   "Ziegfeld" is a comedy performance without music.

3. T / F   "Ziegfeld" will be performed on three days.

4. T / F   You must pay $38 to see the show.

Critical Reading

When we read critically, we draw conclusions and make judgments about the reading. We ask questions such as, "What inferences can be drawn from this? Do I agree with the point of view?" We often do this when we read, but in some cases it is more important than others, as, for example, when authors give opinions about important issues or when you are trying to make a decision.

Use the page from the *Denver Post* to answer the following examples of critical reading questions. In later reading in this book, you will do other kinds of critical reading, making judgments about the written arguments. For the questions below, there is no single correct answer; readers' opinions will vary according to their experiences.

Where To Go, What To Do

FRIDAY

Clint Black

One of the hot new artists on the country music scene, **Clint Black**, will perform with one of country music's legends **Merle Haggard** and up-and-comer **Lorrie Morgan** at Red Rocks Amphitheatre. For ticket information, call TicketMaster at 290-8497.
Time: 7:30 p.m.
Tickets: $19.50

'Ziegfeld'

"Ziegfeld: A Night at the Follies" will be presented through Sunday at the Denver Auditorium Theatre. The comedy includes songs by Irving Berlin, Jerome Kern, Cole Porter and Harold Arlen. Call 893-4100 for tickets or for more information.
Time: 8 p.m. today and Saturday; 7 p.m. Sunday.
Tickets: $25-$38

Jazz clarinetist

Clarinetist Eddie Daniels will join the **Colorado Symphony Orchestra** for two concerts at Boettcher Concert Hall, 950 13th St. The program will include classical and jazz works under the direction of guest conductor Carl Topilow. For tickets or more information, call 595-4388.
Time: 8 tonight and Saturday.
Tickets: $8-$26

Sesame Street

Sesame Street Live presents "Silly Dancing" through Sunday at the Denver Coliseum. The show introduces the newest member to the Big Bird gang, Grundgetta, a match for Oscar the Grouch. Call TicketMaster at 290-8497 for ticket information.
Time: 10:30 a.m. and 7:30 tonight; 10:30 a.m., 2 and 5:30 p.m. Saturday; 1:30 and 5 p.m. Sunday.
Tickets: $9.50, $8.50, $1.50 discount for children 12 and under.

Bluegrass artists

Home on the Grange concert series presents top bluegrass artists including the **Bluegrass Patriots** and **Pete and Joan Wernick** performing at Grange Hall in Niwot. For more information, call 444-4537.
Time: 8:30 tonight and Saturday.
Tickets: $6

Stamp show

The **Rompex 1991 stamp show** will be held for three days at the Holiday Inn, I-70 and Chambers Road. Museum displays and exhibits from stamp collecting societies will be featured. For more information, call 755-3817.
Time: 9 a.m.-6 p.m. today and Saturday, 9 a.m.-4 p.m. Sunday.
Tickets: $1, children under 15 free.

'ZIEGFELD': A Night at the Follies will be presented through Sunday at the Denver Auditorium Theatre.

SATURDAY

Riff performance

Riff will perform with **LL Cool J** at Arnold Hall Theater at the U.S. Air Force Academy. Call 1-719-472-2472 for ticket information.
Time: 8 p.m.
Tickets: $18, $15, $10

Aybar concerts

Pianist **Francisco Aybar** will join the **Aurora Symphony** for two concerts at the Aurora Fox Arts Center, 9900 E. Colfax Ave. Aybar will perform Rachmaninoff's Piano Concerto No. 2. Call 361-2910.
Time: 8 p.m. Saturday, 2 p.m. Sunday.
Tickets: $6

Train rides

The **Georgetown Loop Historic Mining and Railroad Park** is open on weekends through May. Passengers may board in either Georgetown or Silver Plume. The train will run daily beginning Memorial Day and continuing through Labor Day. Call 670-1686.
Time: 9:20 a.m.-3:55 p.m.
Tickets: $5-$12.50

Pottery sale

Potters for Peace will hold its fourth annual benefit **pottery sale** at Clayton College, 3801 Martin Luther King Blvd. Works will be available from more than 300 potters. Proceeds will benefit potters in Nicaragua. Call 781-2035.
Time: 9 a.m.-6 p.m. Saturday and Sunday.
Tickets: Free admission.

Jazz concert

The **Ron Miles Trio Plus** will perform in the New Dance Theatre of Cleo Parker Robinson, 119 Park Ave. West. Featured performers include Andrew Cyrille on drums and Joseph Jarman on saxophone and flute. Call 758-6321.
Time: 8:30 p.m.
Tickets: $10, $8 students with ID

Model railroads

A **train show** will be held for two days in the Sheraton Hotel at the Denver Tech Center. Displays, running layouts and train sets for collectors, buyers and traders is offered. Call 696-1386.
Time: 10 a.m.-3 p.m. Saturday and Sunday.
Tickets: $5 per family, $4 per individual.

CARLA SCIAKY and Pete Sutherland will be in concert at Cameron Church at 8 p.m. Saturday.

Acoustic music

Swallow Hill Music Association will present an acoustic concert with **Carla Sciaky** and **Pete Sutherland** at Cameron Church, 1600 S. Pearl St. The concert will include works from Sciaky's latest album, "The Undertow." Call 777-1003.
Time: 8 p.m.
Tickets: $10, $8 Swallow Hill members.

Library party

A 25th anniversary celebration and groundbreaking party for the Arapahoe Library District's new main library will be held at the new site, South Holly Street and East Orchard Road. Free hot dogs, ice cream, cake and entertainment will be included. Call 798-2444.
Time: 11 a.m.-2 p.m.
Tickets: Free.

Breakfast jam

The fourth annual **Boulder breakfast jam** will be held at Boulder Reservoir. Performers include the Left Hand String Band, Mollie O'Brien and the Blue Tips, Big Head Todd and the Monsters and others. Call 449-6007.
Time: 8:30 a.m. to dusk.
Tickets: $15 in advance, $18 at the gate.

Battle of bands

The third annual **Battle at the Square band competition** will be held for two days at Heritage Square in Golden. Bands will compete at the levels of junior and senior high, college and semi-professional in several categories. Prizes will be awarded for best vocalist, drummer, keyboardist and guitarist. Call 674-3341, ext. 567.
Time: 10 a.m.-10 p.m. Saturday and Sunday.
Tickets: $5

Art auction

The third annual **Artists for Colorado Youth Art Auction** keyed to the theme "Passages: Art Today" will be at the Colorado History Museum, 1300 Broadway. A free preview reception will be available Friday. Call 832-9791.
Time: 4-8 p.m. preview Friday; 6-7:15 p.m. silent auction, 7:30-8:30 p.m. live auction Saturday.
Tickets: $25

Showhouse finale

This is the final weekend for the 16th annual **Junior Symphony Guild Showhouse** tours at 350 Humboldt St. The show features a classic Denver home with each room independently decorated by local interior designers. Call 722-4434.
When: 10 a.m.-3 p.m. Friday; 11 a.m.-4 p.m. Saturday and Sunday.
Tickets: $8

SUNDAY

Morning concert

The **Azusa Pacific University Choir and Orchestra** will perform at the Denver First Church of the Nazarene, 3800 E. Hampden Ave. The 150-member choir will perform a variety of classical and popular songs. A free Continental breakfast will be offered before the concert. Call 761-8370.
When: 8:45 a.m. breakfast, 9:45 a.m. concert.
Tickets: Free-will offering.

Help for kids

Colorado Kids Care and **Funplex** are teaming up to help homeless children by accepting donations of baby items including clothing, formula and diapers at Funplex, located at South Kipling Street and West Coal Mine Avenue in Littleton. Each person who brings a donation will receive a free activity pass to Funplex. For more information, call 934-0227.
Time: 11 a.m.-6 p.m.

Auto exhibit

The eighth annual **Concours d'Elegance auto exhibit** will be held in the north parking lot at University Hills Mall, 2700 S. Colorado Blvd. Rare Porsches, Maseratis, Jaguars and racing cars will be featured. All proceeds benefit Denver's United Cerebral Palsy Association. Call 355-7337 for more information.
Time: 9 a.m.-4 p.m.
Tickets: $5

Origami

The Boulder Public Library's Sunday Specials program is presenting an **origami workshop** in the Japanese Garden at the library, 1000 Canyon Blvd. Participants will learn to make birds, boats and other objects using the age-old Japanese paper folding techniques. Call 441-3100.
Time: 3 p.m.
Tickets: Free.

Honor Band

The **Colorado Honor Band** will perform a spring concert at Skyview High School, 9000 York St. in Thornton. Call 778-6693 for more information.
Time: 2:30 p.m.
Tickets: Free.

MERLE HAGGARD: Country music legend performs at Red Rocks tonight.

Weekend

Diane Carman
Entertainment Editor
Tom Walker
Assistant Entertainment Editor

Weekend is published every Friday. Send all correspondence to **Weekend**, The Denver Post, 1560 Broadway, Denver 80202. Phone 820-1452. Items for Calendar must be received at least 10 days prior to publication. Copyright 1991, The Denver Post Corp.

1. What types of activities and events appear to be important to people in Denver? _____

_____

2. T / F   If you are interested in gardening, you won't want to miss the "bluegrass artists" Friday night in Niwot.

3. T / F   If you were interested in buying a used car, you should look at this page.

4. Read about the Sunday morning concert at the First Church of the Nazarene.

   a. What kind of music do you think they will be playing? _____

   b. T / F   The concert is free.

   c. T / F   This would be a good event to take a new friend to.

5. Note that on Sunday there will be an origami workshop in Boulder. Based on the description, what

   do you think origami is? _____

   What is a workshop? _____

6. Circle the items in the *Post* that you would be interested in doing or at least learning more about. With a classmate or two, discuss the items you have circled and decide on something you would like to do together.

Nonprose Reading

Airline Terminal Maps

Below are two maps from a Trans World Airlines (TWA) magazine. The maps are provided to passengers who are flying into the United States so that they will know how to get to the baggage claim area to pick up their suitcases, to another gate to catch another plane, and to the street to catch a taxi or bus.

Answer the following questions according to your understanding of the map. Your teacher may want you to work individually, in pairs, or in small groups. True/False items are indicated by a T / F before a statement. Some questions may have more than one correct answer. Others may require an opinion. Choose the answer you like best; be prepared to defend your choices.

Part 1: Getting Oriented

1. When you get off the airplane, what are some of the first things you need to do in the airport? Look at the maps. Do you find everything you would need, or is there missing information?

2. On the JFK map, find the rest rooms closest to terminal 4A, gate 32.

3. Circle the Immigration area for JFK and Atlanta.

4. Circle the baggage claim areas in both terminals.

Part 2: JFK International Airport, New York City, New York

Use the map of JFK (page 7) to answer questions 5 and 6. TWA uses terminals 4A and 4B at JFK International Airport. Most transatlantic flights arrive and depart from terminal 4A and most domestic (U.S.) flights operate from terminal 4B. The terminals are connected by an enclosed walkway and by a convenient shuttle bus operating between gates 21 and 17. The bus runs every ten minutes between the terminals between 3 P.M. and 8 P.M.

If you arrive at JFK on flight 841 from Rome, you might find yourself at terminal 4A, gate 30.

5. If you are flying to Denver, Colorado, from New York on TWA, which terminal will your flight

   probably leave from? _____ How do you get there? _____

6. Does the map tell you where to catch a taxi or bus to the city? _____ What can you do to get

   information about ground transportation? _____

From "TWA-Atlanta International Airport, Atlanta" and "TWA-JFK International Airport, New York," *TWA Ambassador,* April, 1994, 51–52.

Part 3: Atlanta International Airport, Atlanta, Georgia

Use the map of Atlanta International Airport (page 8) to answer questions 7 through 11.

TWA uses Concourse C, gates 15, 17, 18, and 20 at Atlanta International Airport. The concourse is connected to the airport terminal by a walkway, a moving sidewalk, and a train.

7. If you arrive at gate 17, and you leave in an hour from gate 20, how would *you* decide whether you

   have enough time to go into the terminal? _____

8. If the TWA representative at your gate cannot help you, where would you go to change your ticket?

   _____

9. T / F   The baggage claim area for TWA is located in the South Terminal.

10. T / F   If you want to get into downtown Atlanta, you must rent a car.

TWA - Atlanta International Airport, Atlanta

11. Which airport do you think is more convenient? Why? _____

_____

_____

Word Study

Context Clues

It is impossible to know the exact meaning of every word, but you can improve your ability to guess the general meanings of words from the words and sentences around the word. You have to use your understanding of English grammar and of the author's ideas and purpose. Here are some steps to follow in using context clues.

1. Use the meanings of other words in the sentence or paragraph and the meaning of the sentence as a whole to limit the possible meanings of the word.

2. Use grammar and punctuation clues to understand the relationships among the parts of the sentence.

3. Be happy with a general meaning of the word. The exact definition is not always necessary.

4. Teach yourself to keep reading even if you do not know the meaning of a word; it is not always necessary to know the meaning of all the words in a selection.

Example Each of the sentences in this exercise contains a blank. You are to write a word in each blank using the context clues to guess the possible meanings of the missing word. You may not be able to think of a single word to put in the blank; in these cases, write a brief description or definition of the missing word. There is no single correct answer; the important thing is to improve your ability to guess.

---

1. Unlike his brothers, who are all very tall, Danny is quite _____.

2. George is a _____; he thinks only of money and will not spend a penny on anything if he can get it free.

3. The _____, like many other freshwater fish, is fun to catch and delicious to eat.

4. How could he be so stupid? He must have known that if he threw the ball against the window,

   it would _____.

5. I was tired and needed sleep, but the composition was due the next day, so I picked up a

   _____ and began to write.

6. Sandra is a loving mother; she _____ her daughter Maia.

7. Barbara rode her new _____ to work today. It is a bright red ten-speed, with hand brakes and rearview mirrors and a basket on the front for carrying things.

Explanation   Check your guesses against the following words and explanations. Remember, there is no single correct answer for each item, just good guesses. In most cases, several words are provided, all of which fit the context. If you guessed one of these words or one similar in meaning, you have used the context clues correctly. If not, study the explanation to understand how to improve your guessing ability.

1. Unlike his brothers, who are all very tall, Danny is quite _____.

short
small
squatty
stubby

Danny is the opposite of his brothers, and since his brothers are all tall, Danny must be short. The word *unlike* tells us about the relationship between Danny and his brothers.

2. George is a _____; he thinks only of money and will not spend a penny on anything if he can get it free.

miser
penny-pincher
scrooge

The semicolon (;) following the blank tells us that the two sentences are closely related. A miser is a person who does not spend money. *Penny-pincher* and *scrooge* are less common, but they mean the same thing.

3. The _____, like many other freshwater fish, is fun to catch and delicious to eat.

cutthroat trout
brown trout
bass
perch

You probably did not write *cutthroat trout,* which is the word the author used. In this case, the comma (,) following the blank tells us that the word is defined or its meaning described in the words that follow, so we know that the missing word refers to a type of fish. Most native speakers would not know this word either. But since you know that the word is the name of a type of fish, you do not need to know anything else. This is an example of how context can teach you the meaning of an unfamiliar word.

4. How could he be so stupid? He must have known that if he threw the ball against the window, it would _____.

break
shatter

You recognized the cause-and-effect relationship in this sentence. If you throw a ball against a window, it will likely break. This is an example of how the general meaning of a sentence defines the meaning of a word.

5. I was tired and needed sleep, but the composition was due the next day, so I picked up a _____ and began to write.

pen
pencil
laptop computer

The number of things that can be picked up in your hand and used to write with are few. You probably guessed pen or pencil immediately. Here, the relationship between the object and its purpose are so close that you have no difficulty guessing the meaning.

6. Sandra is a loving mother; she _____ her daughter Maia.

dotes on
(pours love on;
spends time with;
watches fondly)

Sandra is a loving mother. We all have an idea about how loving mothers treat their children, and this is the general meaning that we put in the blank. Punctuation helps us guess the meaning of the missing word. In this case, the semicolon (;) between the sentences tells us that the second sentence explains the first sentence in some way. *Dotes on* is not a common phrase, but when it is used it generally carries this specialized meaning. The phrases in parentheses may not fit in the sentence grammatically, but if you guessed the meaning of the missing word using these phrases, you know the meaning well enough to continue reading without going to a dictionary.

7. Barbara rode her new _____ to work today. It is a bright red ten-speed, with hand brakes and rear-view mirrors and a basket on the front for carrying things.

bicycle
bike

The description in the second sentence gives you all the information you need to fill the blank. This is an example of why you need to read beyond the word.

Exercise 1

In this exercise, do not *try to learn the meanings of the italicized words. Work to develop your ability to guess the meanings of the words using context clues. Read each sentence carefully, and write a definition, synonym, or description in the space provided. Do not leave any item without a guess. The only bad answer in this exercise is no answer.* Guess, guess, guess!

1. _____   We watched the cat come quietly across the field to where the bird *perched* on the wire. But just as it seemed that the cat would certainly catch him, he flew away.

2. _____   The Wilsons could not have children of their own, so they decided to *adopt* a baby.

3. _____   Elephants are in danger of disappearing completely. They are killed for their *tusks,* which people use to make jewelry.

4. _____   Goettleman was an angry old man, who could often be heard complaining and shouting and arguing about some part of modern life that he disagreed with. Just yesterday, for example, I heard him *railing* against women who work outside the home.

5. _____   The snake *slithered* through the grass.

6. _____ Ross is a very unpleasant person. The other day some of us were having a conversation in the hall when he came up and started arguing about politics and religion. As he became more and more excited, he pushed closer to me until I was backed up against the wall. Then he started *poking* me in the chest with his finger, as if he were punctuating a sentence on my shirt.

7. _____ My uncle is a *periodontist,* so when he comes to stay with us we have to be careful to brush our teeth after every meal. If we don't, he tells long stories about his patients, whose teeth have fallen out because they do not brush regularly.

8. _____ Just like his *taciturn* father, Jon rarely says anything at family gatherings.

9. _____ After not eating all day, Joyce was *ravenous.* She wanted to eat everything in sight.

10. _____ Eating a lot of rich food is unhealthy. The doctor told John he would have to *curb* his eating if he did not want to risk heart disease.

Word Study

Stems and Affixes

Using context clues is one way to discover the meaning of an unfamiliar word. Another way is word analysis. In word analysis, you look at the meanings of parts of a word. Many English words have been formed by combining parts of older English, Greek, and Latin words. If you know the meanings of some of these word parts, you can often guess the meaning of an unfamiliar English word, especially in context.

Think, for example, about the word *report*. *Report* is formed from *re*, which means *back*, and *port*, which means *carry*. *Scientist* comes from *sci*, which means *know* and *ist*, which means *one who.*

Port and *sci* are called stems. A stem is the basic part on which groups of related words are built. *Re* and *ist* are called affixes, that is, word parts that are attached to stems. Affixes like *re* that are attached to the beginnings of stems are called prefixes. Affixes attached to the ends of stems, like *ist*, are called suffixes. Generally, prefixes change the meaning of a word, and suffixes change its part of speech. Here are some more examples:

Stem	pay (verb)	honest (adjective)
Prefix	*re*pay (verb)	*dis*honest (adjective)
Suffix	*re*pay*ment* (noun)	*dis*honest*ly* (adverb)

Word analysis is not always enough to give you the exact definition of a word you find in a reading passage, but often, if you use context clues too, it will help you to understand the general meaning. It will let you continue reading without stopping to use a dictionary.

In this unit, you will work with a group of common prefixes. In later units, you will study stems, suffixes, and other prefixes.

Below is a chart showing some common prefixes that indicate *amount* or *number*. Next to each prefix is its meaning and words that include that prefix. Study the chart. Your teacher may ask you to give examples of other words you know that include these prefixes. Then, do the exercises that follow.

semi-	half	semicircle, semisweet
mono-	one	monarch, monopoly
uni-	one	unite, universe
bi-	two	bicycle, binary
tri-	three	triangle, triple
multi-	many, several	multiple, multiply
poly-	many, more than one	polytechnic, polynomial

Exercise 1

Use the chart to help you answer these questions. Your teacher may want you to do this exercise orally or in small groups.

1. A person who speaks only one language is monolingual.

   A person who speaks two languages is _____.

   A person who speaks three languages is _____.

2. Match each word with the picture it describes:

___ unicycle, ___ bicycle, ___ tricycle.

a.   b.   c.

3. a. When Leslie was 43, she had to get new eyeglasses so that she could see clearly both near and far. Her eye doctor told her she should buy bifocal glasses. What do bifocals look like? Draw a picture below.

   b. Some people even need to wear trifocals. What do trifocal glasses look like? Draw a picture below.

4. *Monogamy* means having only one marriage partner at a time. In the United States, monogamy is legal, but polygamy is against the law. What do you think *polygamy* means?

   _____

5. *Car, man, book,* and *shop* are monosyllabic words because each has only one syllable. Circle all of the words in the following list that are polysyllabic.

   automobile   truck   computer   woman
   television   sister   son   syllable

6. Binoculars are an instrument used to see things far away. Which of these two pictures do you think shows a pair of binoculars?

   a.   b.

7. Draw a picture of a triangle. Use word analysis to explain the meaning of triangle.

_____

8. Which of these triangles do you think is an equilateral triangle? (Hint: *later* is a stem that means *side.*)

   a.   ◺   b.   △   c.   ◿

9. Some factory workers know how to use special, complicated machines. Others work on the simpler machines. Which kind of worker is called "skilled," and which kind of worker is called "semiskilled"?

_____

_____

10. In a hospital, rooms for only one patient are called private rooms. A room for many patients is called a ward. What are semiprivate rooms?

_____

11. California is a multicultural state because of the large number of citizens from Latin America and Asia and other areas who live there. Describe what *multicultural* means.

_____

12. The United States is a multiracial society. What does *multiracial* mean? _____

_____

13. Twins are born about one time out of every 90 births, but triplets are much more unusual. What are triplets?

_____

_____

14. Many people, for example, police officers and soldiers, must wear uniforms when they are working.

    Use word analysis to explain the meaning of *uniform.* _____

_____

15. Would you rather be a millionaire or a multimillionaire? Why? _____

_____

16. The United States was established in 1776. It celebrated its centennial in 1876. When did it

celebrate its bicentennial? _____

17. What would a multicolored shirt look like? Are you wearing one now? _____

_____

18. To keep her camera absolutely still, the photographer put her camera on a tripod. What is a tripod?

(Hint: *pod* is a stem meaning *foot*.) _____

_____

19. Which of these circles is bisected? (Hint: It is the picture that shows semicircles.)

a.   b.   c.

Exercise 2

Word analysis can help you to guess the meaning of unfamiliar words. Using context clues and what you know about prefixes, write a definition, synonym, or description of the italicized words.

1. _____ The magazine used to be published only once a year, but now it is printed *semiannually*.

2. _____ The new school has 20 classrooms, a library, an office area, and a large *multipurpose* room that can be used as a lunchroom, gymnasium, and theater.

3. _____ The English actor's *monocle* hung on a string around his neck. When he read, he held it to his eye.

4. _____ Bill hopes he will get the new job he applied for. The new salary would be *triple* the amount of money he makes now.

5. _____ Many people never expected to see the *unification* of West Germany and the German Democratic Republic.

6. _____ Al should not be in the choir; he sings in a *monotone*.

7. _____ This team will probably win the *semifinal* game, but I would be very surprised if the players are good enough to win the final, championship game tomorrow.

8. _____ According to the *bilateral* trade agreement, both countries will sell more of each other's products.

9. _____ The bank wanted to build a *multistory* building downtown, but the people of the small town did not want such a tall building on Main Street.

10. _____ In the *semidarkness* of the theater, I had a hard time finding my seat.

Sentence Study

Introduction

When you have difficulty understanding a passage, just reading further will often make the passage clearer. Sometimes, however, comprehension of an entire passage depends on your being able to understand a single sentence. Sentences that are very long, sentences that have more than one meaning, or sentences that contain difficult grammatical patterns often cause comprehension problems for readers. The Sentence Study exercise that follows as well as similar ones in later units helps you practice strategies for understanding difficult sentences.

   Although there is no easy formula for understanding complicated sentences, you should keep the following points in mind.

1. Try to determine what makes the sentence difficult.

   a. If the sentence contains a lot of difficult vocabulary, you may be able to understand it without knowing the meaning of every word. Try crossing out unfamiliar vocabulary:

   > It's a wonderful world that we live in—a world filled with rainbows and rockets, with ~~echoes and~~ electric ~~sparks~~, with ~~atomic particles and~~ planets, with ~~invisible~~ forces ~~and vibrations~~ that affect us without our even knowing they exist.

   b. If the sentence is very long, try to break it up into smaller parts:

   > It's a wonderful world that we live in. The world is filled with rainbows and rockets. It is filled with echoes and electric sparks. It is filled with atomic particles and planets. It is filled with invisible forces and vibrations. These forces and vibrations affect us without our even knowing they exist.

   c. Also, if the sentence is very long, try to determine which parts of the sentence express specific details supporting the main idea. Often clauses that are set off by commas or dashes, or introduced by words like *which, who, that,* are used to introduce extra information or to provide supporting details. Try crossing out the supporting details in order to determine the main idea:

   > Our world—~~filled as it is with rainbows and rockets, with echoes and electric sparks, with atomic particles and planets, with invisible forces and vibrations that affect us without our even knowing they exist~~—is truly marvelous.

Be careful! A good reader reads quickly but accurately.

2. Learn to recognize important grammatical and punctuation clues that can change the meaning of a sentence.

   a. Look for single words and affixes that can change the entire meaning of a sentence:

   > Snowstorms are *not un*common.
   > The *average* daytime *high* temperature is *approximately* 56°.

b. Look for punctuation clues:

> Jane writes ☺poetry☺ every morning.
> Peter said, "Ron was elected president②"

Note that all of the italicized words or affixes and the circled punctuation above affect the meaning of the sentences; if any of these are left out, the meaning of the sentence changes.

c. Look for key words that tell you of relationships within a sentence:

> The school has grown *from* a small building holding 200 students *to* a large institute that educates 4,000 students a year.

From . . . to indicates the beginning and end points of something (here, the growth of the school).

> Many people feel that he is *not only* a wonderful researcher and writer *but also* a fine teacher.

Not only . . . but also indicates that both parts of the sentence are of equal importance.

> *In order to* receive a grade in this course, you will need to finish each of the five assignments.

In order to is like *if;* it indicates that some event must occur before another event can take place.

> He thought he would have to apologize to each of his brothers and sisters; *instead* they arrived at his house with presents.

Instead indicates that something unexpected happened.

> *As a result of* all of the newspaper and television attention, the problem of the rain forest has become well known.

As a result of indicates a cause-and-effect relationship. The clause that follows *as a result of* is the cause of some event. The newspaper and television attention is the *cause;* the fact that the problem is now well known is the *effect.*

> *Because of* these phenomena, which include rainbows and rockets, echoes and electric sparks, atomic particles and planets, and invisible forces and vibrations that affect us without our even knowing they exist, our world is a rich and wonderful place to explore.

Because of indicates a cause-and-effect relationship. The world is wonderful to explore as a result of these phenomena. The information between the word *which* and the final comma (,) refers to these phenomena.

> *Apart from* the fact that he had traveled in that part of the world, there was no reason to think that he could speak the language.

In this sentence, *apart from* indicates that there is no other reason except that one. It means "except for."

> *Despite* what many people believe, writing is more than a matter of putting one's ideas into words.

    Despite indicates that the second part of the sentence will not agree with the first.

d. Look at the pronouns in the sentence. Pronouns are words (like *he, she, it, their, those*) that refer to some person, some thing, or some idea expressed elsewhere in the sentence. Try to determine exactly what person, what thing, or what idea each pronoun refers to.

> *Seventeen million people in the United States,* more than half of all the people who speak a language other than English, speak Spanish. *That* is ten times as many as speak French.

Sentence Study

Comprehension

Read the following sentences carefully. The questions that follow are designed to test your comprehension of complex grammatical structures. Select the best answer.

Example

Cliff said he doesn't mind going to the grocery store if his roommate is too busy to go tonight.

We know that . . .

___ a. Cliff is too busy to go.

___ b. Cliff doesn't want to go.

___ c. Cliff's roommate is too busy to go.

___ d. Cliff may go to the store.

Explanation

___ a. According to the sentence, the person who might be too busy to go is Cliff's *roommate,* not Cliff.

___ b. The sentence says that Cliff "doesn't mind going," that he is willing to go. It does not say Cliff doesn't want to go to the store.

___ c. The sentence says "*if* his roommate is too busy." *If* indicates that the roommate may or may not be too busy. We don't know that he is too busy.

✓ d. The sentence says that Cliff is willing to go to the store if his roommate doesn't go, so we know that Cliff may go to the store.

1. and 2. Mrs. Dawson, who had just gone upstairs to change clothes, heard a sudden shout as she passed the old lady's door.
   Who shouted?
   ___ a. Mrs. Dawson
   ___ b. the old lady
   ___ c. We don't know.
   ___ d. Someone who had just gone upstairs.

Who was passing outside the door?
___ a. Mrs. Dawson
___ b. the old lady
___ c. someone who shouted
___ d. We don't know.

3. Albert was sitting next to Julia in the outer office when Alice returned after her meeting with Miss Cain.
    Who had a meeting?
    ___ a. Albert and Julia
    ___ b. Julia and Miss Cain
    ___ c. Julia and Alice
    ___ d. Alice and Miss Cain

4. Joan, following the instructions of the new manager, took a calculator from the desk drawer and started to work out the new monthly rent figures for Mrs. Koester's and Mrs. Pye's rooms.
    Who was doing the calculations?
    ___ a. Joan
    ___ b. the manager
    ___ c. Mrs. Koester
    ___ d. Mrs. Pye

5. If it wasn't bad enough that Kevin left the dinner early, I found out that he left with my coat instead of his.
    What do we definitely know about Kevin?
    ___ a. He ate dinner early.
    ___ b. He should have left early.
    ___ c. It wasn't bad that he left.
    ___ d. He left his coat.

6. and 7. Other wildlife in which Charles was particularly interested and which he worked to save with the World Wildlife Fund were the Javan bison in Indonesia and the Tamaraw buffalo and the monkey-eating eagle (the largest eagle in the world), both of which are found in the Philippines.
    Which animals are found in the Philippines?
    ___ a. the monkey-eating eagle and the world's largest eagle
    ___ b. the Tamaraw buffalo and the monkey-eating eagle
    ___ c. the Javan bison and the world's largest eagle
    ___ d. the Javan bison and the monkey-eating eagle

    What did Charles do?
    ___ a. He worked to help animals.
    ___ b. He tried to save the World Wildlife Fund.
    ___ c. He discovered the largest eagle in the world.
    ___ d. He found Tamaraw buffalo in the Philippines.

8. If any final proof were needed of Joanna's remarkable abilities, it could be found in the way she performed on the difficult three-hour entrance examination.

   How did Joanna do on the examination?

   ___ a. She did very well.

   ___ b. She found the examination difficult.

   ___ c. She could do all except the final proof.

   ___ d. After three hours she hadn't finished.

9. Ms. Haar announced the winner of the contest once Mr. Wilson had arrived.

   What happened first?

   ___ a. The winner was announced.

   ___ b. Mr. Wilson arrived.

   ___ c. Mr. Wilson won the contest.

   ___ d. Ms. Haar won the contest.

10. Obviously, there was a tremendous amount of research that needed to be done, and that would require more money than was available by way of government funding.

    What was money needed for?

    ___ a. to study government funding

    ___ b. to get government funding

    ___ c. to conduct research

    ___ d. to repay the government

Paragraph Reading

Main Idea

In this exercise, you will practice finding the main idea of a paragraph. Being able to understand the main idea of a passage is a very useful reading skill to develop. It is a skill you can apply to any kind of reading. For example, when you read for enjoyment or for general information, it is probably not important to remember all the details of a passage. Instead, you want to quickly discover the general message—the main idea of the passage. For other kinds of reading, such as reading textbooks, you need both to determine the main ideas and to understand how they are developed.

The main idea of a passage is the thought that is in the passage from the beginning to the end. In a well-written paragraph, most of the sentences support, describe, or explain the main idea. It is sometimes stated in the first or last sentence of the paragraph. Sometimes the main idea must be inferred; it is not stated.

In order to determine the main idea of a piece of writing, you should ask yourself what idea is common to most of the text. What is the idea that connects the parts to the whole? What opinion do all the parts support? What idea do they all explain or describe?

Read the following paragraphs quickly to discover the main idea. Remember, don't worry about the details in the paragraphs. You only want to determine the general message. After you read each paragraph, circle the letter next to the sentence that best expresses the main idea.

Study the example paragraph carefully before you begin. When you have finished, your teacher may want you to work in small groups for discussion.

Example

To scan is to look for specific information quickly without reading word by word. You have to know what you're looking for before you begin. When you scan, look for key words, names, dates, or other specifics that mean you have found the information you are looking for. Don't stop to read everything on a page slowly and carefully. Instead, scan until you come to the information you need; then read carefully.

Which sentence best states the main idea of the paragraph?

___ a. Scanning is reading quickly to find specific information.

___ b. Before you read a passage, you should scan it.

___ c. It is not a good idea to read word by word.

___ d. Scanning is a useful reading skill.

Study the explanations following to understand how these sentences relate to the paragraph.

Example paragraph adapted from *The Research Paper: Process, Form, and Content,* by Audrey J. Roth, 6th ed. (Belmont, CA: Wadsworth, 1989), 112.

Explanation

✓ a. This statement, a brief explanation of the process of scanning, is the main idea. All the other sentences in the paragraph give more details about the process of scanning—what it is and how to do it.

— b. The paragraph does not say or imply that we should always scan a passage before reading it, so this statement is false. Therefore, it cannot be the main idea.

— c. This statement is too narrow to be the main idea. It talks only about a part of the scanning process. It does not tell about the whole process of scanning that is described in the paragraph.

— d. This statement is too general. Although it is true, the focus of the paragraph is more specific. The purpose of the paragraph is to describe the process of scanning.

Paragraph 1

A *process* is a natural series of actions and reactions that leads to specific results. All of us participate in a variety of processes every day. We digest our food, heal ourselves by making new skin cells, distribute resources through our bodies by breathing, and use our five senses. Natural processes go on all around us as well. Plants produce their own food through photosynthesis, storms build and move, volcanoes erupt, and fertilized eggs mature—the list seems endless.

Which sentence best states the main idea of the paragraph?

— a. We all take part in many processes every day.

— b. Natural processes that go on around us include photosynthesis.

— c. A series of actions and reactions that leads to certain results is called a process.

— d. Natural processes take place within our bodies.

Paragraph 1 from *Technical Writing,* by Frances B. Emerson (Boston: Houghton Mifflin, 1987), 170.

Paragraph 2   "How will it play in Peoria?" This question was asked in the United States in the 1920s when singers, dancers, and other entertainers performed in traveling musical shows. Performers thought that if the citizens of a typical U.S. town such as Peoria, Illinois, liked their show it would probably be popular across the country. If Peorians disliked it, the entertainers believed the show would fail. This "Peoria test" is still applied to the people of the state of Illinois. Illinoisans' likes and dislikes seem to mirror those of people across the land. Perhaps this is true because of Illinois' central location; it is a crossroads between east and west, north and south. Or perhaps it is because Illinoisans come from such different backgrounds and follow such a wide variety of lifestyles.

Which sentence best states the main idea of the paragraph?

___ a. Illinois is located in the central part of the United States.

___ b. Illinoisans come from different backgrounds.

___ c. The "Peoria test" is the name of a famous show.

___ d. Illinoisans' opinions seem to mirror the beliefs of people throughout the United States.

Paragraph 3   If you ask most people to explain why they like someone when they first meet, they'll tell you it's because of the person's personality, intelligence, or sense of humor. But they're probably wrong. The characteristic that most impresses people when meeting for the first time is physical appearance. Although it may seem unfair, attractive people are frequently preferred over less attractive ones.

Which sentence best states the main idea of the paragraph?

___ a. Judging people by their appearance is unfair.

___ b. Physical appearance is more important to what we think of others than we believe it is.

___ c. Personality, intelligence, and sense of humor are important in deciding whether you like someone or not.

___ d. Most people deceive themselves.

___ e. People should spend more time combing their hair.

Paragraph 2 from *America the Beautiful: Illinois,* by R. Conrad Stein (Chicago: Childrens Press, 1987), 7.

Paragraph 3 from "The Eye of the Beholder," by Thomas F. Cash and Louis H. Janda, *Psychology Today,* December 1984. Reprinted in *Our Times: Readings from Recent Periodicals,* by Robert Atwan (New York: St. Martin's, 1989).

Paragraph 4   All communication is a two-way process involving a speaker or writer and listeners or readers (the audience). In written communication, because the audience is not present, the audience is easy to ignore. However, the kind of audience you write for determines what you write and how you write. In describing the World Series baseball championship to a British reader, you would have to include definitions, explanations, and facts that a reader in the United States would not need. Similarly, if you write about cricket (a British sport) for an audience in the United States, you would need to include a lot of basic information. If you wrote about the international banking systems for bankers, your language and information would be more technical than in a paper written for readers who don't know much about the subject. A discussion of acid rain written for an audience of environmentalists would be quite different from one written for factory owners.

Which sentence best states the main idea of the paragraph?

___ a. Communication is a process that involves speakers and writers.

___ b. British readers would need special information to understand an article on the World Series.

___ c. Listeners and readers are called the audience.

___ d. It is important to consider your audience when you write.

Paragraph 5    Researchers at the University of Michigan are studying the effects of nicotine on the brain. Nicotine is the major drug in cigarettes. The scientists' long-term goal is to improve methods for helping people quit smoking. Recently they have found that cigarettes give several "benefits" to smokers that may help explain why quitting smoking is so hard. The nicotine in cigarettes seems to help smokers with problems of daily living. It helps them feel calm. Nicotine also causes short-term improvements in concentration, memory, alertness, and feelings of well-being.

Which sentence best states the main idea of the paragraph?

___ a. Researchers at the University of Michigan are studying how to help smokers stop smoking.

___ b. Nicotine improves concentration, memory, and alertness.

___ c. Some "benefits" of smoking may help explain why smokers have a hard time quitting.

___ d. Researchers at the University of Michigan have developed a new program to help people stop smoking.

Paragraph 4 from *The Macmillan Guide to Writing Research Papers,* by William Coyle (New York: Macmillan, 1990), 8.
Paragraph 5 adapted from "Anxiety and Smoking," *Research News,* September–October, 1990, 22.

Paragraph 6   The United States faces a transportation crisis. U.S. highways and airways are getting more and more crowded. In the next 20 years, the time that automobile drivers lose because of crowded highways is expected to increase from 3 billion to 12 billion hours a year. During the same time period, the number of airplane flights with delays of more than eight minutes is predicted to triple. For both highway and air travel, the estimated cost of delay to passengers will rise from $15 billion a year today to $61 billion 20 years from now.

Which sentence best states the main idea of the paragraph?

___ a. Airplanes will not be delayed as much as cars will be.

___ b. Transportation problems in the United States are increasing.

___ c. Twenty years from now, drivers will be delayed 12 billion hours a year.

___ d. Transportation delays now cost travelers billions of dollars.

Paragraph 7    Shizuo Torii, a professor at Toho University in Japan, has studied the sense of smell. He studied the effects that odors have on the feelings and behaviors of humans. By measuring the brain waves of people after they smelled a particular odor, Torii found that some odors produced a brain wave pattern that showed the people were calm. Other odors produced a pattern that showed excitement. It was discovered, for example, that lemon and peppermint have an exciting effect; nutmeg and lavender reduce stress; and a mix of rosemary and lemon will improve concentration. Some Japanese corporations are using the results of this research to make the workplace more productive and pleasant.

Which sentence best states the main idea of the paragraph?

___ a. People's brain waves are different when they smell lemon than when they smell rosemary.

___ b. Japanese corporations want to make the workplace more pleasant and efficient.

___ c. Shizuo Torii is a Japanese professor paid by corporations to improve the workplace environment.

___ d. A Japanese researcher has discovered that smells affect people's brain waves.

Paragraph 6 adapted from "Levitating Trains: Hope for Gridlocked Transportation," by Richard A. Uher, *Futurist* 24, no. 5 (September–October, 1990): 28.
Paragraph 7 adapted from "Aromacology: The Psychic Effects of Fragrances," *Futurist* 24, no. 5 (September–October, 1990): 49.

Paragraph 8   In the United States, old people who no longer have an income or who suffer from a loss of physical abilities are often forced to give up living alone. They must leave their homes and depend on someone else to give them a place to live and to take care of their physical needs: they must either live with relatives or live in homes for the aged. This loss of independence is a major problem for the aged.

Which sentence best states the main idea of the paragraph?

___ a. Being unable to live alone is a serious problem for old people in the United States.

___ b. Old people in the United States who are poor or sick cannot live alone.

___ c. Old people who are poor or sick should live with their relatives, not in homes for the aged.

___ d. In the United States, old people who are poor or sick are forced to live in homes for the aged.

Paragraph 9   Not all of the islands in the Caribbean Sea are the tops of a volcanic mountain range that begins under the sea. Some are the tops of older, nonvolcanic mountains, mountains that have been covered in coral. Coral is a hard, rocklike material that is made of the shells of sea animals called coral polyps. When coral polyps are alive, they attach to any base they can find, such as old mountaintops under the sea. When the polyps die, they leave their shells behind as a rocky covering. Then, new polyps attach to this covering. The result is a coral island. Many of the smaller islands in the Caribbean are coral islands.

Which sentence best states the main idea of the paragraph?

___ a. Some of the islands in the Caribbean Sea are the tops of old, underwater volcanoes.

___ b. There are many small islands in the Caribbean Sea.

___ c. Many of the Caribbean islands are the tops of old mountains that are covered with coral.

___ d. Coral is formed by sea animals called coral polyps.

___ e. There are many mountains in the islands of the Caribbean Sea.

Paragraph 8 adapted from *Psychology,* by Robert E. Silverman (New York: Appleton-Century-Crofts, 1971), 823.
Paragraph 9 adapted from *A World View,* by Clyde P. Patton, Arlene C. Rengert, Robert N. Saveland, Kenneth S. Cooper, and Patricia T. Caro (Atlanta, GA: Silver Burdett and Ginn, 1988), 116.

2

Reading Selection 1

Newspaper Article

Before You Begin   1. Have you ever eaten at McDonald's?

Since the 1950s, when the first McDonald's opened, the restaurant has been serving its hamburgers to millions of customers quickly and cheaply. The workers are usually cheerful and speedy, but have you ever given any thought to their working conditions or salaries? The following newspaper story examines the employment situation at McDonald's. Some people say that the restaurant is a good place for young people to get a start; others say that McDonald's pays little and works people too hard.

2. What do you think? Is McDonald's a good place to work? Do you have an opinion based on your own experience?

Read the article and form your own opinion. Your teacher may want you to do Vocabulary from Context exercise 1 on page 32 before you begin.

Is McDonald's Fair?

1   Three months ago, Mariza Castro left Honduras. Today, she is in the United States, and she has a job. Castro works behind the counter at McDonald's. Speed is an important part of her work life. Fast-food counter workers are expected to serve customers in less than a minute. At McDonald's they say, "Work fast or you don't last."

2   Are McDonald's workers lucky to have their jobs? Or are they being exploited? The answer depends on who you talk to.

3   McDonald's does many good things. For example, no other company hires more young people than McDonald's. More than half of its workers are under 20 years old. McDonald's also has a good record of hiring minority workers. Thirteen percent of its workers are black. This is better than any other U.S. company.

4   But the burger house has its critics as well. The pay bothered Edward Rodriguez. He worked for nearly a year at a Los Angeles McDonald's. During that time he got only one 10-cent raise. "I used to joke that working for McDonald's is the closest thing to slave labor in the U.S. today," he says. Today, most McDonald's pay about $5.00 an hour. They hire new workers constantly. The restaurant has no other choice because 70 per-cent of its workers quit or are fired every year.

5   But McDonald's also gets its share of praise. Its best workers move up quickly. Just talk to 17-year-old Ameer Abdur-Razaaq of Harlem, New York City. "They call me 'Young Crew Chief' around my block," he says. "Where else can I go at my age and be in charge of this many people?" He sees the job as the first step in his career.

6   However, most McDonald's crew members never make it to manager because the job pressure is so intense and the rewards so few. As one worker put it, "They expect a lot and they don't pay you much."

Excerpted from *News for You,* May 16, 1990.

Comprehension

Answer the following questions according to your understanding of the passage. Your teacher may want you to work individually, in small groups, or in pairs. True/False items are indicated by a T / F before a statement. Some questions may have more than one correct answer. Others require an opinion. Choose the answer you like best; be prepared to defend your choices.

1. What type of restaurant is McDonald's? _____

2. Consider the sentence in paragraph 1, "Work fast or you don't last."

    T / F   At McDonald's you will be fired if you do not work fast.

3. T / F   McDonald's workers come from different countries.

4. What percentage of McDonald's workers are African American? _____

5. How much do most McDonald's workers make an hour? _____

6. T / F   Most of McDonald's workers quit or are fired every year.

7. T / F   McDonald's hires more old than young workers.

8. Why did Edward Rodriguez say that working at McDonald's is like slave labor? _____

_____

9. T / F   Ameer Abdur-Razaaq is happy to be a crew chief.

Discussion

The following questions are intended to help you form a critical opinion about McDonald's and about this article. Your teacher may want you to work in pairs or small groups as you answer these questions. You may want to take notes to use in writing a short composition on working conditions at McDonald's.

1. Where did the writer get information about McDonald's? Do you think it is accurate? Consider the figures cited in paragraph 4; where would a writer get this sort of information? And what about Ameer Abdur-Razaaq? Do you think the writer talked to many workers like him? On what do you base your answer?

2. Is McDonald's a good place to work? (Would you like to work at McDonald's?) List the advantages and disadvantages based on the reading and your own experience.

Discussion/Composition

Some people say that McDonald's represents what is good about the United States. Do you agree or disagree? Give information from the reading and your own experience to support your opinion.

Vocabulary from Context

Exercise 1

Both the ideas and vocabulary in the exercise below are taken from "Is McDonald's Fair?" Use the context provided to decide on meanings for the italicized words. Write a definition, synonym, or description in the space provided.

1. _____ Critics of McDonald's say that the workers are *exploited* by the restaurant. The workers are often young, uneducated, and either immigrants or minorities who cannot easily get other jobs and therefore have to take whatever work they can find. Some workers claim that McDonald's exploits this situation by making them work long hours with little pay.

2. _____ My son Benjamin says workers are treated no better than *slave labor.* He claims that the bosses act as if they own you, just like in the early days of the United States when rich farmers bought and sold black workers from Africa. Because of this, he refuses to work for McDonald's.

Dale and his boss did not get along well. The other night, after Dale
3. _____ broke some dishes, the boss said, "That's it! You're *fired!* Take your last paycheck and leave!" But Dale was just as angry as his boss. He shouted back, "Don't worry! I'm leaving! You can't fire me, because I
4. _____ *quit!*"

From the time they arrive until quitting time, McDonald's workers work very hard. The restaurant wants to serve every customer in less
5. _____ than one minute, so the job pressure is *intense.* The workers have no time to rest—they run from one thing to the next with no time to relax or think of anything else.

Although McDonald's has been criticized, it has also received a lot of
6. _____ *praise.* For example, Ameer Abdur-Razaaq says that he thinks McDonald's is a good company because it gives young people the chance to earn money and learn important job skills.

Exercise 2

This exercise should be done after you have finished reading "Is McDonald's Fair?" The exercise will give you practice deciding on the meaning of unfamiliar words. Give a definition, synonym, or description of each of the words below. The number in parentheses indicates the paragraph in which the word can be found. Your teacher may want you to do these orally or in writing.

1. (1) counter _____

2. (3, 4) hire _____

3. (4) critics _____

Reading Selection 2

Technical Prose

Before You Begin   Check your impressions of the United States.

1. What percentage of people living in the United States do you think speak English as their native language?

2. Do you think the percentage of native English speakers in the United States has increased or decreased over the last ten years?

3. You may know that, after English, Spanish is the most common native language of U.S. residents. But what would you guess are the next three most common native languages of U.S. residents?

4. How many U.S. residents do you think have the same native language as yours?

Answers to questions like these can be found in reports written by the U.S. Census Bureau, a government office responsible for counting (every ten years) the number of people in the country. The following newspaper article and table are based on information collected by the Census Bureau. Read them to see if your impressions are correct.

USA Today

Language Mirrors Immigration, Provides Key to Nation's Past, Present

1   The number of residents whose native language is not English has risen 34% in the last ten years to approximately 32 million, according to a recent Census Bureau report. Now one in every seven U.S. residents, or about 14% of the total U.S. population, speaks a language other than English at home.

2   According to the Census Bureau report, there are 329 different languages spoken in U.S. homes. The most common language other than English is Spanish. Seventeen million people, more than half of all the residents who speak a language other than English, speak Spanish. That is ten times as many as speak French, the second most common language, used by 5.3%

of those who don't use English at home. The others of the top five most common languages are German, 4.9%; Italian, 4.1%; and Chinese, 3.9%.

3   Almost 90% of those who speak a language other than English at home communicate in one of the 20 most common of these 329 languages. Many of the 309 other languages are used by very small numbers of people in the United States. For example, there are 750 speakers of Papia Mentae, a Portuguese creole* language, and 73 speakers of Woleai-Ulithi, a Micronesian language.

4   The number of speakers of each language shows the changing pattern of immigration to the United States over the last 100 years. Many European languages

are becoming less common, as immigrants who came to the United States during the first half of the 1900s die. In the last ten years, the number of German speakers decreased 4%, to 1.5 million. The number of Italian speakers decreased 20% to 1.3 million. Polish, the fifth most common foreign language ten years ago, dropped to the seventh most common. The number of Yiddish speakers decreased 33.5% to 213,000.

5   Languages of newer immigrants, on the other hand, are becoming more widely used in the United States. The number of Chinese speakers rose 98% to 1.2 million. The number of speakers of Tagalog, the language of the Philippines, rose 87% to nearly

*creole: a language formed as a result of speakers of several languages coming together and creating a new language by which to communicate

850,000. The number of people who speak Kru, an African language, rose 169% to 65,800.

6 More than half of those who do not speak English at home live in just three states, California, New York, and Florida. However, there are non-native English speakers in all states. Often, speakers of particular foreign languages live mainly in just a few states. For example, almost half of the United States's 355,150 Arabic speakers live in California, Michigan, and New York. French speakers are concentrated in Maine, New Hampshire, and Louisiana. A majority of the 429,860 Portuguese speakers can be found in Massachusetts, California, and New Jersey.

7 Most people age 5 or older who speak a foreign language at home also speak at least some English. Fifty-six percent, or 17.9 million people say they speak English "very well," and 23% say they speak it "well." With the help of relatives or foreign-language Census forms, 15.2% answer "not well," and 5.8%–or 1.8 million people–say they don't speak English at all.

8 How well immigrants speak English often reflects how long they've been in the United States. For example, two-thirds of Italian speakers say they know English "very well," compared with just 22% of speakers of Miao. Miao is the language of the Hmong, a people from Laos, most of whom immigrated to the United States after 1975.

The 25 Most-Commonly Spoken Languages in the United States after English

Language	Rank	Number of Speakers	Percentage Change from 10 Years Ago	State with Highest Percentage of Speakers
Spanish	1	17,339,172	+ 50.1	New Mexico
French	2	1,702,176	+ 8.3	Maine
German	3	1,547,099	– 3.7	North Dakota
Italian	4	1,308,648	– 19.9	New York
Chinese	5	1,249,213	+ 97.7	Hawaii
Tagalog	6	843,251	+ 86.6	Hawaii
Polish	7	723,483	– 12.4	Illinois
Korean	8	626,478	+127.0	Hawaii
Vietnamese	9	507,069	+149.8	California
Portuguese	10	429,860	+ 19.1	Rhode Island
Japanese	11	427,657	+ 25.0	Hawaii
Greek	12	388,260	– 5.3	Massachusetts
Arabic	13	355,150	+ 56.4	Michigan
Hindi	14	331,484	+155.0	New Jersey
Russian	15	241,798	+ 38.2	New York
Yiddish	16	213,064	– 33.4	New York
Thai/Lao	17	206,266	+131.8	California
Persian	18	201,865	+ 85.2	California
French Creole	19	187,658	+650.6	Florida
Armenian	20	149,694	+ 46.8	California
Navaho	21	148,530	+ 20.8	New Mexico
Hungarian	22	147,902	– 17.5	New Jersey
Hebrew	23	144,292	+ 45.7	New York
Dutch	24	142,684	– 2.3	Utah
Mon-Khmer	25	127,441	+696.5	Rhode Island

Source: Based on data from the U.S. Census Bureau, *USA Today,* and the *New York Times.*

This article is adapted from two articles by Margaret L. Usdansky: "Language Mirrors Immigration, Provides Key to Nation's Past, Present," *USA Today,* April 28, 1993, 11A, and "Census: Languages Not Foreign at Home," *USA Today,* April 28, 1993, 1A. Copyright © 1993, USA TODAY. Reprinted by permission.

Comprehension

Use information from the article and the table to answer the following questions. True/False items are indicated by a T / F preceding a statement.

1. T / F   Thirty-four percent of all U.S. residents do not speak English as their native language.

2. T / F   The number of U.S. residents whose native language is not English increased by about one-third in the last ten years.

3. T / F   About one-third of the people in the United States whose native language is not English are Spanish speakers.

4. T / F   There are fewer U.S. residents who are native speakers of Mon-Khmer than of any other language.

5. T / F   Most of the U.S. residents who don't speak English at home speak one of only twenty other languages.

6. T / F   The Census Bureau only reported information about languages that are spoken by more than 100 residents.

7. Which language had the greatest percentage increase in the last ten years? _____

8. Which language is the second-fastest growing native language in the United States? _____

9. T / F   Ten years ago, the top five languages (after English) were the same ones as the top five now.

10. T / F   There are fewer native speakers of French in the United States now than there were ten years ago.

11. T / F   There are fewer native speakers of Italian in the United States now than there were ten years ago.

12. Why are there fewer speakers of European languages in the United States now than there were fifty years ago?

    _____

    _____

13. More than half of the residents who don't speak English at home live in which three states?

    _____

14. T / F   About half of the U.S. residents who speak Arabic live in Michigan.

15. T / F   About 38 percent of the U.S. residents who speak Russian at home live in New York.

16. T / F   More than three-fourths of U.S. residents whose native language is not English say they speak English "well" or "very well."

17. T / F   In general, the longer immigrants have been in the United States, the better they say they speak English.

18. T / F   The Census Bureau gets information from U.S. residents who do not speak English very well.

19. Why isn't Indonesian one of the languages listed on the chart? _____

_____

20. How many people in the United States speak your native language in their homes? _____

Discussion/Composition

1. Are there languages in this table that you think will not be among the "top 25 languages" ten years from now? What languages might be added to the chart in ten years? For which other languages do you think the number of speakers will increase or decrease?

2. Some people say that a country is weakened when its residents do not speak the same language. Others believe that a multilingual society strengthens a country. What do you think? Give reasons and examples to support your opinion.

3. Should elementary schools in the United States teach children in the language they speak at home? Be sure to support your opinion.

Reading Selections 3A–3C

Popular Social Science

Before You Begin:
Establishing Your
Point of View

The changing family is a popular topic in magazines, newspapers, and social science texts in North America. These readings often begin by discussing popular definitions of the family. Before you read the articles that follow, consider your own beliefs.

1. Throughout history, people around the world have had different ideas of what a family is. List the people in your family. What is your definition of a family?

Before You Begin:
Comparing Your
Point of View
with Others'

The following description is from a special issue of *Life* magazine on the American Family.

> In a recent study on family and family values, Americans were asked for their definition of the family. Only 22 percent thought a family was "a group of people related by blood, marriage or adoption." The definition preferred by 74 percent was much broader. A family, the majority felt, was "a group of people who love and care for one another."

1. According to the preferred definition, check (✓) those groups below that could be a family.

   ___ people who live together
   ___ people and their pets
   ___ neighbors
   ___ people who belong to the same church

2. Does the definition in the study surprise you? Do you agree or disagree with it?

The following reading selections discuss families and relationships. Your teacher may want you to do the Vocabulary from Context exercise on pages 39 and 41 before you begin.

Selection 3A   **Trade Book**

Trade books are written on popular topics and are intended for a general audience. Although they sometimes discuss academic topics, these books require no specialized knowledge. The following passages are taken from a trade book called *Families: A Celebration of Diversity, Commitment, and Love.* You will begin by developing a first impression of this book.

From *Life* (Collector's Edition: The American Family), 1992, 4.

Critical Reading

When evaluating a passage, readers often develop a first impression of the point of view of the author and compare it with their own. *Families: A Celebration of Diversity, Commitment, and Love* was written for children about other children's lives so they could see many kinds of human families. Below is a paragraph from the acknowledgments, written by the woman who collected these children's stories. Read it to get your first impression of her.

> Many thanks are due to . . . my own family, for what I have learned from them: my parents, my brother and niece, my ex-husband and his family, my ex-and-thankfully-forever mother-in-law, my children and stepchildren and their spouses, my partner and his family, and, not least, my dearest friends.

1. What is your first impression of the writer?

2. What is your impression of her family?

3. Do you think you will mostly agree or disagree with this writer?

On page 40 is the Introduction to the book. It contains a number of statements about families, some of which you may agree with and others perhaps not. After each paragraph, decide which ideas you agree with and which you disagree with. Underline those with which you agree; circle those with which you disagree. Your teacher may want you to compare your reactions with those of your classmates.

Vocabulary from Context

The vocabulary in the exercise below is taken from various sections of *Families: A Celebration of Diversity, Commitment, and Love* that you will be reading. Use the context provided to decide on meanings for the italicized words. Write a definition, synonym, or description in the space provided.

1. _____ Bill and Jane work together every day, but they have never met each other's *spouses*. John's wife and Jane's husband both work out of town, so they can never come to company parties and meet the people their spouses work with.

2. _____ Jane doesn't always get along with her *mother-in-law*, and when her husband Steve asked if his mother could move in with them, Jane was slow to agree.

3. _____ Jane and Steve live in a large family. Along with the mother-in-law, they have two biological children and two children by Steve's previous marriage. Jane's biological children and her *stepchildren* get along very well.

Introduction

Families — what are they? Your family is the people who take care of you, who care about you. Your family may be the person who adopted you. Your family may be your birth mother or father. Your family may include people who joined you, like stepparents and stepbrothers and stepsisters. Your family may be your grandparents, your aunt or uncle, or your guardian. Some kids are able to ask friends to act as family for them — sometimes temporarily — and this can be a big help.

Families change over time. This can be painful, if you miss someone who's moved out of your life. In other ways, it's fine. At different times in your life, when you will have new needs and interests, you may find new people to call on.

Families are spread out over space. Members may move all over the world. You may be able to write to, or telephone, or visit, relatives who live in different kinds of places. It can be a big network you have, a way of learning about places far from your hometown.

Some people think a family is supposed to be a mom and a dad and their children. This can cause a lot of hurt feelings. In school, you may be asked to make a Mother's Day card; but lots of kids don't live with their mothers. You may be asked to bring your dad to work on the school playground for a day; but lots of kids don't live with their dads. Most kids know

that, really, families are often very different from "Mom 'n' Dad".

And that "very different" can be a fine thing. A family of two can be close and cozy. A big family can mean there are many people to go to for help or for fun. A family that changes over time means there are different people to be with over your life. A family whose members are very different from each other means you can learn a wide variety of things.

What do *you* think a family is?

Here are some kids' answers to the question.

Excerpts from *Families: A Celebration of Diversity, Commitment, and Love,* by Aylette Jenness (Boston: Houghton Mifflin, 1990), 8, 22–23, 30–31, 32–33, 42, 46–47.

4. _____   Although I do not know them well, I have the *impression* that Jane and Steve are very happy.

5. _____
6. _____   Bill and his wife Sally were not able to have children. Recently, they decided to *adopt* a child whose parents had been killed in an accident. They could have become only the child's *guardians,* but they wanted to do more than take care of her. They wanted her to be legally their daughter, to be part of their family.

7. _____
8. _____   Jane's brother Paul is *gay.* He and his lover John live very near Jane and Steve and see them often for dinner. Although Paul and John are not legally married, the men have made a lifetime *commitment* to stay together.

9. _____   Today in North America there is a great *diversity* in the kinds of families that people live in. Of course, some people live in traditional families—with husbands or wives and biological children. But others live in a variety of situations—with in-laws and stepchildren, with gay partners and adopted children, with friends and religious groups.

10. _____   When Jane wrote the *acknowledgment* in the beginning of her book, she thanked all the members of her large extended family.

Selection 3B   **Trade Book**

Following are four descriptions from *Families: A Celebration of Diversity, Commitment, and Love.* For each description think about the following questions.

1. In what ways is this a traditional family?

2. In what ways is it untraditional?

3. By your definition, do you consider that the child lives in a "family"?

4. What special problems does this child face?

5. What are some good aspects of this kind of family?

Your teacher may want you to answer these questions individually, in pairs, or in groups. Your teacher may suggest that you discuss these after each description or wait until you have read them all.

Discussion/Composition

Consider your answers to questions 1–5, above. What are similarities and differences among the families? Which of these four families would you want to live in? Why?

Jaime

Jaime's father came to the United States from Mexico twelve years ago. At first he stayed with his uncle, and worked on a farm. There he began to learn English, and later he moved to California. Jaime's mother came from Mexico a little later, living with her brother until she met and married Jaime's father.

Now they have five sons — Jaime, Salvador, Javier, Gabriel, and Hector. Jaime and Salvador go to school, and Javier goes to a nursery school where both of his parents help the teacher each week. Gabriel and Hector are at home with their mother, where she is busy all the time, washing clothes, cooking, and cleaning for her big family.

Jaime's father has two jobs — he works full time in a restaurant, and part time as a janitor. He says, smiling, "Five kids — I've got to work a lot!"

A few months ago Jaime's whole family went back to Mexico for the first time to visit relatives. Jaime's father says, "I drove nearly fifty hours — two nights and three days." The boys got to know many family members they had never met, especially their grandparents.

Here in the United States, Jaime's family members speak Spanish to each other and to their Mexican-American friends. They speak English to people who can't understand Spanish. Jaime's father wants the boys to do well in school here. He says, "Some people like to get money, and that's it. I don't like that.

School is important. Maybe the boys will have a job like a mailman — or, why not, maybe a doctor or a lawyer."

Jaime likes his school, especially math class and using the computers. After school, he plays with his brothers. Sometimes he helps take care of his littlest brother, Hector. "I pick him up, give him toys, play games with him. Sometimes I help my mother — I clean my room. Sometimes I *don't* help my mother."

"I like playing with my friends — hand wrestling, tag, hide and seek, and soccer." Jaime is on a soccer team, and he practices twice a week after school.

What does he want to be when he grows up? He smiles at his father and says, "I want to be a lawyer."

Elliott

Elliott's family is his two fathers — his "Papa," Dmitri, and his "Daddy," Tom. Dmitri says, "Families come in all shapes and sizes. We happen to be gay men, two men who love each other, but we do the same things that other families do — we make oatmeal for Elliott, we give him baths."

"Dmitri and I knew when we first got together nine years ago that we wanted to be parents," Tom explains. "We started to prepare for a family long before Elliott was born. That's why we bought our house."

"Elliott was adopted at birth," Dmitri says. "His birth mother wasn't able to raise him. Elliott knows her. He sees her from time to time, and he'll be able to ask her questions when he wants to. He'll always have a relationship with her.

"We were in the hospital when Elliott was born, and we brought him home, here, from the hospital. I think that our way of being open about our family helped people accept us. We'd be out pushing the baby carriage in our neighborhood, and neighbors would say, 'Oh, you've got a baby? Congratulations!' We try to make ourselves approachable, so people can ask us questions if they want to.

"We've split up taking care of Elliott pretty evenly," Dmitri continues. "If he gets hurt, he'll run to one of us, say me — I'll pick him up, and then he'll turn to Tom." Dmitri goes to work very early each morning, so Tom helps Elliott get dressed and takes him to his day-care center.

"I like my teachers," Elliott says. "I like it when we read stories in school, and I like drawing and tracing and coloring." Dmitri picks Elliott up and spends the afternoon with him.

"After school I play with my Lego farm," says Elliott. "I paint at my easel. I have a smock. And I like to play Sesame Street on the computer. I can put in the disk. Then I push ENTER. I can make numbers and animals on the computer. I can spell my name, E-L-L-I-O-T-T. You have to be careful. You never shake the computer!"

When Tom comes home, he cooks Elliott's dinner and puts him to bed. "And every night, we sing 'Goodnight, Sweetheart,' " Dmitri says. "Together.

"You know," Dmitri goes on, "I'd like to have six kids. I came from a family of four kids, and I love my siblings. I want Elliott to have that, too. The most I've gotten Tom to commit to is four; I may

have to come down a little. Maybe five."

Tom and Dmitri have begun to make it known that they're available to adopt another child who needs a family. "I want a baby brother!" says Elliott.

Right now they're looking for a bigger house with a bigger yard. Big enough for their three dogs. And — who knows — maybe five kids.

Dmitri says. "We're really not so different from other families. Sometimes adults have more preconceived notions than kids do. The other day I was picking up Elliott at school, and a little girl came up to me. She said, 'Are you Elliott's daddy?' I said, 'Yes.' She said, 'Then who's Tom?' I said, 'He's Elliott's daddy, too.' 'Oh,' she said. Then, almost to herself, 'Elliott's got two daddies. I haven't got any!' "

Eve

"I mostly live with my mom," Eve says, "but about two nights a week I go to my dad and my stepmom's house, and I live there and I go to school from there. I have my own room in each house, and in both houses I have desks where I can do my homework.

"I have two brothers, but they're both away at school. And I have a dog, Lion.

"In Dad's house, it's Dad's way, and in Mom's house, it's Mom's way. I've realized that they're different parents, and I shouldn't treat them the same. But sometimes it gets into problems for myself. If I like rules from one house better than the other, I feel like saying, 'I

like it better when you do it *this* way.' But I try to work it out. I usually say, 'Well, I know this is your rules, but I wonder if you would rewrite the rules a little, because I'm disagreeing with some of them.'

"My mom pushes me a lot in my homework, and it helps, 'cause she really makes me do it. At my dad's it's a little bit like, 'Okay, let's do this together.' At my mom's there's more expected of me, and at my dad's there's more done for me. Those are very different, but they're a nice contrast. I like them both.

"When my dad first got married, it was a little hard, because I thought I was expected to treat my stepmother like Mom, but then I realized I didn't have to. I love them both, but I know more about my mom; I know what's going to happen

more. With my stepmom, I have to think a little more, or ask a little more, because she's a lot newer in my life. My mom likes my stepmother, and how she treats me, and my stepmother respects my mom. I consider myself real lucky."

Jennifer

Jennifer lives with her mother and her sister, Merryn, in a commune — a household of people who have chosen to share a home. Her family includes two other small families right now — and Tiger Lily, her cat. Here Jen and Merryn are sitting on the floor in their living room, with their mother behind Merryn.

"I've lived here in this house since I was three. It's always seemed right to me. I love it. I'd be lonelier if it was just my mom and Merryn and me. In this house you make more friends, you meet more people. Of course, it's hard when people leave — they're family, they really *are* family — and you get really close to them. There's a list of about fifty people who've lived here. They come back to visit.

"We have a hard time trying to find new people to move in, 'cause we have to get to know them, we have to see if they can fit into our family style. And everyone has to agree on someone. And of course, *they* have to like it, too."

Family members share housework, help each other in a variety of ways, and spend a lot of time together. "They help me with schoolwork — Jerry's good at math — and they give me rides. We go shopping together, or to the movies. And I'll do favors for them — I baby-sit for Sam, I help them out.

"I love my family. I can't imagine living anywhere else."

Selection 3C   **Trade Book**

On pages 50–51 is the Postscript from the book *Families: A Celebration of Diversity, Commitment, and Love.* Read it quickly, then return to the Discussion and Discussion/Composition questions on this page.

Discussion

1. Why do you think the author chose to do an exhibit on the topic of families? Why do you think she decided to use parts of the exhibit to write a book about children for children?

2. Peoples' definitions of a family can change over time and can be different depending on where they live. Do you think this book would be popular around the world? Do you think this book could have been written 50 years ago?

Discussion/Composition

1. Pretend you are a reviewer for a newspaper in your community. Write a review of this book based on the parts you have read. Be sure to describe the book and then to evaluate it.

2. The Postscript includes 4 pictures and 7 written comments by visitors to the exhibit. Notice that some of the comments have responses. Write a response to one of the comments or pictures. You may agree or disagree with the point of view, or you may try to be helpful or kind to the person.

Postscript

This book began as a photographic exhibition at The Children's Museum in Boston, Massachusetts. Many families joined the project, allowing me to photograph and interview them, generously sharing their feelings and ideas. Kids spoke of their problems, pleasures, interests, and hopes, and carefully corrected and approved my edited versions of their taped conversations.

In the finished exhibit, a table with paper, crayons, and pencils encouraged visitors to join the show. Kids made drawings and stories about their own families and put them up on the walls. Many were joyous: "I have a family and they love me; that's the way it's going to be." Others expressed the pain of family problems in pictures and words: "I wish I had a nice family. If your parents are divorced, be thankful!"

Adults wrote about their own experiences and opinions, and posted these:

"I've been part of a big family, a single-parent (me) family, and a traditional family. I think it's all the same! . . . I think that if you love someone you have to work at it. That can relate to 1 other person or 100 other people. And we are all in the *human* family."

"Families are precious! The diversity here makes me realize the strength, the willingness and bondedness that hold us together. To be unique, irreplaceable and unrepeatable, that is family. Color, size, denomination or preferences only add flavor and texture to a beautiful commodity."

One visitor asked, "I have only one question. Is it wrong to be idealistic and want a traditional family with a mom and dad, a couple of kids, a dog and a cat, and grandparents who live in St. Louis?"

And another replied, "No. This exhibit makes no judgment in regard to right and wrong. It acknowledges that there are many kinds of families in addition to the traditional one."

One teenager found help: "When I first found out about my daddy being gay I was very upset, but after seeing what you have about being gay I feel a lot better about his sexual preferences. Thank you sooo much."

And many people voiced this sentiment: "The photographs show that the traditional family unit is changing; however, this transition is preserving the only really important ingredient to make a family — love."

Reading Selection 4

Technical Prose

The families you have just read about show changing lifestyle patterns in the United States. Below is a statistical discussion of changes in marriage patterns. It is based on a U.S. Census Bureau* report.

Overview

Read the first two paragraphs of "Marriage Taking a Back Seat, Says Census" to get a general idea of its content. Indicate if each statement below is true (T) or false (F) according to your understanding of these paragraphs.

1. T / F   The average age of marriage for both men and women is higher now than it was 20 years ago.

2. T / F   More people are living together without being married today than did 20 years ago.

3. T / F   Most young people today will never marry.

4. T / F   Most children in the United States live with only one parent.

Now, look at the full article to answer the Comprehension questions on page 53. Your teacher may want you to do the Vocabulary from Context exercise on page 54 before you begin.

Marriage Taking a Back Seat, Says Census

UNITED PRESS INTERNATIONAL

1 WASHINGTON—Men and women are waiting longer than ever to marry, a Census Bureau report said yesterday, and the number of unmarried couples living together has more than quadrupled in the past 20 years.

2 At the same time, the report said the number of children affected by divorce, separation, and out-of-wedlock births continues to rise and fewer than three-quarters of all children now live with both parents.

3 According to the report, an examination of marital status and living arrangements showed that the median age for a man's first marriage is 26.2 years, breaking the previous high of 26.1 years set in 1890.

The median age for a woman's first marriage is 23.8, higher than any previously recorded level.

4 "At the beginning of the 20th century, the median age at first marriage started a decline that ended in the mid-1950's," the report said, "reaching a low in 1956 of 20.1 years for women and 22.5 years for men."

5 Delays in marriage are also reflected by increases in the proportion of men and women who have not yet married for the first time.

6 The proportion of men and women in their 20s and early 30s who have never married grew substantially.

7 In the last 20 years, "the proportion never married at ages 20 to 24 increased by 75 percent for women and 41 percent for men," the report said.

8 "The proportion for those in the 25–29 age group tripled for women and more than doubled for men. For those in the 30–34 age group, the never-married proportions tripled for both men and women."

9 At the same time, the report

Adapted from "Marriage Taking a Back Seat," *Seattle Post-Intelligencer,* July 12, 1990, A16.

*The U.S. Census Bureau takes a population count every ten years. Census questionnaires provide a variety of information about people living in the United States.

showed that the number of unmarried-couple households continued to rise, from 523,000 20 years ago to 2.8 million today.

10   The majority of partners in unmarried-couple relationships—59 percent—had never been married, while 32 percent were divorced, 4 percent widowed and 5 percent were separated from their spouses.

11   "The typical age of the partners was 25 to 34 years, 27 percent were under age 25, and 17 percent were age 35 to 44," the report said.

12   "In 6 of 10 unmarried households, both partners were under 35 years of age."

13   The proportion of children under 18 years living with two parents has declined considerably as divorce, separation, and births to unmarried mothers have become more common.

14   In the past 20 years, the proportion living with two parents declined while the proportion living with one parent doubled from 12 percent to 24 percent, the report said.

Comprehension

Indicate if each statement below is true (T) or false (F) according to your understanding of the article.

1. T / F   Six times as many unmarried couples are living together today as did 20 years ago.

2. T / F   Today, three-quarters of all children are affected by divorce.

3. T / F   The oldest average age for men marrying was recorded in 1890.

4. T / F   The youngest average age at which men and women married was recorded in 1956.

5. T / F   Over the past 20 years, the proportion of people who have never married increased by 75 percent for women and 41 percent for men.

6. T / F   The increase in the proportion of people who have never married has been greater for younger people than for older people.

7. T / F   Most people living in unmarried-couple relationships are divorced.

8. T / F   Most people living in unmarried-couple relationships are between 25 and 34 years of age.

Critical Reading

Why do you think the article refers to people who have never married as "waiting longer to marry" (paragraph 1) and people "who have not yet married for the first time" (paragraph 5)? Do you think this is a good choice of words?

Discussion/Composition

1. List three reasons why a person might choose not to marry. Why are some people concerned about others not marrying—Religious reasons? Worries about the care of children? Concern that old people won't be taken care of? Can you think of other reasons? Are these causes of concern for you?

2. What are the effects on children of changing family patterns? Are new freedoms that encourage more diversity in families helpful or harmful to children? Use examples from your reading and personal experience.

3. When the results of a study are only briefly reported, it is sometimes necessary to use your general knowledge to try to interpret the results. This article reports that people in the United States began to marry at a younger age at the beginning of the 20th century; then the average age for marriage began to rise in the mid-1950s. Why do you think the marriage age declined? Why do you think it rose again?

Vocabulary from Context

The vocabulary in the exercise below is taken from "Marriage Taking a Back Seat, Says Census." Use the context provided to decide on meanings for the italicized words. Write a definition, synonym, or description in the space provided.

1. _____
2. _____

When Sally and Tom got married, people thought they were the perfect couple. But things didn't work out. First they tried a *separation*. Living apart made them realize that they should never have gotten married. In May, their marriage ended in *divorce*.

3. _____
4. _____

5. _____

6. _____

When Jesse and Rachel got married, they knew they wanted to live in a traditional *nuclear family*—mother, father, and biological children. Each of them had come from other family *arrangements,* and they had decided that a more traditional arrangement was what they wanted. Rachel had been born *out of wedlock*. Because her parents had never married, she had never met her biological father. Jesse's mother had been *widowed*. His father's early death made Jesse want to have a large family.

7. _____

When Doris and Henry decided to get married, their friends were surprised. Doris and Henry were only 20 years old, and their friends expected that the couple would *delay* marriage at least until they finished college.

8. _____

At the beginning of the 20th century the average age at which people married began to *decline*. There are a number of reasons why people began to get married earlier, many of which are related to industrialization.

9. _____

Sue doesn't see why anyone else should care whether or not she is married. When strangers ask her whether she is married, she tells them that her marital *status* is none of their business.

10. _____

The *proportion* of people who never marry has been increasing. Many people, including gay men and lesbians, no longer feel that they must marry.

Reading Selection 5

Literature

The following selection is adapted from *Silas Marner,* a famous nineteenth-century English novel by George Eliot. Marner is a weaver, a person who makes cloth from cotton or wool on a large machine called a loom. He lives alone and works day and night without thought of rest or friends. He just sits at his loom and weaves cloth for the people of Raveloe. Because he has no family, he spends all of his time thinking about his money, which he collects in a metal pot hidden under his floor. He is lonely and thinks only about his money, but he is not completely without feeling.

As you read this selection, decide what you think of Silas Marner.

—Do you think you would like Silas Marner?

—Do you know anyone who is like him? Can you understand the way he acts?

Read the selection through completely without stopping to look up unfamiliar words. Your teacher may want you to do the Vocabulary from Context exercise on pages 57–59 before you begin.

Excerpt from Silas Marner
George Eliot

1   Year followed year, and still Silas lived alone. The gold coins rose in the metal pot. He watched them and he worked. That was his life. No other thought, no other person had any part in it. The loom curved his back and his arms and legs, so that when he left it, the curves remained. It also gave his eyes a strange look. He was not forty years old, but his face was dry and yellow like an old man's. The children always called him "Old Master Marner."

2   But love was not quite dead in his heart. Every day he had to bring water from a well and for this purpose he bought a small brown pot. Indeed, it was one of the few things for which he had taken money from his metal pot. The pot was his most prized possession. He took pleasure in the touch of its round, smooth surface and firm handle as much as he enjoyed the satisfaction of having the cool, clear water ready for use. It had been his friend for twelve years, always standing in the same spot, always waiting for him to go to the well in the morning. Then one day, as he was returning from the well, he dropped it and it broke into three pieces. He picked up the pieces with a broken heart and stuck them together. Even though the pot would be of no use, he set it in its spot as a memorial for a lost friendship.

3   This is the history of Silas Marner until the fifteenth year after he came to Raveloe. The whole day he spent at his loom, his ears filled with the boring click of his weaving, his eyes bent close down on the threads, his arms and legs moving

Adapted from *Silas Marner,* by George Eliot (New York: Dodd, Mead, and Co., 1948), 25–27.

thoughtlessly in the same motions. But at night came his celebration. He closed and locked the door, shuttered the windows, and took out his gold. Long ago the pile of coins had become too large for the iron pot and he had made two thick leather bags. Out poured the gold and silver pieces! How bright they shined! There was more gold than silver, and he spent the shillings and other small silver coins on his few necessities. His favorites were the gold pounds, but he loved them all. He spread them out in piles and bathed his hands in them; then he counted them and set them up in regular columns, and felt their rounded outline between his thumb and fingers, and thought fondly of the gold that was only half earned in his loom. "These are not all," he thought. "Others are on the way, like children not yet born. Year will follow year and still they will come."

4   But about Christmas of that fifteenth year a great change came over Marner's life, and his history became part of the histories of his neighbors.

Comprehension

Answer the following questions according to your understanding of the passage. Your teacher may want you to work individually, in small groups, or in pairs. True/False items are indicated by a T / F before a statement. Some questions may have more than one correct answer. Others require an opinion. Choose the answer you like best; be prepared to defend your choices.

1. T / F   Silas had a large circle of family and friends.

2. Why was the loom so important in Silas's life? _____

_____

3. How old was Silas at this point in the story? How did he look? _____

_____

4. How long had he lived in Raveloe? _____

5. What does the brown pot tell us about Silas Marner? (Check all that are correct.)

___ a. He spends very little money on his comforts.
___ b. He has no running water in the house.
___ c. He is a skilled potter.
___ d. He appreciates beauty.
___ e. He keeps only tools that are useful.
___ f. He is capable of love.

6. T / F   A shilling is worth more than a pound.

7. Silas compares his coins to children. What does this tell us about him? (Check all that are correct.)

  ___ a. He is lonely.
  ___ b. He has come to love his coins as if they were his family.
  ___ c. He does not need people to be happy.
  ___ d. He is an honest man.

8. What does the author mean in paragraph 3 by "he bathed his hands" in the money? _____

_____

9. a. Draw a picture of a pile of coins.

  b. Now draw a picture of a column of coins.

Discussion

1. This selection is part of a novel. Do you think it occurs at the beginning, middle, or end of the novel? Explain your answer.

2. In paragraph 4, it says that Marner's "history became part of the histories of his neighbors." What do you think this means? What "great change" do you think will happen in Marner's life?

Discussion/Composition

Write a paragraph to begin the next chapter in *Silas Marner*. Use the ideas and the vocabulary from this selection. In your paragraph give some idea about the change that you think will occur in Marner's life.

Vocabulary from Context

Both the ideas and the vocabulary in the exercise below are taken from the excerpt from *Silas Marner*. Use the context provided to decide on meanings for the italicized words. Write a definition, synonym, or description in the space provided.

1. _____

Silas Marner lived by himself and spent all of his time working, caring for nothing but making money. In the evening, after he had collected payment for his cloth, he would sit by candlelight and count the piles of *pounds and shillings* that he earned for his work.

2. _____

3. _____

The *loom* where he worked stood in the corner by the fireplace. Apart from the table and one chair it was the only piece of furniture in his house, and he spent most of the hours of his life seated at it, *weaving* cloth for the women of Raveloe.

4. _____

Marner did not own much—the clothes he wore every day, some pots and pans for cooking, the loom. But he did have one *possession* that was very important to him: the brown pot that he used to carry water from the well.

5. _____

You could say that Marner was a sad and unhappy person, a man without *pleasures,* even simple ones such as walks in the forest, or reading, or listening to music. Unlike most people, he did not do things for enjoyment.

6. _____

There was only one thing that made him happy, and this was collecting and saving money. This one *satisfaction* was the only pleasure he allowed himself, and as the years passed he became more and more focused on this task.

7. _____

He had no use for religion and, if anyone had asked, he would have said that he had no use for anything or anyone. But when his little brown pot broke, he put it back together and placed it on the shelf, like a *memorial* to the twelve years that it had served him. Like the stones in the cemetery that marked the final resting place of the dead, the broken pot reminded him of something he had loved.

8. _____

Most people would consider Marner's life to be *boring;* it never changed from day to day, and nothing happened to bring him happiness or excitement.

9. _____

As he worked at his loom, all that could be heard was the small *click* of the pieces of the machine as they hit against each other. No other sound in the silence: *click, click, click* as he worked throughout the day and into the night.

10. _____

He was, of course, a very good weaver. This was to be expected, since he did nothing else all day long. In his hands the cotton and wool *threads* became, as if by magic, whole pieces of cloth that the women of Raveloe would make into shirts or dresses for their families.

11. _____

Marner observed no holidays. Not Christmas, nor birthdays, nor any other *celebration.* He took no time away from his work for such enjoyment.

12. _____

But he did have one special celebration: the counting of his money. At night, when he was finished working for the day, and just before he went to bed, he would close the house up tight so that no one would see him. He would shut the door and *shutter* the window, and pull his money from its hiding place to count it.

13. _____

He would pour the money out on the table and run his fingers through the gold and silver coins. He would count every pound and shilling, and stack the money into little *columns* that stood like the buildings of a small city in front of him.

14. _____

Marner had no other possessions, no family, no friends, no one to love. But he was as *fond of* his money as any of the villagers were of their children.

3

Nonprose Reading

Campus Map

When you make your first visit to a college or university in North America, you will usually be given a map of the campus. Sometimes the map will also include other useful information. On pages 62–64 you will find information that originally appeared with a map of the University of British Columbia (UBC), located in Vancouver, British Columbia. Founded in 1915, UBC provides instruction, research, and public service. As you can see, the university offers a wide variety of activities, programs, and services. The map itself is at the back of the book.

Answer the following questions about UBC. Your teacher may want you to work individually, in pairs, or in small groups. True/False items are indicated by a T / F before a statement. Some questions may have more than one correct answer. Others require an opinion. Choose the answer you like best; be prepared to defend your choices.

Part 1

Pages 62–64 provide a list of places to go and things to do. Refer to these pages as you answer questions 1–4.

1. Under how many sections is the information listed? _____

2. Under which section would you expect to find the libraries and bookstores listed? _____

3. Under which section would you look to find information about something to eat? _____

4. Circle the places that interest you the most.

Part 2

Notice the letters and numbers to the left of each listing. This refers to the location on the map where each place can be found. For example, under "More Literate," the listing for the UBC library shows it is located in section D3 on the map. Use the map and the listings to answer the following questions.

5. Circle the main library on the map; how far is it from the bookstore? _____

6. Does the University have tennis courts? _____

7. a. What road takes you from the library to the Tennis Bubble? _____

   b. Would you take a bus between the two? _____

   c. If you get hurt playing tennis, where could you get medical attention on campus? _____

   _____

8. After getting help at the University Hospital, you decide to get something to eat. What is the closest place with food? What phone number would you call to get more information?

   _____

9. Can you take a bus from the University Hospital to the Botanical Gardens? _____

10. Find the Old Barn Coffee Shop on the map. Can you drive to it from the main library? _____

11. If you need the telephone number of a campus office, what number would you call? _____

12. a. What number should you call if you want to know the telephone number of an office on

    campus? _____

   b. What would *you* do on Saturday if you needed to know a number? _____

   _____

BETTER PREPARED

D3 **Executive Programmes** (Angus Bldg.)
Seminars and workshops to help executives and
professionals maintain and upgrade management skills.
Courses in marketing, human resources, finance, strategic
planning, personal communications and management.
Catalogue. 822-8400.

A3 **Extra-Sessional Studies**
Winter and Term I summer evenings, Term II summer
day-time courses, plus directed studies abroad. Course fees
are the same as winter session. Calendar. 822-2657.

B1 **Centre for Continuing Education**
Courses in the arts, humanities, sciences, personal and career
development, communications, languages and travel. All
programs are non-credit; most have no prerequisites. Classes
on campus, year-round. Calendar. 222-2181.

UBC Women's Resources Centre
Career and personal counselling services for women and
men. Vocational testing, job-search skills, assertiveness
training and building self-esteem. Year-round. Located at
#1–1144 Robson St., Vancouver. 685-3934

F2 **UBC Access** (Library Processing Centre)
Guided independent study. Degree-credit courses in
agricultural sciences, arts, education, forestry and post-RN
nursing. Information throughout B.C., 8:30 a.m.–4:30 p.m.
Long distance, call collect. 822-6565.

E4 **Distance Education–Faculty of Education**
Continuing education opportunities for practicing B.C.
teachers through: off-campus direct instruction courses;
video study and Knowledge Network courses; summer
institute courses; and special projects. Credit and non-credit.
822-2013.

MORE LITERATE

D3 **UBC Library**
Second-largest library in Canada, 17 branches, 2.9 million books,
journals, newspapers, maps, microforms, government
publications, classical records, taped books for the blind and
more. Open to all. Cards $50 per year, $10 per year for seniors.
822-2077. ♿ Partial

E3 **UBC Bookstore**
Excellent selection of over 70,000 titles, including children's and
general-interest material; UBC souvenirs, stationery, computers
and more. Weekdays 8:30 a.m.to 5:00 p.m.; Wednesday until 8:30
p.m.; Saturday 9:30 a.m.–5:00 p.m. 822-2665. ♿

C4 **University of British Columbia Press** (Old Auditorium)
Second-largest scholarly press in Canada. Published works
include the Atlas of British Columbia, popular Canadian
biography and history, Pacific Rim studies and more. Authors
include UBC faculty, international scholars and lay authors.
Catalogue. 822-5959.

MORE WORLDLY

C4 **International House**
Student centre with services and programs for both international
and Canadian students. Services for international students
include reception, orientation, housing and resource information,
and year-round educational, cultural and social activities.
822-5021.

C4 **Asian Centre**
Special events and programs to increase understanding and
awareness of Asia. The Asian library is Canada's national
repository for Japanese government publications. Facilities may
be rented for public events with an Asian theme. 822-2746. ♿

THOROUGHLY ENTERTAINED

C4 **UBC School of Music**
Memorable performances by students, faculty and special guests.
Series' run September through March, with a major opera
performed in the spring; summer concerts in July and August.
Free admission to most concerts. 822-3113. ♿ Passable

C4 **Frederic Wood Theatre**
Training ground for some of Canada's award-winning theatre
people. Four plays per season in the 400-seat proscenium theatre.
Evening performances during winter and summer sessions.
Subscription package available. 822-3880.

D3 **Fine Arts Gallery** (Main Library)
Mounts exhibitions of contemporary art on a regular basis.
Programs include lecture series, publications and special events.
822-2759. ♿ Passable

MORE RELAXED

J5 **UBC Botanical Garden**
A 70-acre living museum features plants from all the temperate
regions of the world. 822-4208. The Shop in the Garden has a
wide range of books and garden gifts. 822-4529. ♿ Passable

University of British Columbia Campus Map

C5 **Nitobe Memorial Garden**
Considered one of the finest Japanese gardens outside Japan. Near the Museum of Anthropology. 822-6038. Season passes and group rates for all gardens. Free admission Wednesdays.

E4 **Neville Scarfe Children's Garden**
West Coast forest grotto, clover meadow, stream, pond, vegetable and flower gardens which appeal to daycare, pre-school and school groups. Visitors welcome anytime. 822-3767. ♿

MORE AWARE

F4 **M.Y. Williams Geological Museum**
4.5 billion years of mineral and fossil treasures, including the mineral collection and the incredible 80-million-year-old Lambeosaurus dinosaur. Year-round, weekdays, 8:30 a.m.–4:30 p.m. Free. Collector Shop, Wednesdays 1:30–4:30 p.m. 822-5586. ♿

B4 **UBC Museum of Anthropology**
Stunning display of Northwest Coast Indian art, including Bill Reid's massive sculpture "Raven and the First Men;" outstanding 15th- to 19th-century European ceramics collection; award-winning building of soaring glass and concrete, overlooking mountains and sea. Guided tours for groups. Gift shop. Admission charge. Tuesday 11:00 a.m. to 9:00 p.m.; Wednesday to Sunday 11:00 a.m. to 5:00 p.m. Closed Mondays. 822-3825. ♿

GROWN WISER

UBC Research Farm
Self-supporting, 700-hectare dairy, forage and forestry research facility. Weekday tours; salmon rearing and spawning channel and small hatchery; open house in July. Free. Oyster River, Vancouver Island. 923-4219. ♿ Partial

Malcolm Knapp Research Forest
32 kilometres of foot trails over a 5,150-hectare research forest. Deer and other wildlife frequently sighted by visitors. Free. About 60 kilometres east of UBC, north of Haney, along 232nd St. to end of Silver Valley Rd., Maple Ridge. 463-8148. ♿

Alex Fraser Research Forest
This 9,000-hectare forest with eight lakes is a great destination for summer camping. Weekdays 8:00 a.m.to 4:30 p.m.; weekends by appointment. Free. Williams Lake, B.C. 392-2207.

IN BETTER SHAPE

H2 **Thunderbird Winter Sports Centre**
Three ice rinks, a curling rink, two racquetball and four squash courts, a lounge with large sports screen and a private banquet room. Year-round. 822-6121.   ♿ Partial

H2 **Community Sport Services** (Thunderbird Winter Sports Centre)
Year-round programs for the whole family. UBC's summer hockey school draws thousands of young people from around the world. Also gymnastics, fencing, badminton, soccer, cycling, field hockey, golf, sports camp and more. 822-3688.

H2 **UBC Tennis Centre**
Year-round training facility for adults and juniors. Ten outdoor and four indoor courts. Pro shop and full racquet-stringing service. 822-2505. ♿

D2 **UBC Aquatic Centre**
More than 300,000 people a year splash down in UBC's two award-winning, olympic-size pools — one indoor, one outdoor. Weightlifting area downstairs. 822-4521. ♿

For information about and results of UBC athletic events, call 222-BIRD.

READY FOR TOMORROW

F4 **UBC Astronomical Observatory**
Telescopes open for free public viewing most clear Saturdays, year-round, dark to midnight. Always call ahead: 822-6186. Tours, day-time viewing and group observing sessions by appointment: 822-2802.

F4 **UBC Geophysical Observatory**
Every tremble in Vancouver is recorded on the Lower Mainland's most sensitive earthquake network, displayed here at UBC. Find out about *The Big One*, watch gravity change and more. Guided and self-guided tours. Free. 822-2802. ♿

K1 **TRIUMF**
World's largest cyclotron, used to study the properties of subatomic particles and to find practical uses for them. Experiments conducted by 400 to 500 scientists each year from 24 countries. Tours. 222-1047. ♿ Partial

K1 **Dairy Cattle Teaching and Research Centre**
Barn tours bring dairy agriculture to life for school children. For curious adults and agri-professionals, a glimpse of research facilities and technology that are second to none. 822-4593. ♿

MORE SOCIABLE

D4 **UBC Food Services** (Ponderosa)
Many unique locations throughout the campus can accommodate every dining need, from our famous cinnamon buns to gourmet catering. Some locations open for the academic term only. Subway Cafeteria in SUB open year-round. 822-2616. ♿ Subway

A3 **Cecil Green Park**
Book your next reception, meeting or wedding in the rosewood and oak elegance of a bygone era. Panoramic view of English Bay and Howe Sound. Superior catering. 822-6289. ♿

D2 **SUB: Student Union Building**
Hub of student cultural, social and recreational activities and a year-round conference centre with 22 meeting rooms, UN-style board room, movie theatre, bar and pub facilities, plus cafeteria and full catering. 822-2901. Bookings 822-3456/3465. ♿

C1 **UBC Conference Centre** (Gage Residences)
Largest university conference centre in Canada. Available for meetings ranging in size from 10 to several thousand, May through August. Over 500 meeting rooms and accommodation for more than 3,000 people in three residences. 822-5442. ♿

Visitor Accommodation: Inexpensive accommodation for groups and individual visitors year-round. 822-2963.

H2 **The Thunder Deck**
Enjoy your favorite refreshments and food at the south end of the Winter Sports Centre overlooking the playing fields, tennis courts and Georgia Strait. May to September. 822-6121.

MORE IN TOUCH

Campus Telephone Directory Assistance
Monday through Friday, 8:00 a.m. to 4:30 p.m. 822-2211.

C4 **Community Relations Office** (Old Administration Bldg.)
General information on publicly accessible UBC events, programs and facilities. Weekdays, 8:30 a.m. to 4:30 p.m. On campus, look for UBC Reports, a bi-weekly tabloid of campus news and events. 822-3131.

C4 **UBC Speakers Bureau** (Old Administration Bldg.)
You choose the topic, UBC provides the speaker. Faculty and professional staff available to address your club, association, class, conference or business group, September through April. 822-6167.

D2 **Summer Campus Tours** (Student Union Bldg.)
Our gardens, museums and recreational facilities are especially scenic during the summer. Friendly student guides lead free drop-in or pre-booked walking tours. Specialized tours for seniors, children, English-as-a-second-language groups, persons with disabilities and other groups. May through August. 822-3131. ♿

F2 **University Hospital–UBC Site**
One of Vancouver's major hospitals is located right on campus. UBC enjoys a special relationship with this centre as many of UBC's medical faculty teach and practice in this fully equipped hospital. 822-7121. Emergency Service. 822-7222. ♿

C2 **Legal Clinic** (Curtis Bldg.)
Legal services and advice provided by supervised second- and third- year UBC law students for those unable to afford a lawyer. 822-5911. ♿

F1 **Dental Clinic** (MacDonald Bldg.)
Dental services from routine to specialized performed by supervised UBC dentistry students for a reasonable charge. Emergency Clinic runs September to April. 822-2112. ♿ Passable

C2 **School and College Liaison Office** (Brock Hall)
Information about undergraduate programs, admission requirements and student services. Free, guided walking tours of campus for prospective students offered most Friday mornings. 822-4319. ♿

E1 **Office of the Registrar** (General Services Administration Bldg.)
Coordinates admissions, registration and graduation for UBC students. Publications available: Admissions Guide; College-University Transfer Guide; and University Calendar. Year-round hours 8:30 a.m. to 4:00 p.m., weekdays. 822-2844. ♿

J5 **Hortline** (Botanical Garden Centre)
Horticulture advice and information. Monday through Wednesday, 12:00 p.m. to 3:30 p.m., May through August. Tuesday and Wednesday, 12:30 p.m. to 3:30 p.m., September through April. 822-5858.

A3 **Alumni Association** (Cecil Green Park)
Links the university with the community through UBC graduates. To participate in any of the association's activities, call 822-3313. ♿

B3 **Development Office** (Mary Bollert Hall)
Works to advance the goals of the university by increasing private funding. Individuals, corporations, foundations and service organizations contribute to UBC's development through annual, special and major campaign gifts. Monies raised are used for buildings, scholarships, endowed chairs, library acquisitions, equipment and other academic projects. 822-8900. ♿ Passable, phone ahead

B4 **Parking and Security**
Manages all on-campus parking as well as patrolling the campus and providing information and security services. 822-4721. ♿

WELL TRAVELLED

Enjoy the breathtaking scenery of beaches, mountains and the University Endowment Lands on your way to UBC. Bicycle racks throughout the campus and large carparks at each of the four corners. 822-4721.

Five major bus routes will get you here. From downtown: No. 4 UBC via 4th Ave., No.10 UBC via Broadway and 10th Ave. From Burnaby: No.25 King Edward, beginning at Brentwood Mall. From South Vancouver: No.41 via 41st Ave. and Southwest Marine Dr.; No.49, from Metrotown Skytrain Station via 49th Ave.

Word Study

Stems and Affixes

Below is a chart showing some commonly occurring stems and affixes.* Study their meanings, then do the exercises that follow. Notice that the stems all refer to common actions. Your teacher may ask you to give examples of other words you know that are derived from these stems and affixes.

Prefixes

de-	away, down, reverse the action of	depart, deport, dehumanize, defrost, desalt
e-, ex-	out, away	export
in-, im-	in, into, on	import, income
pre-	before	prehistoric, prepare
re-, retro-	again, back	replay, return
tele-	far, distant	telephone
trans-	across	trans-Atlantic

Stems

-audi-, -audit-	hear	audience, auditorium
-dic-, -dict-	say, speak	predict
-fact-, -fect-, -fic-	make, do	factory
-graph-, -gram-	write, writing	telegram
-mit-, -miss-	send	emit, missionary
-pon-, -pos-	put, place	position
-port-	carry	transport
-scrib-, -script-	write	manuscript
-spect-	look	spectator, inspect
-vid-, -vis-	see	vision, visit
-voc-, -vok-	call	vocal, revoke

Suffixes

-able, -ible, -ble (adj.)	capable of, fit for	doable, visible
-er, -or (noun)	one who	reader, spectator
-ion, -tion (noun)	state, condition, the act of	description
-ize (verb)	to make, to become	vocalize

---

*For a list of all stems and affixes taught in *Choice Readings,* see the Appendix.

Exercise 1

1. What does *in retrospect* mean in the following sentence?

   In retrospect, I think I made a good decision to study engineering.

   a. looking back   c. speaking honestly

   b. recently   d. surprisingly

2. Use your knowledge of stems and affixes to explain how the following words were formed.

   television _____

   telegram _____

   transportation _____

3. The prefix *pre-* (meaning before) often combines with simple verbs to create new verbs (for example, *pre-* + *view* becomes *preview*). List three words you know that use *pre-* in this way.

   _____

4. *-Sap-,* or *-sag-* is a root that means wise or knowing. It appears in *homo sapiens,* the scientific name for humans. It also appears in *sage,* a wise person. What do you think a *presage* is? Here is a sentence to give you some context clues:

   The dark skies were a *presage* of the coming storm.

   _____

5. *Migrate* means to move from one place to another. Explain the difference between *immigration* and *emigration.*

   _____

6. *Re-,* with the meaning *again,* is a commonly used prefix. Circle the words below in which *re* is a prefix and means again.

   | repaint | rear | reread | reuse | reborn |
   | ready | reform | religion | remake | real |

Exercise 2

Word analysis can help you to guess the meaning of unfamiliar words. Using context clues and what you know about word parts, write a definition, synonym, or description of the italicized words.

1. _____ Maria plans to study *vocal* music at the university.

2. _____ Because he likes to watch television in the kitchen and the bedroom, Steve bought a *portable* TV.

3. _____ We can't hear that radio station here; it can only *transmit* its signal 30 miles.

4. _____ Cameras outside the front door of the bank *videotape* everyone who goes in or out.

5. _____ It is difficult to travel by train when there are very few *porters* to help travelers get their suitcases on and off the train.

6. _____ The director *dictated* a letter into a tape recorder.

7. _____ The photographer used a *telephoto* lens to take a picture of the movie stars swimming at their private pool.

8. _____ The U.S. *imports* many automobiles from other countries.

9. _____ All the teachers have a key for the room where the *audiovisual* equipment is kept.

10. _____ The king *imposed* heavy new taxes on the people of his country to pay for building his new palace.

11. _____ The students damaged the top of the wooden desk by *inscribing* their names on it with a pocket knife.

12. _____ My television was *manufactured* in Korea.

13. _____ Xian had trouble *visualizing* what it would be like to live in a foreign country for four years.

14. _____ The children ran up to the soccer star, holding out pencils and paper and asking for his *autograph*.

15. _____ Good readers make *predictions* about what a passage will say before they read it.

16. _____ We cannot move into the apartment unless we *prepay* three months' rent.

17. _____ Please *remit* your payment to the address shown at the top of your telephone bill.

18. _____ The *emissions* from automobiles make the air unhealthy.

19. _____ There was a crowd of *spectators* at the scene of the accident.

20. _____ According to the *edict* of the *dictator* on December 1, it is illegal to
21. _____ say anything bad about the government.

22. _____ The king was *deposed* by revolutionaries who wanted to control the
government themselves.

23. _____ Looking through my old family photographs *evokes* wonderful
memories of my childhood.

24. _____ The *deforestation* of the world's rain forests is a serious problem.

25. _____ Before each new car leaves the *factory, inspectors* examine it
26. _____ carefully, looking for any problems in how it looks or how it works.

27. _____ The President's speech was *televised* at 8:00 P.M.

28. _____ My uncle *remarried* a year after his first wife died.

29. _____ Oakland University told Jim to *reapply* for admission next year.

30. _____ The pilot asked the ground workers to *de-ice* the wings of the plane
before he tried to take off in the winter storm.

31. _____ The mountain climbers told us that the *vista* from the top of the
mountain was beautiful.

Word Study

Dictionary Use

Discuss the following questions.

1. When do you use a dictionary?

2. What kind of information does it give you?

3. When reading English, do you use a monolingual (English-English) or bilingual dictionary?

4. What are the advantages and disadvantages of a bilingual dictionary? Of a monolingual dictionary?

5. Are there times when you do not know what a word means and you do not use a dictionary?

The dictionary provides many kinds of information about words. Below is an excerpt from an English language dictionary. Study the entry carefully; notice how much information the dictionary presents under the word *discount.*

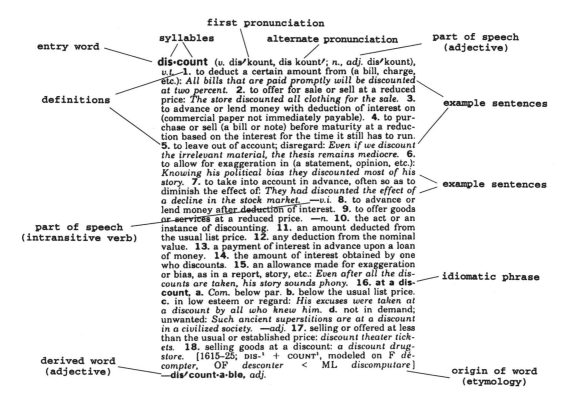

From *Random House Unabridged Dictionary* (New York: Random House, 1967), 563.

Your dictionary may use a different system of abbreviations or different pronunciation symbols. It is important for you to become familiar with your English dictionary and with the symbols it uses.

Look up *discount* in your dictionary and compare the entry to the entry above. Did you notice any differences? If so, what are they?

Exercise 1

Use the sample entry (page 69), the dictionary page (page 71),* and your own dictionary to answer the following questions. Your teacher may want you to work alone, in pairs, or in small groups.

1. When the dictionary gives more than one spelling or pronunciation, which one should you use?

   _____

2. Look at the sample entry.

   a. How many syllables are there in *discount*? _____

   b. What symbol does this dictionary use to separate the syllables? _____

   c. Why would you want to know where a word is divided into syllables? _____

   _____

3. *Discount* can be pronounced with the stress on either syllable when used as a verb.

   a. Which syllable is stressed in the first pronunciation of *discount*? _____

   b. Practice pronouncing *discount* with the stress on the first and on the second syllable.

4. How many different meanings are given for the verb *discount*? _____

   How many definitions are there for the noun *discount*? _____

5. T / F   *Discount* comes from Old German.

6. What are derived words? _____

   What is the derived adjective form of *discount*? _____

7. Where is the pronunciation guide on the dictionary page? _____

   a. What is the key word for the *ou* sound in *discount*? _____

   b. This key is the concise pronunciation key. Where do you think you might find the complete pronunciation key?

   _____

---

*From *Random House Unabridged Dictionary, Second Edition* (New York: Random House, 1993), 478; Concise Pronunciation Key is from page 479.

atia, differing from Serbian chiefly in its use of the Latin alphabet. [1545–55; CROATI(A) + -AN]

croc (krok), *n. Informal.* crocodile. [1880–85; by shortening]

Cro·ce (krô′che), *n.* **Be·ne·det·to** (be′ne det′tô), 1866–1952, Italian statesman, philosopher, and historian.

cro·ce·in (krō′sē in), *n. Chem.* any of several acid azo dyes producing orange or scarlet colors. Also, **cro·ce·ine** (krō′sē in, -ēn′). [< L *croce(us)* saffron-colored (see CROCUS, -EOUS) + -IN[2]]

cro·chet (krō shā′; *Brit.* krō′shā, -shē), *n., v.,* **-cheted** (-shād′; *Brit.* -shād, -shēd), **-chet·ing** (-shā′ing; *Brit.* -shā ing, -shē ing). —*n.* **1.** needlework done with a needle having a small hook at one end for drawing the thread or yarn through intertwined loops. —*v.t., v.i.* **2.** to form by crochet. [1840–50; < F: knitting needle, lit., small hook, dim. of *croche, croc* < ME or Scand. See CROOK[1], -ET] —**cro·chet·er** (krō shā′ər; *Brit.* krō′shā ər, -shē-), *n.*

crochet′ hook′, a needle with a hook at one end, used in crochet. Also called **crochet′ nee′dle.** [1840–50]

cro·chet·work (krō shā′wûrk′; *Brit.* krō′shā wûrk′, -shē-), *n.* needlework done by crocheting. [1855–60; CROCHET + WORK]

cro·cid·o·lite (krō sid′l īt′), *n. Mineral.* a bluish, asbestine variety of riebeckite. Also called **blue asbestos.** [1825–35; < Gk *krokid-* (s. of *krokís*) nap, wool + -o- + -LITE]

crock[1] (krok), *n.* **1.** an earthenware pot, jar, or other container. **2.** a fragment of earthenware; potsherd. [bef. 1000; ME *crokke,* OE *croc(c), crocca* pot; c. ON *krukka* jug]

crock[2] (krok), *n.* **1.** a person or thing that is old, decrepit, or broken-down. **2.** *Slang.* a person who complains about or insists on being treated for an imagined illness. **3.** an old ewe. **4.** an old worn-out horse. —*v.t.* **5.** *Brit. Slang.* to disable or injure. [1300–50; ME *crok* old ewe, perh. akin to CRACK (v.) and obs. *crack* whore; cf. LG *krakke* broken-down horse]

crock[3] (krok), *n.* **1.** *Brit. Dial.* soot; smut. **2.** excess surface dye from imperfectly dyed cloth. —*v.t.* **3.** *Brit. Dial.* to soil with soot. —*v.i.* **4.** (of cloth) to give off excess surface dye when rubbed. [1650–60; orig. uncert.]

crock[4] (krok), *n. Slang.* a lie; exaggeration; nonsense: *The entire story is just a crock.* [orig. unclear, though often taken as a euphemism for *a crock of shit*]

crocked (krokt), *adj. Slang.* drunk. [1925–30, *Amer.;* CROCK[2] + -ED[2]]

crock·er·y (krok′ə rē), *n.* crocks collectively; earthenware. [1710–20; CROCK[1] + -ERY]

crock·et (krok′it), *n. Archit.* a medieval ornament, usually in the form of a leaf that curves up and away from the supporting surface and returns partially upon itself. [1300–50; ME *croket* hook < AF, equiv. to *croc* hook (< Gmc; see CROOK[1]) + *-et* -ET. See CROCHET, CROTCHET]

crockets on coping of a gable

Crock·ett (krok′it), *n.* **David** (*Davy*), 1786–1836, U.S. frontiersman, politician, and folklore hero.

Crock·pot (krok′pot′), *Trademark.* a brand of electric slow cooker.

croc·o·dile (krok′ə dīl′), *n.* **1.** any of several crocodilians of the genus *Crocodylus,* found in sluggish waters and swamps of the tropics. **2.** any reptile of the order Crocodylia; crocodilian. **3.** the tanned skin or hide of these animals, used in the manufacture of luggage and accessories, as belts, shoes, and wallets. **4.** *Chiefly Brit.* a file of people, esp. schoolchildren, out for a walk. **5.** *Archaic.* a person who makes a hypocritical show of sorrow. [1250–1300; < L *crocodīlus* < Gk *krokódeilos* crocodile, orig. a kind of lizard, said to be equiv. to *krók(ē)* pebble + -o- -O- + *drîlos, dreîlos* worm (though attested only in sense "penis"), with *r* lost by dissimilation r. ME *cocodrille* < ML *cocodrilus*] —**croc·o·dil·oid** (krok′ə dil′oid, krok′ə dī′loid), *adj.*

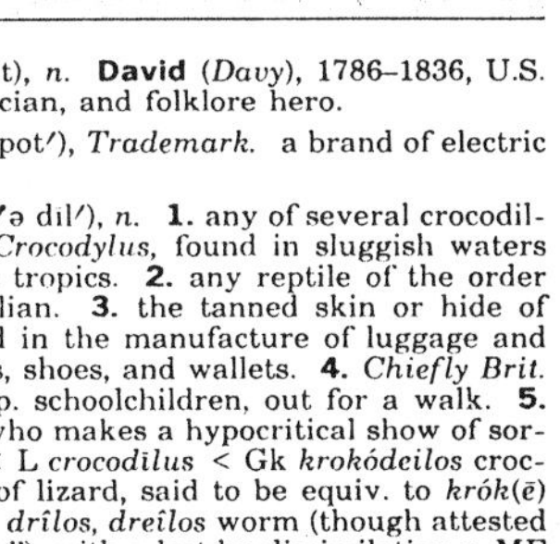

Nile crocodile, *Crocodylus niloticus,* length 20 ft. (6 m)

CONCISE PRONUNCIATION KEY: *act, cāpe, dâre, pärt; set, ēqual; if, īce; ox, ōver, ôrder, oil, bŏŏk, bōōt, out; up, ûrge; child; sing; shoe; thin, that;* zh as in *treasure.* ə = *a* as in *alone, e* as in *system, i* as in *easily, o* as in *gallop, u* as in *circus;* ° as in *fire* (fī°r), *hour* (ou°r). l and n can serve as syllabic consonants, as in *cradle* (krād′l), and *button* (but′n). See the full key inside the front cover.

croc′odile bird′, an African courser, *Pluvianus aegyptius,* that often sits upon basking crocodiles and feeds on their insect parasites. [1865–70]

Croc′odile Riv′er, Limpopo.

croc′odile tears′, 1. a hypocritical show of sorrow; insincere tears. **2.** *Pathol.* spontaneous tearing initiated by tasting or chewing food, occurring as a result of facial paralysis. [1555–65; so called from the the ancient belief that crocodiles shed tears while eating their victims]

croc·o·dil·i·an (krok′ə dil′ē ən), *n.* **1.** any reptile of the order Crocodylia, comprising the true crocodiles and the alligators, caimans, and gavials. —*adj.* **2.** of, like, or pertaining to a crocodile. **3.** hypocritical; insincere. [1625–35; CROCODILE + -IAN]

cro·co·ite (krō′kō īt′, krok′ō-), *n.* a yellow, orange, or red mineral, lead chromate, $PbCrO_4$, formed by replacement. Also called **cro·co·i·site** (krō′kō ə zīt′, krok′ō-). [1835–45; < Gk *krokó(eis)* saffron-colored + -ITE[1]; see CROCUS]

cro·cus (krō′kəs), *n., pl.* **-cus·es. 1.** any of the small, bulbous plants of the genus *Crocus,* of the iris family, cultivated for their showy, solitary flowers, which are among the first to bloom in the spring. **2.** the flower or bulb of the crocus. **3.** a deep yellow; orangish yellow; saffron. **4.** Also called **cro′cus mar′tis** (mär′tis). a polishing powder consisting of iron oxide. [1350–1400; ME < L < Gk *krókos* saffron, crocus < Sem; cf. Ar *kurkum* saffron] —**cro′cused,** *adj.*

cro′cus sack′, *Southern U.S.* (*chiefly South Atlantic States*). a burlap bag. Also called **cro′cus bag′, croker sack.** [1780–90; orig. uncert.]
—**Regional Variation.** See **gunnysack.**

Croe·sus (krē′səs), *n., pl.* **-sus·es, -si** (-sī) for 2. **1.** died 546 B.C., king of Lydia 560–546: noted for his great wealth. **2.** a very rich man.

croft[1] (krôft, kroft), *n. Brit.* **1.** a small farm, esp. one worked by a tenant. **2.** a small plot of ground adjacent to a house and used as a kitchen garden, to pasture one or two cows, etc.; a garden large enough to feed a family or have commercial value. [bef. 1000; ME, OE: small field]

croft[2] (krôft, kroft), *n.* a small, portable filing cabinet of table height, having drop leaves for use as a table. [named after the Rev. Sir Herbert *Croft* (1757–1816), lexicologist, its inventor]

croft·er (krôf′tər, krof′-), *n. Brit.* a person who rents and works a small farm, esp. in Scotland or northern England. [1250–1300; ME; see CROFT[1], -ER[1]]

Crohn's′ disease′ (krōnz), *Pathol.* a chronic inflammatory bowel disease that causes scarring and thickening of the intestinal walls and frequently leads to obstruction. Also called **regional ileitis, regional enteritis.** [named after Burrill Bernard *Crohn* (1884–1983), U.S. physician, one of the authors of a description of the disease published in 1932]

croi·sette (krô set′, kro-), *n.* crossette.

crois·sant (*Fr.* krwä säɴ′; *Eng.* krə sänt′), *n., pl.* **-sants** (*Fr.* -säɴ′; *Eng.* -sänts′). a rich, buttery, crescent-shaped roll of leavened dough or puff paste. [1895–1900; < F: lit., CRESCENT]

Croix de Guerre (krwäd° ger′), a French military award for heroism in battle. [1910–15; < F: lit., cross of war]

cro′ker sack′ (krō′kər). *Southern U.S.* (*chiefly Gulf States*). a crocus sack. Also called **cro′ker bag′.** [1875–80; *croker,* alter. of CROCUS]
—**Regional Variation.** See **gunnysack.**

Cro-Mag·non (krō mag′nən, -non, -man′yən), *n.* **1.** an Upper Paleolithic population of humans, regarded as the prototype of modern *Homo sapiens* in Europe. Skeletal remains found in an Aurignacian cave in southern France indicate that the Cro-Magnon had long heads, broad faces, and sunken eyes, and reached a height of approximately 5 ft. 9 in. (175 cm). See illus. under **hominid. 2.** a member of the Cro-Magnon population. [1865–70; named after the cave (near Périgueux, France) where the first remains were found]

Cro·mer (krō′mər), *n.* **1st Earl of.** See **Baring, Evelyn.**

crom·lech (krom′lek), *n. Archaeol.* (no longer in technical use) a megalithic chamber tomb. Cf. **chamber tomb, dolmen, passage grave.** [1595–1605; < Welsh, equiv. to *crom* bent, curved, crooked (fem. of *crwm*) + *lech,* comb. form of *llech* flat stone]

cro′mo·lyn so′dium (krō′mə lin), *Pharm.* a substance, $C_{23}H_{14}Na_2O_{11}$, used as a preventive inhalant for bronchial asthma and hay fever. [1970–75; contr. and rearrangement of the chemical name]

cro·morne (krō môrn′, krə-), *n.* crumhorn. [1685–95; < F, alter. of G *Krumhorn;* see CRUMHORN]

Cromp·ton (kromp′tən), *n.* **Samuel,** 1753–1827, English inventor of the spinning mule.

Crom·well (krom′wəl, -wel; *for 1–3 also* krum′-), *n.* **1. Oliver,** 1599–1658, English general, Puritan statesman, and Lord Protector of England, Scotland, and Ireland 1653–58. **2.** his son, **Richard,** 1626–1712, English soldier, politician, Lord Protector of England 1658–59. **3. Thomas, Earl of Essex,** 1485?–1540, English statesman. **4.** a town in central Connecticut. 10,265.

Crom′well Cur′rent. See **Equatorial Countercurrent.** [after Townsend *Cromwell* (1922–58), U.S. oceanographer]

Crom·wel·li·an (krom wel′ē ən, krum-), *adj.* **1.** of, pertaining to, or characteristic of the politics, practices, etc., of Oliver Cromwell or of the Commonwealth and Protectorate. **2.** noting or pertaining to a style of English furnishings of the middle 17th century, characterized by austerity, the use of oak and leather, and simple, decorative moldings. [1715–25; CROMWELL + -IAN]

Cromwel′lian chair′, *Eng. Furniture.* an upright oaken chair, often with arms, having all pieces turned and a seat and back panel of leather or cloth attached with brass-headed nails. [1900–05]

crone (krōn), *n.* a withered, witchlike old woman. [1350–1400; ME < MD *croonie* old ewe < ONF *caronie* CARRION] —**cron′ish,** *adj.*

Cro·nin (krō′nin), *n.* **A(rchibald) J(oseph),** 1896–1981, Scottish novelist and physician in the U.S.

Cron·jé (*Du.* krôn′yā), *n.* **Piet Ar·nol·dus** (*Du.* pēt är-nôl′dŏŏs), 1835?–1911, Boer general.

cronk (krongk, krôngk), *adj. Australian Slang.* sick or feeble. [1875–80; < Yiddish or G *krank,* MHG *kranc* weak]

Cro·nus (krō′nəs), *n. Class. Myth.* a Titan, son of Uranus and Gaea, who was dethroned by his son Zeus. Cf. **Saturn.**

cro·ny (krō′nē), *n., pl.* **-nies.** a close friend or companion; chum. [1655–65; alleged to be university slang; perh. < Gk *chrónios* for a long time, long-continued, deriv. of *chrónos* time; cf. CHRONO-]
—**Syn.** pal, buddy.

cro·ny·ism (krō′nē iz′əm), *n.* the practice of favoring one's close friends, esp. in political appointments. [1830–40; CRONY + -ISM]

Cro·nyn (krō′nin), *n.* **Hume,** born 1911, Canadian actor in the U.S.

crook[1] (krŏŏk), *n.* **1.** a bent or curved implement, piece, appendage, etc.; hook. **2.** the hooked part of anything. **3.** an instrument or implement having a bent or curved part, as a shepherd's staff hooked at one end or the crosier of a bishop or abbot. **4.** a dishonest person, esp. a sharper, swindler, or thief. **5.** a bend, turn, or curve: *a crook in the road.* **6.** the act of crooking or bending. **7.** a pothook. **8.** Also called **shank.** a device on some musical wind instruments for changing the pitch, consisting of a piece of tubing inserted into the main tube. —*v.t.* **9.** to bend; curve; make a crook in. **10.** *Slang.* to steal, cheat, or swindle: *She crooked a ring from that shop.* —*v.i.* **11.** to bend; curve. [1125–75; ME *crok(e)* < ON *krāka* hook]

crook[2] (krŏŏk), *adj. Australian.* **1.** sick or feeble. **2.** ill-humored; angry. **3.** out of order; functioning improperly. **4.** unsatisfactory; disappointing. [1875–80; perh. alter. of CRONK]

crook·back (krŏŏk′bak′), *n.* a hunchback. [1400–50; late ME. See CROOK[1], BACK[1]] —**crook′backed′,** *adj.*

crook·ed (krŏŏk′id *for 1-4, 6;* krŏŏkt *for 5*), *adj.* **1.** not straight; bending; curved: *a crooked path.* **2.** askew; awry: *The picture on the wall seems to be crooked.* **3.** deformed: *a man with a crooked back.* **4.** not straightforward; dishonest. **5.** bent and often raised or moved to one side, as a finger or neck. **6.** (of a coin) polygonal: *a crooked sixpence.* [1200–50; ME *croked;* see CROOK[1], -ED[2]] —**crook′ed·ly,** *adv.* —**crook′ed·ness,** *n.*
—**Syn. 1.** winding, devious, sinuous, flexuous, tortuous, spiral, twisted. **3.** misshapen. **4.** unscrupulous, knavish, tricky, fraudulent.

Crookes (krŏŏks), *n.* **Sir William,** 1832–1919, English chemist and physicist: discovered the element thallium and the cathode ray.

Crookes′ dark′ space′, *Physics.* the dark space between the cathode glow and the negative glow in a vacuum tube, occurring when the pressure is low. Also called **Crookes′ space′.** [1890–95; after Sir W. CROOKES]

crookes·ite (krŏŏk′sīt), *n.* a rare mineral, selenide of copper, thallium, and silver, $(Cu, Tl, Ag)_2Se$, occurring in steel-gray, compact masses. [1865–70; after Sir W. CROOKES; see -ITE[1]]

Crookes′ radiom′eter, *Optics.* radiometer (def. 1). [1880–85; after Sir W. CROOKES]

Crookes′ tube′, *Electronics.* a form of cathode-ray tube. [1880–85; after Sir W. CROOKES]

crook·neck (krŏŏk′nek′), *n.* **1.** any of several varieties of squash having a long, recurved neck. **2.** any plant bearing such fruit. [1750–60, *Amer.;* CROOK[1] + NECK]

crook′ raft′er. See **knee rafter.**

croon (krōōn), *v.i.* **1.** to sing or hum in a soft, soothing voice: *to croon to a baby.* **2.** to sing in an evenly modulated, slightly exaggerated manner: *Popular singers began crooning in the 1930's.* **3.** to utter a low murmuring sound. **4.** *Scot. and North Eng.* **a.** to bellow; low. **b.** to lament; mourn. —*v.t.* **5.** to sing (a song) in a crooning manner. **6.** to lull by singing or humming to in a soft, soothing voice: *to croon a child to sleep.* —*n.* **7.** the act or sound of crooning. [1350–1400; ME *cronen* < MD: to lament] —**croon′er,** *n.* —**croon′ing·ly,** *adv.*

crop (krop), *n., v.,* **cropped** or (*Archaic*) **cropt; cropping.** —*n.* **1.** the cultivated produce of the ground, while growing or when gathered: *the wheat crop.* **2.** the yield of such produce for a particular season. **3.** the yield of some other product in a season: *the crop of diamonds.* **4.** a supply produced. **5.** a collection or group of persons or things appearing or occurring together: *this year's crop of students.* **6.** the stock or handle of a whip. **7.** Also called **riding crop.** a short riding whip consisting of a stock without a lash. **8.** Also called **craw,** *Zool.* **a.** a pouch in the esophagus of many birds, in which food is held for later digestion or for regurgitation to nestlings. **b.** a chamber or pouch in the foregut of arthropods and annelids for holding and partly crushing food. **9.** the act of cropping. **10.** a mark produced by clipping the ears, as of cattle. **11.** a close-cropped hair style. **12.** a head of hair so cut. **13.** an entire tanned hide of an animal. **14.** *Mining.* an outcrop of a vein or seam. —*v.t.* **15.** to cut off or remove the head or top of (a plant, grass, etc.). **16.** to cut off the ends or a part of: *to crop the ears of a dog.* **17.** to cut short. **18.** to clip the ears, hair, etc., of. **19.** *Photog.* to cut off or mask the unwanted parts of (a print or negative). **20.** to cause to bear a crop or crops. **21.** to graze off (the tops of plants, grass, etc.): *The sheep cropped the lawn.* —*v.i.* **22.** to bear or yield a crop or crops. **23.** to feed by cropping or

8. Now look for the pronunciation guide in your dictionary. Where is it located? _____

   Is it as easy to use as this one? _____

9. Dictionaries sometimes contain usage labels such as "regional," "informal," and "slang." Why are these labels useful?

   _____

10. Read the definitions of *discount.* Below are several sentences in which *discount* is used. In the space provided, write the number of the definition for that usage.

    ___ a. Because it is the end of the ski season, you can buy most ski equipment at a *discount.*

    ___ b. Most stores know that if they do not *discount* all of the ski equipment, they will not be able to sell it.

    ___ c. Because he never told me the truth before, I *discounted* his story about the accident.

Exercise 2

In this exercise you will scan the dictionary page (p. 71) to find the answers to specific questions. These questions will introduce you to several kinds of information to be found in a dictionary. Read each question, find the answer as quickly as possible, then write it in the space provided. Your teacher may want you to work individually and then discuss your answers with classmates in pairs or small groups.

1. The two words at the top of the page are called guide words. They are the first and last words defined on the page; only words that occur alphabetically between *croc* and *crop* will be found on this page.

   a. T / F   You will find *crook* on this page.

   b. T / F   You will find *critical* on this page.

   c. T / F   You will find *cropper* on this page.

2. How many syllables are there in *crocidolite?* _____ What are they? _____

3. Which syllable is stressed in *cronyism?* _____

4. Look at the entry for *crocus.*

   a. T / F   A *crocus* is a type of small crocodile.

   b. What is the key word that tells you how to pronounce the *o* in *crocus?* _____

   c. What is the key word that tells you how to pronounce the *u* in *crocus?* _____

   d. Pronounce *crocus* aloud.

5. How do the British pronounce *crochet?* _____

6. Write the correct form of the italicized words in the sentences below.

   a. Yesterday I _____ the twin's hair. Tomorrow I'll *crop* yours.

   b. "Those pictures look *crooked* to me." "You're right, they are hung _____."

   c. The mayor has been criticized for his *cronyism*. It seems that no matter what the job is, he always finds one of his friends to take it. This office, for example, is full of his _____.

7. T / F   Samuel Crompton is an American inventor who lives in Boston.

8. Write the languages from which the following words came:

   a. *croissant* _____

   b. *cronk* _____

   c. *crochet* _____

   d. *crony* _____

9. What word must you look up to find the meaning of *riding crop?* _____

10. a. How many synonyms are listed for *crooked?* _____

    b. How many antonyms? _____

Sentence Study

Comprehension

Read the following sentences carefully.* The questions that follow are designed to test your comprehension of complex grammatical structures. Select the best answer.

1. Despite all the money it spent on advertising the new car, the company isn't having much success selling it.
   What do we know about the company?
   — a. It spent a lot of money on advertising.
   — b. Its advertisements have had much success.
   — c. It has had a lot of success selling its new car.
   — d. It has had a lot of success selling its advertising.

2. So many of the test questions are so difficult that no student should feel ashamed of not knowing the answers.
   What does the writer say about students?
   — a. They should feel ashamed if they can't answer the difficult test questions.
   — b. They should know the answers to many of the difficult questions on this test.
   — c. No students will do well on the test.
   — d. They should not feel ashamed if they miss some questions on this test.

3. The project would have failed even with Theresa's help.
   What do we know about the project?
   — a. It failed because Theresa didn't help.
   — b. Theresa did not help, and it failed.
   — c. Theresa helped, so it didn't fail.
   — d. It will fail without Theresa's help.

4. It is surprising that doctors don't know whether many drugs found effective for men will also help women.
   What does the writer think is surprising?
   — a. That many drugs that help men also help women
   — b. That many drugs that help men don't help women
   — c. That doctors don't know whether some drugs help men
   — d. That doctors don't know how some drugs affect women

5. As a doctor at Harper Hospital, Susan Wilson is a part of a team of cancer experts advising other doctors about their patients and teaching medical students.
   Who is Susan Wilson?
   — a. A doctor who is an expert on cancer
   — b. A cancer patient whose doctor is at Harper Hospital
   — c. A medical student working with cancer experts
   — d. An adviser who works part time at Harper Hospital

---

*For an introduction to sentence study, see Unit 1.

6. If it goes the way the boss hopes it will, John will start his new job no later than June 1, when Ellen leaves.
   The boss wants . . .
   __ a. Ellen to leave after June 1.
   __ b. John to start by June 1.
   __ c. to go away before June 1.
   __ d. to start his new job by June 1.

7. Aside from her work with the movie director D. W. Griffith, Lillian Gish's acting in *The Wind* is her best.
   Gish's best performance was . . .
   __ a. in *The Wind*.
   __ b. aside from her work.
   __ c. with D. W. Griffith.
   __ d. not as good as D. W. Griffith's.

8. Sam, the worst player on the team, passed the ball to Pete who, as the best player, had a better chance to score.
   What happened in the game?
   __ a. Sam got a better chance to score.
   __ b. Pete threw the ball to the best player.
   __ c. Sam threw the ball to the best player.
   __ d. Pete threw the ball to the worst player.

9. For J. D. Woods, the long-term worry is not that there will be too many airplanes at the small airport, but too few.
   J. D. Woods worries that . . .
   __ a. there will not be enough airplanes.
   __ b. there will be too many airplanes.
   __ c. the airport will be too small.
   __ d. it will take a long time to land at the airport.

10. With the exception of AT&T, each of the many long-distance telephone companies in this country is a relative youngster.
    What does the author say about AT&T?
    __ a. It is a relatively young company.
    __ b. It is older than the other long-distance companies.
    __ c. It no longer operates in this country.
    __ d. It has a long relationship with other companies.

11. The thing that surprised me is not the number of attacks by lions on humans in the Vancouver area but how really few there have been.
    What does the author say about the attacks?
    __ a. He expected there would be more.
    __ b. He expected there would be fewer.
    __ c. He didn't expect there would be any.
    __ d. He isn't sure how many there were.

12. Although the dance looks easy to do, it isn't; just ask John!
    What do we know about the dance?
    ___ a. It isn't easy to do.
    ___ b. It is easy to do.
    ___ c. John knows how to do it.
    ___ d. John asked how to do it.

Paragraph Reading

Restatement and Inference

The paragraphs in this exercise are taken from the book *Helen Keller: Crusader for the Blind and Deaf.* So that you will know something about Helen before you begin reading, here is a summary of the book that appears on its cover:

> Helen Keller was born in 1880. From the age of a year and a half, she could not hear. She could not see, and she did not speak. She lived in a dark and lonely world—until Annie Sullivan came to teach her. Annie spelled letters and words in Helen's hand and made Helen realize she could "talk" to people. Helen threw herself into her studies. She decided to teach others about the special training deaf and blind children need. Helen traveled all over the world and raised money to start schools for deaf and blind children. Her courage and desire to help others overcome their problems earned her the respect and love of people all over the world.

Before You Begin   1. Have you heard of Helen Keller before?
2. What do you know about her based on your previous knowledge and information from the summary paragraph you just read?

Each paragraph below about Helen Keller's life is followed by four statements. The statements are of four types:

1. Some of the statements are restatements of ideas in the original paragraph. They give the same information in a different way.

2. Some of the statements are inferences (conclusions) that can be drawn from the information given in the paragraph.

3. Some of the statements are not true based on the information given.

4. Some of the statements cannot be proved true or false based on the information given.

Put a check (✓) next to all restatements and inferences (types 1 and 2). Note: do not check a statement that is true of itself but cannot be inferred from the paragraph. There is not always a single correct set of answers. Be prepared to discuss your choices with your classmates.

Example

One morning Helen woke early. She could not see the daylight, but she smelled bacon and eggs cooking. She knew it was time to get up. Her mother hurried Helen through breakfast and dressed her carefully. Helen did not know what was happening. Still she felt excited. When her father lifted her into the carriage she wondered where they were going.

___ a. Helen could not see, but there was nothing wrong with her sense of smell.
___ b. Helen had bacon and eggs every day for breakfast.
___ c. There was something unusual about this morning.
___ d. Helen was not very smart.

Explanation

  ✓ a. This is a restatement of the second sentence. Helen could not see the daylight, but she could smell the bacon (there was nothing wrong with her sense of smell).

  ___ b. This cannot be inferred from the paragraph. Helen obviously recognizes bacon as something she eats for breakfast, but we do not know that she eats it every day.

  ✓ c. This can be inferred from the paragraph. Helen did not know what was happening. Also, the fact that Helen's mother wants her to finish breakfast quickly but dresses her carefully suggests that something important or special is about to happen. Helen feels excited, and she and her father are going someplace.

  ___ d. This is false. Although she is blind, Helen is able to use the other information around her (smells and feelings) to understand the world.

Paragraph 1

     Whatever they did, Annie spelled letters into Helen's hand. When they petted the cat, Annie spelled "C-A-T." Helen quickly learned to copy the movements of Annie's fingers. "Helen is like a clever little monkey," Annie wrote. "She has learned the signs to ask for what she wants but she has no idea that she is spelling words."

  ___ a. Finger spelling is only for saying what you want.

  ___ b. Helen didn't know that the sign for cat spelled the word for cat.

  ___ c. Monkeys can copy actions without understanding their real meaning.

  ___ d. People who make signs don't understand what they are doing.

But Helen needed to learn more. One morning while cold water poured over Helen's hand, Annie spelled the word W-A-T-E-R in the other hand. Suddenly Helen understood that this was a word and pointed to things around her, wanting to know how they were all spelled.

Paragraph 2

     Helen and Annie were both excited. They ran to the house to find Mrs. Keller. When Helen threw herself in her mother's arms, Anne spelled "M-O-T-H-E-R" into her hand. When Helen nodded to show that she understood there were tears of happiness in Mrs. Keller's eyes.

  ___ a. Helen understood that the finger spelling of M-O-T-H-E-R was the word for the person, mother.

  ___ b. Helen's mother was happy because Helen hugged her.

  ___ c. Helen's mother was a very emotional person.

  ___ d. Helen's mother understood that Helen would now be able to learn.

Paragraphs adapted from *Helen Keller: Crusader for the Blind and Deaf,* by Stewart and Polly Anne Graff (New York: Dell Young Yearling/Bantam Doubleday Dell, 1965), 7, 13–14, 17, 28, 30, 36, 39–40, 41, 46–48, 56–57.

Now Helen had discovered language. But there were other things that Helen needed to learn as well. Helen had become used to doing things her own way. For example, she ate with her fingers and she refused to do anything that was difficult or new.

Paragraph 3   At the dinner table, Annie made Helen sit in her own chair and eat from her own plate. Helen was furious. When Annie gave her a spoon, Helen threw it on the floor and kicked the table. They spent a whole afternoon fighting while Annie insisted that Helen fold her napkin before leaving the table.

___ a. Annie believed in always being neat and clean.
___ b. Annie did not love Helen.
___ c. Helen did not usually sit at the table and eat from her plate.
___ d. Folding the napkin represented something important to Annie.

Annie became Helen's special teacher and lifelong friend. When Helen was eight years old, it was time for Helen (and Annie) to go to school. Helen learned to read braille, the system of raised dots that blind people read with their fingers.

Paragraph 4   In Helen's second year at Perkins school she heard of a little blind-deaf boy named Tommy Stringer. He had no family and no one to teach him.

___ a. Helen spent only two years at the Perkins school.
___ b. Tommy Stringer probably did not know how to read braille.
___ c. Helen could hear Tommy Stringer speak.
___ d. Tommy Stringer was at Perkins school when Helen heard of him.

Helen helped raise money for Tommy Stringer to come to Perkins school. All the while, Helen continued to study. When she was ten years old, she was taught to speak by Sarah Fuller, a teacher at the Horace Mann School for the Deaf in Boston.

Paragraph 5   First Helen would put her hand on Miss Fuller's face when she talked. Then Helen would try to copy the way Miss Fuller's lips and tongue moved. It was hard work. Over and over Helen tried to make sounds, but she could not hear the sounds she made. She did not know when her voice sounded strange to others. After each lesson, Helen practiced with Annie. At last, one day, she could speak a whole sentence that Annie could understand.

___ a. Helen could not feel Miss Fuller's face very well.
___ b. Helen's voice sometimes sounded strange to others.
___ c. Annie could always understand what Helen was trying to say.
___ d. It was hard work learning to talk.

When she was in her teens, Helen decided that she wanted to attend college. To prepare, she studied hard at school and had private teachers. She learned to use a braille typewriter to keep her study notes and a regular typewriter too for school papers. Helen entered Radcliffe College in 1900. Her special teacher, Annie Sullivan, went with her.

Paragraph 6   When college classes began, Annie sat next to Helen. She spelled what the teachers said into Helen's hand. Annie looked up words in the dictionary for Helen. She read Helen books that were not printed in braille.

___ a. Annie read books aloud to Helen.
___ b. Annie finger spelled dictionary definitions for Helen.
___ c. Annie finger spelled some books for Helen.
___ d. Annie did Helen's homework for her.

After graduating from college, Helen had to decide whether to become a teacher herself or to work for blind and deaf children in other ways.

Paragraph 7   Helen wanted to pass on the gift of teaching that Annie had given her. But at last she decided she could help best by writing and lecturing. "I can tell more people about the special training that deaf and blind children need," she told Annie. "I can teach them what you taught me—that children must not be treated differently because they are blind and deaf. They can learn to work and be happy."

___ a. Helen could teach by writing and lecturing.
___ b. Deaf and blind children are not different from other children.
___ c. Helen could not speak in public because her voice was too strange.
___ d. Helen gave special training to blind and deaf children.

Helen worked to try to get more books printed in braille because she knew that many blind people did not have enough to read. She went to Washington, D.C. to ask the U.S. government for help.

Paragraph 8

In 1913 there was important news. The National Library for the Blind was started. Helen and Annie went to Washington for the opening. President Taft of the United States was present at the opening of the new library.

__ a. President Taft began the library.
__ b. The library was in Washington, D.C.
__ c. The library had braille books.
__ d. The library mostly had books about blind people.

During one period, when Helen and Annie needed money, Helen acted in a movie about her life, and she and Annie appeared in theaters. Finally, they earned the money they needed.

Paragraph 9

Now Helen could work again for others. She was happy with news from Washington. Congress had voted money for many more books for the blind. Some could be played on records. They were called "talking books."

__ a. Talking books were a way for the deaf and blind to hear.
__ b. The library for the blind was only for blind people who could hear.
__ c. The library for the blind had only a few books before.
__ d. The library for the blind was supported by the U.S. government.

But Helen wanted to help people all over the world. She had already helped children in Japan, and the Emperor himself had thanked her. Now she hoped to help more children worldwide.

Paragraph 10

In May 1959, the Helen Keller World Crusade was begun at the United Nations building in New York City. It would help blind and deaf children all over the world. Helen was very proud. She had lived through two terrible world wars. She had always hoped for world peace. Now it made her happy to know that people of different countries and races would work together to help children.

__ a. Helen Keller did not believe in war.
__ b. The Helen Keller World Crusade helped all blind and deaf children who needed help.
__ c. Before the Helen Keller World Crusade, some blind and deaf children had no help.
__ d. Before the Helen Keller World Crusade, people throughout the world had not worked together to help children.

Discourse Focus

Careful Reading / Drawing Inferences

Readers all around the world love mystery stories. Have you heard of Sherlock Holmes? Have you read some of the cases of Agatha Christie's famous detectives Miss Marple and Hercule Poirot? Do you have a favorite character in mysteries written in your native language?

One reason mysteries are so popular is that reading a mystery story is a kind of game with questions. Readers try to find out why something happened or who did something. In one type of mystery story, a famous detective is called to try to answer questions that no one else has been able to answer. Readers watch the detective study the problem. They learn all that the detective learns. The game for readers is to understand what happened before the detective explains it.

The stories that follow are mysteries solved by a police detective named Dr. Haledjian. He is known for solving the most difficult cases. As you read each story, see if you are as good a detective as Dr. Haledjian. Read each mystery carefully, and then answer the question that follows it. Your teacher may want you to work with your classmates to answer the question. Be prepared to defend your answers with details from the story. (If you have trouble solving a mystery, you'll find additional clues on pages 85–86.)

Mystery 1: The Case of the Big Deal

Dr. Haledjian had just ordered a drink at the bar in the Las Vegas hotel when a young stranger with sun-bleached golden hair and suntanned cheeks sat down next to him.

After asking for a drink, the sunburned young man looked towards Dr. Haledjian. "I'm Clive Vance," he said pleasantly. "It's sure great to be back in civilization."

The famous detective introduced himself. "You've been out in the desert for a long time, have you?"

"Got back yesterday," said Vance. "Washed the dust out of my ears, and had a barber shave off seven months of beard and cut my hair. Then I bought all new clothes. I didn't even have to pay for them yet. All I had to do was to show the owner of the clothes store this piece of paper," he said as he showed Haledjian a report that showed he had found gold. "I sure am ready to celebrate."

"You found gold in the desert?"

"Right you are." Vance rubbed his suntanned chin thoughtfully. He lowered his voice to a whisper:

"Listen," he said. "If I can find someone to pay to get the gold out of the ground, I'll make enough to buy ten hotels like this one.

"Of course," he added, "I'm not trying to interest *you* Doctor. But if you know somebody who'd like to make a million dollars or two, let me know. I'm staying in room 210. I can't talk about all the details here, you understand."

Mysteries are adapted from *Two-Minute Mysteries,* by Donald J. Sobol (New York: Scholastic Book Services, 1967): "The Big Deal," 13–14; "The Case of the Blackmailer," 17–18; "The Case of the Bogus Robbery," 19–20; "The Case of the Buried Treasure," 27–28; "The Case of the Dentist's Patient," 49–50.

"I understand," said Haledjian, "that you should tell a better story if you want some fool to give you money."

How did Dr. Haledjian know that Vance was lying?

Mystery 2: The Case of the Lying Gardener

"Dr. Haledjian, I have had some problems since my father died and left me all his money," said Thomas Hunt. "Do you remember Martin, the man who took care of my father's gardens for many years?"

"A smiling, overly polite fellow, right?" said Haledjian as he poured his young friend a drink.

"That's the man. I told him his job ended the day my father died. Well, three days ago he came to my office, smiling as always, and demanded that I pay him $100,000.

"He claimed to have been taking care of the trees outside my father's room when Dad prepared another will, leaving all of his money to his brother in New Zealand."

"You believed him?"

"I admit the news surprised me. Sometime during the last week in November, Dad and I had argued about my plans to marry Elizabeth. Dad did not want us to marry, so it seemed possible that he had decided to change his will and leave all his money to his brother instead of to me.

"Martin said he had my father's second will and offered to sell it to me and keep it a secret for one hundred thousand dollars. He told me that the second will would be considered legal because it was dated November 31, the day after the will that left my father's money to me.

"I refused to be blackmailed. He tried to bargain, asking $50,000, and then $25,000."

"You paid nothing, I hope?" asked Haledjian.

"Nothing at all. I told him to get out of my house."

"Quite right," approved Haledjian. "The story is clearly not true!"

What was Martin's mistake?

Mystery 3: The Case of the Fake Robbery

Mrs. Sidney was so rich that she could do almost anything she wanted, but she could not do what she wanted most. Although she had tried many times, she never had been able to fool the great detective, Dr. Haledjian.

Haledjian knew she was trying once more when at two o'clock in the morning he got a call from Mrs. Sidney who cried, "My jewels have been stolen."

Entering Mrs. Sidney's bedroom, the famous detective closed the door and quickly looked around the room.

The window was open. Across the room, to the left of the bed, stood a table with a book and two lighted candles. The candles had burned down to three inches and had dripped down the side facing the windows.

A bell lay on the thick green carpet. The top drawer of the bedside table was open.

"What happened?" asked Haledjian.

"I was reading in bed by candlelight when the wind blew the window open," said Mrs. Sidney. "I could feel a cool breeze, so I rang the bell to call James, the butler, to come shut it.

"Before he arrived, a man with a gun entered and forced me to tell him where I kept my jewels. As he put them in his pocket, James entered. The thief tied both of us up with pairs of my stockings.

"As he left, I asked him to close the window because the wind was so cold. He just laughed and left it open.

"It took James 20 minutes to free himself and untie me. I will have a terrible cold in the morning!" said Mrs. Sidney.

"Congratulations," said Haledjian, "on a clever, well-planned crime; and you have been fair to give me the clue that proves the crime never happened."

How did Haledjian know that there had been no robbery?

Mystery 4: The Case of the Buried Treasure

"From the look on your face, I would guess you are about to get rich quick," said Dr. Haledjian.

"Clever of you to notice," said Bertie Tilford, a young man who was too lazy to work. "If I had just $10,000, I could make a million! Do you have $10,000 to invest?"

"What's your trick this time?" demanded Haledjian. "Gold coins at the bottom of the ocean? Treasure, gold and silver buried under the sands of some desert island?"

Bertie opened a bag and pulled out a shining silver candlestick. "Pure silver," he sang. "Look at what's written on the bottom."

Haledjian turned the candlestick over and read the name *Lady North*. "Wasn't that the ship that sank in 1956?"

"The *Lady North* sank, but not all the sailors on board died as most people believed," replied Bertie. "Four men escaped with a fortune in silver before the ship sank in the storm.

"They hid the silver in a cave in the side of a mountain on Gull Island," continued Bertie. "But the storm started a rock slide and closed off the entrance, burying three of the sailors inside the cave. The fourth, a man named Pembroot, escaped. Pembroot's been trying to raise $10,000 to buy the land on which the cave is located."

"You provide the money, the cave will be opened, and the treasure will be divided between you and Pembroot. Wonderful," said Haledjian. "Only how do you know Pembroot isn't trying to trick you?"

"Earlier tonight he took me to the cave," said Bertie. "This sack was half buried in the bushes, and I nearly broke my leg tripping over it. I took one look and brought the candlestick here immediately. You've got to agree it's real silver."

"It is," admitted Haledjian. "And there's no doubt that Pembroot placed it near the cave to fool you."

How did Haledjian know that the silver candlestick did not come from the Lady North?

Mystery 5: The Case of the Dentist's Patient

Dr. Chris Williams, a London-born New York dentist, was preparing to check the teeth of her patient, David Hoover. Silently the door behind her opened. A gloved hand holding a gun appeared.

Two shots sounded. Mr. Hoover fell over, dead.

"We've got a suspect," Inspector Winters told Dr. Haledjian at his office an hour later. "The elevator operator took a nervous man to the 15th floor—Dr. Williams has one of six offices on the floor—a few moments before the shooting. The description fits John Burton.

"Burton was recently let out of prison," continued the inspector. "I had a police officer go to his hotel and bring him in. Burton thinks I just want to ask him about whether he has been following the rules since he left prison."

Burton was brought into the room. "What's this all about?" he demanded angrily.

"Have you ever heard of Dr. Williams?" asked the inspector.

"No, why?"

"David Hoover was shot to death less than two hours ago as he sat in a chair in Dr. Williams' office."

"I was sleeping all afternoon."

"An elevator operator says he took a man who looks like you to the 15th floor just before the shots."

"It wasn't me," shouted Burton. "I look like a lot of guys. I haven't been near a dentist's office since I was in prison. This Williams, I bet she never saw me, so what can you prove?"

"Enough to send you to prison for the rest of your life," exclaimed Dr. Haledjian.

Why was Haledjian so sure that Burton was the murderer?

Additional Clues

If you had trouble solving any of the mysteries, here are additional clues. True/False items are indicated by a T / F before a statement.

Mystery 1: Try answering these questions:

  a. Why was Clive Vance's hair blond?
  b. T / F   Clive had just had his beard shaved off.
  c. T / F   Clive's face was brown from the sun.

Now can you explain why Dr. Haledjian did not believe Vance?

Mystery 2: No luck? Try these questions:

    a. What was the date of the will that Martin had?
    b. Why is the date important to the solution of the mystery?
    c. How many days are there in November?

Mystery 3: Do you want some more clues?

    a. How long had the windows been open?
    b. What did the candles look like when Haledjian came into the room? Where had the wax dripped?
    c. T / F   The wind was blowing into the room.

Mystery 4: Maybe answering these questions will help:

    a. Where had the candlestick been since 1956?
    b. What was the condition of the candlestick Bertie had?
    c. What happens to the appearance of silver as time passes?

Mystery 5: If you're not sure, answer these questions:

    a. Does Burton know whether Williams is a man or woman?
    b. How does Burton know that Williams is a dentist and not a foot doctor?

Reading Selection 1

Newspaper Article

Before You Begin   1. If you could live anywhere, where would it be?

2. What kind of a house would you live in?

These are questions that Ernest Dittemore had thought about before his house burned down. When that happened he knew what he wanted to do. . . . (Your teacher may want you to do the Vocabulary from Context exercise on pages 89–90 before you begin.)

The Seattle Times/Seattle Post-Intelligencer

Farmer Calls Hole His Home

KENDALL J. WILLS, ASSOCIATED PRESS

Associated Press

Ernest Dittemore wipes some dirt from his eye while tending his 80-acre Kansas farm, where he lives in a hole in the ground that he dug with a shovel after his house burned down 18 years ago.

1   When fire destroyed Ernest Dittemore's six-room farmhouse 18 years ago, his neighbors got together to buy the 60-year-old bachelor a trailer house.

Dittemore was grateful. He thanked his friends, filled the trailer with food, then spent the night in a 4-by-10-foot hole that he'd dug in the ground with a shovel.

2   Now just months before his 78th birthday, Dittemore still goes into the hole every night, using the trailer just for storage.

"I'd been thinking about living underground for quite a while, even before the house burned," Dittemore said. "It's a lot easier to heat."

3   His underground house has dirt walls and a dirt floor. He sleeps on a bed of newspapers and uses a wood-burning stove for heat.

A skylight built into the piece of concrete that is his ceiling has been darkened by the smoke, but it still allows a little light in. There are no lights or electricity.

4   Dittemore is unconcerned about anybody who thinks he's odd. "As long as I like it, that's all that matters. I don't ask them what they think, and I don't care," he said.

At first people nearby in the small town of Troy, about 15 miles west of St. Joseph, Missouri, were confused. But they seem to have accepted Dittemore's unusual lifestyle.

From the *Seattle Times/Seattle Post-Intelligencer,* March 7, 1993, A8.

Some affectionately call him the "cave man of Doniphan County."

5   To get to his underground room, Dittemore lifts the ceiling. Steps lead to the floor 7 feet below. He says it's comfortable enough, even when the temperature outside goes below freezing.

6   Two bad knees force Dittemore to use canes made from tree branches to get around. Even so, he takes care of 30 head of cattle, six horses, a dozen chickens, and a few cats and dogs on his 80-acre farm.

7   His money from Social Security* and cattle sales is enough to pay for what he needs.

Neighbors say Dittemore is not crazy. He sends birthday and Christmas cards to his relatives and friends. And when his legs were better, he helped them on their farms.

Neighbor Larry Jones returns this favor by bringing Dittemore food for him and his animals.

8   Jim Gilmore, who grew up on the farm next to Dittemore's, said his friend is just different, not a hermit trying to hide from the real world.

"A lot of guys you read about, they seem to get mean living by themselves," Gilmore said. "But Ernie is the nicest guy you'll ever meet.

"One day we'll find him dead in the hole. But he'll die happy."

---

*Social Security: A U.S. government program that gives money monthly to older people and those who are not able to work.

Comprehension

Indicate if each statement below is true (T) or false (F) according to your understanding of the article.

1. T / F   Ernest Dittemore lives in a 6-room farmhouse.

2. T / F   Dittemore is 60 years old.

3. T / F   Sometimes Dittemore lives in a trailer given to him by his neighbors.

4. T / F   Dittemore's hole is 10 feet deep.

5. T / F   There is a wood-burning stove in Dittemore's hole.

6. T / F   There is a little electric light in Dittemore's hole.

7. T / F   Because of his bad knees, Dittemore is no longer able to take care of his farm.

8. T / F   Dittemore's neighbors think he is trying to hide from the world.

Critical Reading

Below is a list of words and phrases. You will decide which of these describe Ernest Dittemore. There is no single correct set of answers. Your teacher may want you to discuss this exercise in pairs or small groups. Be prepared to support your choices with examples from your personal experiences and the text.

1. First, check (✓) all the descriptions below that Ernest Dittemore's *neighbors* would use to describe him. Be sure you can support your choices with parts of the article you have read.

__ crazy   __ nice   __ a hermit
__ odd   __ lonely   __ a farmer
__ mean   __ happy   __ a good neighbor

2. Now look at the list again. Check (✓) all those descriptions that *you* think describe Ernest Dittemore. Again, be prepared to defend your choices.

  — crazy   — nice   — a hermit
  — odd   — lonely   — a farmer
  — mean   — happy   — a good neighbor

3. Were your answers the same in question 1 and question 2? If not, why not?

4. Why do you think this article was written? That is, why would readers find this article interesting? Do you think Ernest Dittemore would find this article interesting?

Discussion/Composition

Choose one of the statements below and tell why you agree or disagree with it. Use information from the article and from your own experience.

a. We should all be more like Ernest Dittemore. He is doing what he wants to do. He lives the way he wants to live, and he doesn't hurt anyone.

b. Ernest Dittemore is crazy.

c. Sometimes we need to save people from themselves. Ernest Dittemore should not be allowed to live alone in his dangerous home.

Vocabulary from Context

The vocabulary in the exercise below is taken from "Farmer Calls Hole His Home." Use the context provided to decide on meanings for the italicized words. Write a definition, synonym, or description in the space provided.

1. _____   John never wanted to get married; he always said he enjoyed being a *bachelor.*

2. _____   Mary couldn't afford a regular house, so she lived in a *trailer.* It had everything a house has—bathroom, bedrooms, kitchen—but, of course, it had wheels.

3. _____   The ground was very hard and full of rocks. The workers broke three *shovels* trying to dig holes.

4. _____   Doug missed seeing the stars at night when he was indoors. At first, he tried painting a picture of the sky on his *ceiling,* so he could lie in bed at night and see the stars. But then he had a better idea. He made a

5. _____   hole through his ceiling and roof, and he put in a glass *skylight.* Now he had more light in the daytime and could watch the stars at night.

6. _____   Most sidewalks are made of *concrete*. When they are being built, children can write their names in the wet concrete so people can see them forever.

7. _____   Celia owns so many things that there isn't enough room in her house for all of them. Instead of keeping her car in the garage, she uses the garage for *storage*.

8. _____   Bill always worries about what other people think. In contrast, Sue is completely *unconcerned* about the opinions of others.

9. _____   Paula is a warm, loving person who likes all of her students. Every morning she greets each of them *affectionately*.

10. _____   Barb helped Mary by giving her a ride to work. The next day, Mary returned the *favor* and drove Barb.

11. _____   Ken lives by himself and tries never to see other human beings. Although he is a *hermit*, he isn't lonely.

12. _____   The children don't like Mr. Jones because he is so *mean*. In fact, because of his hateful ways, he has no friends.

Reading Selection 2

Popular Social Science

Before You Begin   T / F People should never say things that aren't true.

1. Check (✓) all those situations below in which you would say something that is not true. When you are finished, compare your responses to your classmates'.

___ a. Your friends want to come over, but you'd rather not see them.

___ b. You are tired of talking to friends on the telephone but don't want to hurt their feelings.

___ c. Your host serves you a terrible dinner and asks if you liked the meal.

___ d. In a job interview, you are asked if you have experience doing something you know only a little about.

___ e. Your friend copied from you on a test, and you are asked by the teacher why the two test answers look the same.

___ f. A crime has been committed. Your friend is not involved but cannot tell the police where he has been. He asks you to say that he was with you.

___ g. You are separated from your husband or wife, and you think it will be a big problem if your friends or family find out.

2. A *lie* is an untrue statement. But people disagree whether all untrue statements are bad and whether all untrue statements should be called lies. Some people think that there is a difference between "little lies" and "lies." And some think that "little lies" shouldn't be thought of as lies at all. Look again at the items you checked in question 1. Put an *L* next to all those that you think are "little lies." Would you call these untrue statements "lies"?

Read the following article to find out why people "lie." Your teacher may want you to do the Vocabulary from Context exercise 1 on page 95 before you begin.

Lies Are So Commonplace, They Almost Seem Like the Truth

Terry Lee Goodrich
Fort Worth Star-Telegram

1   Everyone lies. Little lies, perhaps, which may not cause serious problems, but still they are lies. We fudge on how old we are, how much we weigh, what we are paid. Some people tell their children that Santa Claus will come on Christmas Eve.

2   Consider the last time you got a phone call from someone you didn't want to talk to. Did you perhaps claim falsely that you were just on your way out the door? That your newborn (you're childless) needed you?

Did you ever promise anyone, "We'll do lunch," when you knew that you'd never get together?

Did you ever reach for the phone to call in sick to work, then leap from bed to enjoy the day?

Did you ever tell someone you owed money to that the check was in the mail when it wasn't?

3   Few behaviors serve as many purposes as lying. We grow up to use lies—or at least half truths—to avoid things that should be done, to get people to believe us, to get what we want, to buy time, to end conversations, to keep relationships going.

"Lying is also exciting," said Margaret Summy, a professional counselor in Fort Worth, Texas. "It's living dangerously. Besides, we all want to be important, so we change our stories to make them more interesting."

4   "We also lie to make people agree with us, without really realizing that we're doing so," said clinical psychologist David Welsh.

"In working with relationships such as parent-child or husband-wife, each person has a different memory, one which helps them. They'll accuse each other of lying," he said. "But both are telling their own understanding of the truth."

5   Perhaps the most understandable reason people lie is so they don't hurt others' feelings. Most guests at a dinner party wouldn't want to say that they didn't like a specially prepared meal, even if it was terrible.

6   But even though people lie for good reasons, lying can be harmful. If we act on false information, we can be hurt. If we lie and it is discovered, it can destroy the trust necessary for strong relationships. Besides, lying is hard on the brain because one lie leads to another, and we always have to remember our false story. In his "Discourses on Government," Algernon Sidney said, "Liars ought to have good memories."

7   For most of us, though, lying is hard on us physically. We breathe faster, our hearts beat harder, and our blood pressure goes up.

The truth can be hard on the body, too, of course—especially if we're admitting to a lie. Just about the most difficult thing for any human being to do is to tell others that he or she lied to them. It's very stressful.

Comprehension

Exercise 1

Check (✓) all those statements below with which the author would probably agree.

1. __ All untruths are lies.

2. __ Everyone lies.

3. __ We learn to lie as we are growing up.

Adapted from "Lies Are So Commonplace, They Almost Seem Like the Truth," by Terry Lee Goodrich, *Seattle Post-Intelligencer,* October 29, 1990, C1. Reprinted courtesy of the Fort Worth Star-Telegram.

4. __ Lying is exciting.

5. __ Lying is dangerous.

6. __ People should lie in order not to hurt other people's feelings.

7. __ Lying can help us not to hurt others' feelings.

8. __ Lying can hurt relationships.

9. __ Lying is bad for your health.

Exercise 2

Below is a list of reasons for lying taken from the article you have just read. To make an argument stronger or clearer, authors often give specific examples. Following the list of reasons are examples of lying given in the article. Match each example with the letter of a reason given. There may be more than one possible answer, and some letters may be used more than once. Choose what you feel to be the best answer. Be prepared to defend your choice.

a. We lie to avoid doing things we should do.

b. We lie to get what we want.

c. We lie to buy time.

d. We lie to end conversations.

e. We lie because it's exciting.

f. We lie to make our stories more interesting.

g. We lie to make people agree with us.

h. We lie so as not to hurt others' feelings.

Example   *d*   You answer the telephone and falsely say that your newborn needs you.

1. __ We say that we have already put a check in the mail when we haven't.

2. __ You answer the phone and falsely say that you were just on your way out the door.

3. __ We promise that we'll do lunch, but we never get together for lunch.

4. __ We tell people at work that we are sick, then go out and enjoy the day.

5. __ We tell our host that a terrible dinner was fine.

6. __ Parents and children report different understandings of the same event.

Exercise 3

Authors of newspaper articles such as the one you just read often cite "experts," people who know a good deal about the topic the author is writing about. However, articles that mention experts can be based mostly on the personal opinion of the writer. In evaluating texts, it's important to notice whose research and opinions are being reported. Below is the list of reasons from the article for why people lie. Indicate if each one is given by the author (A) or by one of the experts (E) cited by the author.

1. __ a. We lie to avoid doing things we should do.

   __ b. We lie to get what we want.

   __ c. We lie to buy time.

   __ d. We lie to end conversations.

   __ e. We lie because it's exciting.

   __ f. We lie to make our stories more interesting.

   __ g. We lie to make people agree with us.

   __ h. We lie so as not to hurt others' feelings.

2.   If you were writing a research paper on lying, would you cite this article? Why or why not?

Discussion/Composition

1. Below is a dictionary definition of *lie.*

   > *n.* **a.** a statement of something known or believed by the speaker to be untrue with the purpose of giving the hearer the wrong idea. **b.** an untrue statement that the speaker may or may not believe to be true.

   Give your definition of a lie. Explain why some things are lies and others are not.

2. Is it sometimes necessary to lie? Why or why not? Give examples from the article and from your own experience.

3. Do you think there are cultural differences in the definition of lying? Is politeness in one culture a lie in another? Use examples from the article and your own experiences to compare and contrast different ideas about lying.

Vocabulary from Context

Exercise 1

Below is the beginning of the article "Lies Are So Commonplace, They Almost Seem Like the Truth."
Use your general knowledge, your knowledge of stems and affixes, and information from the entire text
below to write a definition, synonym, or description of the italicized word on the line provided. Note
that some of the words appear more than once. Read through the entire passage before deciding on a
definition of each term. By the end of the passage, you should have a good idea of the meaning. You do
not need an exact definition; with only a general idea of the meaning, you will often be able to
understand the meaning of a written text.

Everyone *lies*. Little lies, perhaps, which may not cause serious problems, but
still they are lies. We *fudge* on how old we are, how much we weigh, what we are
paid. Some people tell their children that Santa Claus will come on Christmas Eve.

Consider the last time you got a phone call from someone you didn't want to
talk to. Did you perhaps *claim* falsely that you were just on your way out the
door? That your *newborn* (you're childless) needed you?

Did you ever promise anyone, "We'll *do* lunch," when you knew that you'd
never get together?

Did you ever reach for the phone to call in sick to work, then *leap* from bed to
enjoy the day?

1. lies: _____

2. fudge: _____

3. claim: _____

4. newborn: _____

5. do: _____

6. leap: _____

Exercise 2

This exercise should be done after you have finished reading "Lies Are So Commonplace, They Almost Seem Like the Truth." The exercise will give you practice deciding on the meaning of unfamiliar words. Give a definition, synonym, or description of each of the words below. The number in parentheses indicates the paragraph in which the word can be found. Your teacher may want you to do these orally or in writing.

1. (3) behaviors: _____

2. (3) purposes: _____

3. (3) avoid: _____

4. (4) memory: _____

5. (6) destroy: _____

6. (6) trust: _____

Reading Selections 3A–3C

Popular Press

In recent years, more women have begun to work outside the home, and men seem to have taken on more tasks for families. North American magazines and newspapers have begun to write about the "new man"—whether he really exists and how changes in family life affect women. The articles and cartoons that follow are examples of these discussions from the popular press.

Selection 3A   **Popular Social Science**

For many years, Lou Harris has been questioning people in the United States about their opinions on everything from politics to love. The results of these surveys, known as the "Harris polls," have become an interesting record of popular culture. Recently, Harris published a book describing the results of a number of his surveys. The reading passage below, from a chapter in his volume *Inside America,* describes survey results on the topic of how men and women share housework. Your teacher may want you to do Vocabulary from Context exercise 1 on pages 102–3 before you begin.

Before You Begin   1. When men and women live together, do you think they should share all household tasks equally? If not, which ones should men do and which ones should women do? Why?
2. How do you think most people in the United States would answer this question?

Skimming

When an article presents a lot of statistics, it is often useful to read it first quickly to discover the organization of the article and to get a general sense of the main ideas and information presented. In this article, you will notice that the survey results are not presented in numerical tables. Skim the article first; keep in mind that your next task will be to put the statistics into tables so that they will be easier to understand.* After skimming, then, you will need to return to the article to locate the information necessary to complete the tables in Comprehension exercise 1. Your teacher may want you to do Vocabulary from Context exercise 1 before you begin.

Who's Doing the Work around the House?

1   Most adult women in the United States today work outside the home. And the majority of men and women believe that when men and women live together, household tasks should be shared by men and women. But what really happens?

Adapted from "How Nice to Have a Man Around the House—If He Shares the Chores," in *Inside America,* by Lou Harris (New York: Vintage/Random House, 1987), 98–102.

*For an introduction to skimming, see Unit 1.

2   When asked who does the household chores, 41% of all women report that they do, another 41% say they do a lot and their husbands help some, 15% report the chores being evenly divided, and 2% say the husbands do more. Clearly, there is a gap between deciding that things should be equal and the reality of who, in fact, gets things done.

3   However, it must be noted that in families where both spouses are employed, among husbands, 24% say the wife does nearly all the work around the house, 42% report that the wife does most of it but the husband helps some, 28% report that the work is evenly divided, and 5% that the husband actually does more around the house. Greater sharing within couples is also seen more among young married families under 30 years of age and among those who are college-educated.

Sharing Money

4   When both spouses work, 79% of both men and women report that both salaries are combined and used for all household expenses, personal expenses, and savings. Only 15% of husbands whose wives work say that the spouses keep their money separated after both spouses contribute a part of their salaries for household and living expenses and savings. Obviously, when it comes to money, sharing of both salaries and expenses has become the norm.

Beyond Sharing: Exchanging Roles

5   One possible way for men and women to share family responsibilities is for people to change roles: the men would stay home and the women would become the breadwinners of the family. This possibility has been surveyed since 1970. Back then, 63% said they would have less respect for a husband who stayed home than for one who had a job outside the home, only 8% would respect him more, and 15% said it would make very little difference. By 1980 things had begun to change. A much lower 41% said they would respect the stay-at-home husband less, 6% more, but 42% about the same. Now, only 25% say they would respect a man who stayed home to do household chores less, 12% more, and a big 50% say the same.

6   Thus the number who say they would think less of a husband who exchanges roles with his wife and stays home to take care of the household has declined from 63% to 25% over a generation's time. What is more, the younger people are and the more money they have, the less likely they are to say they will respect a stay-at-home husband less.

The Future: Teenagers on Sharing Chores

7   Attitudes toward change are usually formed early in life or no later than the teens. Therefore, it is significant to find that teenagers today expect to share almost all household and child-rearing chores in married life.

8   Here is what they say about sharing chores:

—On vacuuming the house, only 40% of all teenagers think this should be the responsibility of the wife, compared with 38% who say both should do it, and 20% who believe it doesn't matter who does it. The point is that a 60%–40% majority does not think it is the duty of the wife to vacuum the house.
—On mopping the house, an even 50% think that it is a woman's chore only, but an equal 50% do not think so.

—On preparing meals, 39% of the teenagers think this is a wife's responsibility, but a higher 46% see cooking as a shared future responsibility, 2% see it as primarily a man's task, and the remaining 13% say it doesn't matter.

—On washing dishes, in the past generally only a task for women, no more than 54% of teenagers believe this is a wife's task, and 46%, nearly as many, do not agree that this task should only be done by women.

—On washing the car, traditionally a man's duty, now only 40% of all teenagers think the husband should do it. Thirty-nine percent think the chore should be equally shared (49% of teenage girls feel this way), 2% think the woman should do it, and the rest say it doesn't matter.

—On mowing the lawn, almost always the man's job around the house, a large 64% still agree with tradition and say let the husband do it. But 15% of the young men and a much higher 43% of the young women simply don't agree with that. It is significant that teenage girls lead the way in feeling that many traditional men's chores should now be shared by women.

Caring for Young Children

9   On caring for young children, the teenage view is that the chores should be shared all the way:

—91% of all teenagers believe that playing with children should be an equal responsibility of husbands and wives.

—71% believe that feeding babies and young children should be a joint duty of husbands and wives.

—64% of all teens believe that changing diapers should be shared all the way, although a much higher 78% of teenage girls think this, compared with a lower 50% of teenage boys.

—87% believe that disciplining young children should be a responsibility shared between men and women.

—56% believe that bathing a baby should be the equal and joint responsibility of men and women.

—73% think that putting the baby to bed should be done just as often by husbands and wives.

—68% of all teenagers believe that putting a young child to bed must be the shared responsibility of both spouses in a good marriage.

Observation

10   It seems that the public believes it is very difficult for a young mother to work, take care of the household, and be primarily responsible for raising children. There simply is not enough time to do it all. And there is no doubt that most women in the future are going to choose to work, marry, and be mothers. Therefore, people conclude, tradition must change and male spouses must do many things that their fathers and grandfathers would not have agreed to do.

Women, especially young women, are determined to see the change come about. Even more interesting is that males, particularly teenage boys, agree with the women.

The significance of this is that right in the home, daily, the reality of equality between the sexes is being created. This newfound sharing is not simply something that people say without doing. It is a real revolution.

Comprehension

Exercise 1

Use information from "Who's Doing the Work around the House?" to complete the tables that follow.

TABLE 1.   Sharing Tasks: Reports of Who Does Household Chores (%)

Who Does Chores	Family Arrangement	
	All Families (Women's reports)	Families in Which Both Spouses Work (Men's reports)
Women do nearly all		
Women do most; husbands help		
Task evenly divided		
Husbands do more		

TABLE 2.   Sharing Money: Men's and Women's Reports When Both Work (%)

Salaries combined for all things	
Some money kept separately	

TABLE 3.   Exchanging Roles: Respect for Stay-At-Home Husbands (%)

Respect for the husband	Year		
	1970	1980	Now
Would respect him less			
Would respect him more			
Would respect him the same			

TABLE 4.   Teenagers Sharing Chores (%)

Who Does Chore	Chore					
	Vacuum	Mop	Cook	Wash Dishes	Wash Car	Mow Lawn
Women's work						
Shared work						
Men's work						
Doesn't matter who does it						

___

Exercise 2

Answer the following questions based on your understanding of the passage and the tables you have completed in Comprehension exercise 1.

1. T / F   Based on the Harris Poll, women do most of the housework.

2. T / F   When both men and women work, they say they typically share their salaries and expenses.

3. T / F   Today, most people in the United States have less respect for a stay-at-home husband than for a "working" husband.

4. T / F   Teenagers believe there are no household tasks that should be done only by women.

5. T / F   Most teenagers believe that caring for young children should be shared by men and women.

___

Discussion/Composition

1. These survey results are based on what people say they do or say they believe. How believable do you find these self-reports? Support your opinion with information from your reading or from your personal experience.

2. The author says that based on the teenagers' beliefs about the future, "a real revolution" is happening in U.S. homes. Do you agree? Use information from the article and your own observations about life.

3. The teenagers surveyed hope that they will be able to avoid traditional patterns around the house. But is this possible? On page 102 is a cartoon from the comic strip "Sally Forth." Sally and her husband Ted are a modern couple who both have careers outside the home. They work hard on their

marriage and friendship. It's not always easy to be a "modern couple." But when they have problems, they are able to face these with humor.

In this cartoon, Sally's and Ted's daughter is asking how they decided who would do which tasks in the house. How does Sally feel about this? How does Ted feel? Explain the world from either Sally's or Ted's point of view.

Reprinted with special permission of King Features Syndicate.

4. When men and women live together, should they share all household tasks? Support your opinion with information from the article and your own observations.

5. Using the information in the article and the tables, summarize the major findings in this article. Be sure to compare and contrast different groups and time periods.

Vocabulary from Context

Exercise 1

Both the ideas and the vocabulary in the exercise below are taken from "Who's Doing the Work around the House?" Use the context provided to decide on meanings for the italicized words. Write a definition, synonym, or description in the space provided.

1. _____

2. _____

3. _____

4. _____

Much has been written of late about the sharing of household tasks between men and women. *Chores* once thought to belong only to one sex, for example, fixing cars by men and cooking by women, are now shared—at least by some. But there is a *gap* between what people say should happen and what they actually do. Although most people think chores should be shared, many report this is not what happens. However, some couples are better at sharing the money they earn. Their *salaries* are combined and this is used to pay for all household *expenses,* such as the bills for food, light, and housing.

5. _____   One way of sharing tasks is for men and women to change *roles:* men
                              would do traditional women's jobs, and women would become the
6. _____   breadwinners. People tend to have strong feelings about this. *Attitudes*
                              toward this possibility have been surveyed for about 30 years. People
                              have been asked whether they would have a lower opinion of a stay-
                              at-home husband than of a man who is employed outside the home. A
7. _____   *generation* ago, when the parents of today's adults were asked, they
8. _____   said they would *have less respect for* men who switched roles.

                              Today's teenagers have different views about most things. For
9. _____   example, they no longer think that *child-rearing* is the job only of a
10. _____   mother. They believe the *responsibility* for taking care of children
                              should be shared. Similarly, they no longer believe that correcting or
                              punishing children who misbehave is the job only of a father. Most
11. _____   believe the *disciplining* of children should be shared.

Exercise 2

*This exercise gives you additional clues to the meaning of unfamiliar vocabulary in context. In the
paragraph of "Who's Doing the Work around the House?" indicated by the number in parentheses, find
the word or phrase that best fits the meaning given. Your teacher may want to read these aloud as you
quickly scan the paragraph to find the answer.*

1. (4) What word means *money put away for the future?*

2. (4) What phrase means *typical; average; what most people do?*

3. (5) What word means *people who bring home the money,* that is, *who buy the bread?*

4. (6) What word means *probable?*

5. (8) What word means *responsibility; task; job?*

6. (8) What word means *mostly; mainly?*

7. (10) What phrase means *want very much; have made a decision?*

8. (10) What word means *importance?*

9. (10) What word means *new; newly discovered?*

Selection 3B   **Cartoons**

Before You Begin   1. What do you think would happen if a married couple exchanged household
                        tasks for a day? Do you think each of them might learn something?
                     2. What are things that women do around the house that men might not notice?
                        What things that men do might go unnoticed by women?

The cartoons that follow are taken from the comic strip "Sally Forth." Sally and Ted are a "modern couple" who both have careers outside the home. When they have problems, they try to face these with humor. The comic strips were printed over the course of a week in newspapers throughout North America. Read each strip only for the main idea and the humor, then answer the questions that follow.

Sally Forth

Monday:

SALLY FORTH By Greg Howard

Reprinted with special permission of King Features Syndicate.

1. Why are Sally and Ted going to switch roles for a week?

2. When Ted and Sally switch roles, what is the first job Ted will do? What will Sally do?

Tuesday:

SALLY FORTH By Greg Howard

Reprinted with special permission of King Features Syndicate.

1. What is Ted's household task in today's cartoon?

2. Why does Ted want their daughter to wait until next week to get sick?

Wednesday:

SALLY FORTH By Greg Howard

Reprinted with special permission of King Features Syndicate.

1. What is Ted's task today?

2. The cartoonist says that Sally and Ted are reversing roles. What has been reversed in Wednesday's comic strip?

Thursday:

SALLY FORTH By Greg Howard

Reprinted with special permission of King Features Syndicate.

1. What is Ted's task today?

2. What does his daughter mean when she says, "It's working"?

Friday:

SALLY FORTH By Greg Howard

1. Was the week of switching roles successful?

2. Why does Sally want to kick Ted?

Discussion/Composition

1. We know what tasks Ted did during this week of switching roles. What do you think Sally was doing? Whose role would you want? Why?

2. Think of a household you are familiar with in which a man and a woman could switch roles for a week. What do you think would happen? Be sure to give specific examples.

3. Humor grows from the culture in which it occurs. Did you find this series of cartoons funny? Do you think these cartoon strips would seem funny in your community/country? Why or why not?

Selection 3C   **Magazine Article**

Before You Begin   1. What do you think makes a good father?

2. Are there reasons why some women might not want men to be more active in raising children and taking care of a home?

The magazine article you are about to read argues that there is no single way to be a good father and discusses reasons why all men are not "new fathers." Your teacher may want you to do the Vocabulary from Context exercise 1 on page 110 before you begin reading.

The "New Father"
No Real Role Reversal

1   Although we hear much about the "new father," the man who takes an active role in the day-to-day care of his children, there is no single way to be a good father, claims Michael Lamb, a psychologist with the National Institute of Child Health and Human Development. He says children can do very well in many different situations, and the greater involvement of fathers is probably most important when it makes mothers' lives happier.

2   In the U.S., about half the men questioned reply that if there were no job-related penalty, they would like to spend more time with their children. Looked at another way, the other 50% are satisfied the way things are and are saying that they don't feel any great desire to spend more time with their children than they currently do. The same questionnaires often ask women if they are satisfied with the amount of their husbands' participation in child-rearing. Thirty-five to forty percent say they would like their partners to do more.

3   What is often overlooked, Lamb says, is that about two thirds of the women are happy with their spouses' current level of parental involvement. "The truth is that men are not asking to be more involved with the children, but women are not trying to get them more involved, either. For many reasons, both men and women, on average, are more or less satisfied with traditional responsibilities." The fact that women don't necessarily want men to have more involvement in child-rearing "has a lot to do with power and privilege in this society. Women fear they may lose power and status in the family, which is the one area in which these had never been questioned. At the same time, they do not have equality in the world of work. For many women, it's better to keep their responsibility for parenthood, even if that means they have what might be called role overload, rather than give some of that status, responsibility, and power to a partner."

4   Fathers often say they aren't more active parents because they don't have child-caring skills. "But women are just as frightened by parenthood and just as poorly prepared as men. The difference is that they're expected to know how to do it. From the time the baby is born, everybody acts as if either they know or they better find out fast because no one else is going to do it." If the same thing were expected of men, they, too, would learn. "All the evidence we have suggests that when fathers try caring for children, they can do it just as well as mothers can, with the exception of making milk."

5   What is important, notes Lamb, is that parents be able to divide child care responsibilities in a way that suits their individual needs. If the father doesn't want to be involved and a traditional mother agrees, those children would be better off if the father were not highly involved because that would make everyone more comfortable. It is not better to have a father stay home who doesn't want to be there. "Father involvement has to be looked at in the context of the family arrangements and the value it has for both mothers and fathers."

Adapted from "The 'New Father': No Real Role Reversal," *USA Today,* July, 1989, 11.

Comprehension

Answer the following questions according to your understanding of the passage. Indicate if statements 1–4 are true (T) or false (F).

1. T / F   Most married mothers would be happier if their husbands were more involved in caring for the children.

2. T / F   Most married mothers are happy with their husband's current level of involvement with the children.

3. T / F   Work in the home gives a person no power or status in the United States.

4. T / F   In the United States, women are better prepared to be parents than are men.

5. If a father doesn't want to be involved in caring for his children and the mother wants him to be, what would the author of the article think would be best for the children?

_____

Discussion/Composition

1. The author states that fathers care for children just as well as mothers do. Do you agree? Use examples from reading you have done on this topic and personal experience to support your opinion.

2. The author of this article believes that no single style of family is best for children. Do you agree? Do you think that some "family arrangements" (that is, who does what in the family) are not good for children? Use examples from reading you have done on this topic and personal experience to support your opinion.

3. a. Do people feel the same way about "new fathers" and "new mothers"? On page 109 is a cartoon showing some business people's feelings about "a new kind of father." How do their reactions to the father and mother differ?

   b. Compare difficulties in the workplace faced by working women and by "new fathers." Use information from your discussion of this cartoon and your own knowledge.

4. People in many countries feel that family life is different today than it was in the past. Penelope Leach, author of the popular parenting book *Your Baby and Child,* believes that things do feel different, but she argues that the causes of these feelings are not what we think. According to Leach, what has changed is not that more women have begun to work, but that the *place* where everyone works has changed. Here is a summary of Leach's beliefs from *Time* magazine:

> The change, according to Penelope Leach, comes from the Industrial Revolution, which forced a separation between home and the work place. "Home and its surrounding community used to be the central place where everyone spent the day, with work and play and family pretty much intermixed," she says. "Now work has moved into geographically separate production centers and takes the form of specialized jobs that cannot be shared or done with a baby on your back." Home has become a place where people do little more than sleep, get cleaned up, and change clothes. And as mothers have increasingly left home for the office or factory, children's separation from the adult world has very much increased.

Summarize Leach's views in two or three sentences. Then indicate whether you think her argument is a strong one. Be sure to support your opinion.

_____

Cartoon from *Z Magazine,* July/August 1994, 31.

Paragraph adapted from "The Great Experiment," *Time* (Special Issue), Fall 1990, 74.

Vocabulary from Context

Exercise 1

Both the ideas and the vocabulary in the exercise below are taken from "The 'New Father': No Real Role Reversal." Use the context provided to decide on meanings for the italicized words. Some of these words are also taught with Selection 3A. Write a definition, synonym, or description in the space provided.

1. _____

2. _____

3. _____

4. _____

Much has been written about the so-called new father, the man who takes an active part in taking care of his children. This *involvement* by fathers in *child-rearing* has been shown in questionnaires given to men and women about their participation in child-rearing. The questionnaires show that some men are taking more *responsibility* for their children. But also, many women are still doing more than men in the home even though they are working outside the home. This means that women have two *roles:* the role of parent and of worker. And the heavy responsibilities of both these roles make women very tired.

5. _____

6. _____

This role overload can be explained in part by the fact that not all women want their male spouses to be more involved in child care. Raising children has traditionally been the place where women get power and *status.* Their position in society has come from their role as mothers. And this role has given them the *privilege* to have things their way in the home. It is hard to give up this status and privilege, to let men take over in the home, when women are still not equal in the workplace.

7. _____

8. _____

And not all men want to be more involved at home. Even if this involvement would not hurt men's careers, many say they would not want to be more involved at home. That is, even if there is no job-related *penalty* at work, many men like things the way they are. The *arrangements* whereby family roles and tasks are divided are difficult to change.

Exercise 2

This exercise gives you additional clues to the meaning of unfamiliar vocabulary in context. In the paragraph of "The 'New Father'" indicated by the number in parentheses, find the word that best fits the meaning given. Your teacher may want to read these aloud as you quickly scan the paragraph to find the answer.

1. (2) Which word means *happy; pleased?*

2. (2) Which word means *involvement; taking part?*

3. (3) Which word means *looked past; not noticed; missed; ignored?*

4. (4) Which word means *child-rearing?*

5. (5) Which word means *fits; agrees with; satisfies?*

Reading Selection 4

Magazine Graphic

The maps and charts on the following pages contain information published in *Time* magazine. They provide readers with a picture of problems facing the world. Your teacher may want you to do Vocabulary from Context exercise 1 on pages 120–21 before you begin.

The article presents the information in two ways. Some of the information appears in maps and report cards (pages 115 and 117) that grade selected countries on their efforts to solve environmental problems. Information about problems facing individual countries is presented in brief reports (pages 118–19).

Before You Begin   1. Which parts of the world are you interested in reading about?

2. What sorts of environmental problems do you expect to read about?

Summit to Save the Earth: The World's Next Trouble Spots

with report cards for major countries on . . .

| Air Pollution | Population Growth | Safe Drinking Water | Protected Lands |

What kind of world will our children have to live in? Will they have air to breathe and food to eat? These are among the basic questions that were addressed at the first world meeting on the environment, attended by more than 100 world leaders and 30,000 other scientists, newspeople, and concerned citizens. These complex problems can no longer be solved by individual countries; nations of the world must act together if we are to develop answers that will give a safe and healthy world to our children. Will world leaders have the vision to make the necessary changes in the laws that protect the environment? The answer is not certain, but there is hope.

A number of important problems were examined in the summit conference, all related to quality of life on the planet. As more and more countries become industrialized, air pollution from factories and automobiles worsens, causing an increase in disease and medical costs. Many leaders are concerned about birth rates because the populations of their countries are growing faster than their economies. Clean water is, of course, another concern for all countries, but very often rivers and other water sources are threatened by industrial growth, as factories and other large businesses look for ways to dispose of chemical waste matter. Another area where industry and nature must be balanced is in the use of forests, jungles, grasslands, and deserts; government officials argue that the land is needed for farming, industry, and housing, while environmentalists say that we need to preserve the wild lands.

Environmentalists have "graded" the world on environmental problems. They have provided the "report cards" that appear with the maps. Like the report cards that teachers send home with school children, these give us a better understanding of how we are doing in taking care of the Earth.

Getting Oriented

Study the maps and the report cards on the following pages to understand how the information is organized, then answer the questions below.

1. What are the four environmental problems on which the countries are graded? _____

_____

2. How have the countries of the world been grouped for evaluation? _____

_____

Grading the World

Within each geographical area several countries have been given grades on each of the four environmental problems. The grades are explained in the Key to Report Cards box. Take a few minutes to study the report cards and the key, then answer the questions below. The questions require you to use the maps and report cards. Some may require that you look at the brief reports on pages 118–19. True/False items are indicated by a T / F before a statement. Some questions may have more than one correct answer. Others may require an opinion. Choose the answer you like best; be prepared to defend your choices. Your teacher may want you to work individually, in pairs, or in small groups.

1. Look at the Key to Report Cards.

    a. Notice that air pollution is graded according to "per capita CO_2 emissions".* This means the amount of carbon dioxide in the air compared with the number of people who live in the area. Would you want to live in a country with high CO_2 emissions? Why or why not?

    _____

    b. T / F   Population growth is measured by counting the number of babies born every year.

    c. Areas are graded according to the percentage of the country that is protected. What do you think this means? Protected against what?

    _____

    d. Before looking at the maps, predict the grades that you believe your own area of the world would receive.

    _____

2. T / F   The U.S. has no serious environmental problems.

3. Based on the information provided above, would you rather live in Argentina or Mexico? Why?

    _____

4. T / F   Building the dam in Costa Rica will give jobs to 3,000 Indians.

5. T / F   The tourist industry is not all good for Belize.

6. T / F   The land along the Bio-Bio River in Chile is not liveable.

7. For which two countries in South America is oil a problem? _____

_____

*CO_2 is the chemical formula for carbon dioxide. Carbon monoxide (CO) is a deadly gas that comes primarily from automobiles.

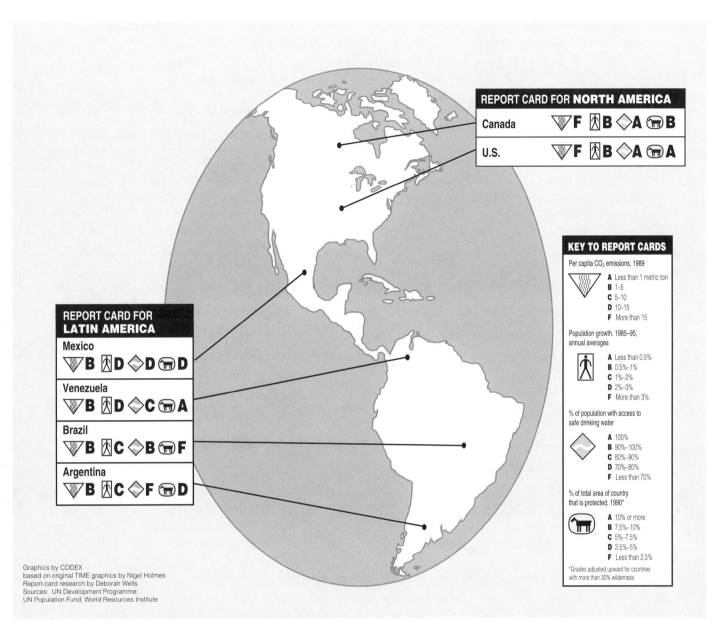

REPORT CARD FOR NORTH AMERICA

| Canada | ▽F | B | ◇A | B |
| U.S. | ▽F | B | ◇A | A |

REPORT CARD FOR LATIN AMERICA

Mexico
▽B D ◇D D

Venezuela
▽B D ◇C A

Brazil
▽B C ◇B F

Argentina
▽B C ◇F D

KEY TO REPORT CARDS

Per capita CO$_2$ emissions, 1989

A Less than 1 metric ton
B 1–5
C 5–10
D 10–15
F More than 15

Population growth. 1985–95, annual averages

A Less than 0.5%
B 0.5%–1%
C 1%–2%
D 2%–3%
F More than 3%

% of population with access to safe drinking water

A 100%
B 90%–100%
C 80%–90%
D 70%–80%
F Less than 70%

% of total area of country that is protected, 1990*

A 10% or more
B 7.5%–10%
C 5%–7.5%
D 2.5%–5%
F Less than 2.5%

*Grades adjusted upward for countries with more than 30% wilderness.

Graphics by CODEX
based on original TIME graphics by Nigel Holmes
Report-card research by Deborah Wells
Sources: UN Development Programme;
UN Population Fund; World Resources Institute

8. Find your own area of the world. What grades did your area receive? Do you agree with the evaluation? Why or why not?

_____

9. Which of the four environmental problems do you worry about the most? Why? _____

_____

10. Which environmental problem appears to be the most serious for countries throughout the world? (Another way to think about this question is to ask yourself which environmental problem received the most F's?)

_____

11. Which countries have the most serious problems with CO_2 emissions? _____

12. T / F   Europe's air is generally cleaner than that of Latin America.

13. Based on the information in the report cards, would you rather live in Spain or Germany? Why?

_____

Reporting on the World

Skim and scan the brief reports (pages 118–19) for answers to the following questions.

1. T / F   Skiers have damaged the Alps.

2. T / F   Bulgaria uses nuclear power to meet the country's energy needs.

3. In many countries, meeting basic needs today (for food and fuel, for example) makes it difficult to plan for the future. Botswana, Ethiopia, and Madagascar are examples.

    a. T / F   In Botswana, the government is working to provide drinking water for the growing population.

    b. T / F   In Ethiopia, more food today may mean less food tomorrow.

    c. T / F   In 35 years, Madagascar will have no forests.

4. Why are Australia's desert bandicoot and lesser bilby extinct? _____

5. T / F   In Nepal, the problem of trash along mountain trails has been solved.

6. T / F   It is possible to do this exercise without becoming sad or angry.

_____
*For an introduction to skimming and scanning, see Unit 1.

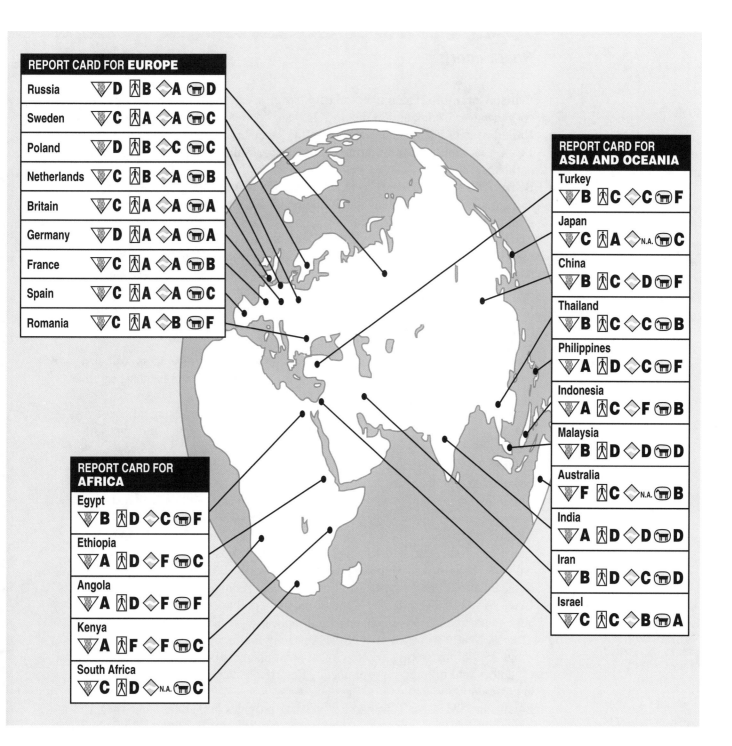

REPORT CARD FOR EUROPE

Russia	▽D	⚇B	◇A	🐑D
Sweden	▽C	⚇A	◇A	🐑C
Poland	▽D	⚇B	◇C	🐑C
Netherlands	▽C	⚇B	◇A	🐑B
Britain	▽C	⚇A	◇A	🐑A
Germany	▽D	⚇A	◇A	🐑A
France	▽C	⚇A	◇A	🐑B
Spain	▽C	⚇A	◇A	🐑C
Romania	▽C	⚇A	◇B	🐑F

REPORT CARD FOR ASIA AND OCEANIA

Turkey	▽B	⚇C	◇C	🐑F
Japan	▽C	⚇A	◇N.A.	🐑C
China	▽B	⚇C	◇D	🐑F
Thailand	▽B	⚇C	◇C	🐑B
Philippines	▽A	⚇D	◇C	🐑F
Indonesia	▽A	⚇C	◇F	🐑B
Malaysia	▽B	⚇D	◇D	🐑D
Australia	▽F	⚇C	◇N.A.	🐑B
India	▽A	⚇D	◇D	🐑D
Iran	▽B	⚇D	◇C	🐑D
Israel	▽C	⚇C	◇B	🐑A

REPORT CARD FOR AFRICA

Egypt	▽B	⚇D	◇C	🐑F
Ethiopia	▽A	⚇D	◇F	🐑C
Angola	▽A	⚇D	◇F	🐑F
Kenya	▽A	⚇F	◇F	🐑C
South Africa	▽C	⚇D	◇N.A.	🐑C

Brief Reports

1   **British Columbia.** The timber industry has clear-cut more than half of the trees on Vancouver Island, and in the next 25 years the rest could be gone.

2   **United States.** The Florida Keys, a marine sanctuary, is dying at the rate of 4% to 10% a year. Pollution from farming and warmer water temperatures is the major problem.

3   **Belize.** This small country's growing tourist industry could harm the coast. Fish and other wildlife, as well as the fragile reef,* are threatened by large numbers of swimmers and pollution from hotels.

4   **Ecuador.** Ecuador's large Cuyabeno National Park provides a safe environment for a wide variety of animals such as pink dolphins, harpy eagles, and jaguars. But the park is endangered by the construction of oil wells and new roads and by the increased use of land for farming.

5   **Costa Rica.** The government wants to dam the Pacuara River for a hydroelectric plant because Costa Rica needs more energy. But the project would flood 3,000 acres of forest and displace numerous groups of Indians.

6   **Chile.** Five new power stations are planned for the Bio-Bio River, as well as a large dam that will flood nearly 11,860 acres of land. Environmentalists say that the land along the river could become unfit for living.

7   **Argentina.** Oil leaks from ships carrying oil off the coast of Patagonia have caused major damage to the marine life. Hunting threatens many rare types of animals.

8   **Poland.** The Dunajac valley is famous for its scenery and castles. A dam will soon be completed on the river, however, that will destroy important natural preserves.†

9   **The Alps.** These famous mountains are scarred by roads, railways, and ski runs. Native plants are dying, the air is polluted, and mudslides are common.

10   **Bulgaria.** The nuclear power plant at Kozlodoy has been called, "the most dangerous in the world." It has had numerous problems with leaks, fires, and failures. The cost for fixing the plant will be over $1 billion, but it supplies 40% of the country's energy needs, so it must be kept running.

11   **Black Sea.** The Sea is fed by some of the most polluted rivers in the world, and large numbers of fish and animals are disappearing from its shores and waters.

12   **Siberia.** Nearly twice the size of the Amazon jungle, Siberia's forests contain about 25% of the world's wood. Government planners hope to increase the amount of lumber sold to foreign governments. Environmentalists fear that this will result in erosion of land that will pollute the rivers.

13   **Botswana.** The large Oksvango River delta‡ provides homes for some of Africa's last wild herds of elephant, Cape buffalo, and zebra. But the area could be hurt by a plan to clean out 23 miles of river to provide drinking water for growing towns. Environmentalists who are against the project say the project is really meant to help the country's diamond mining industry.

Reefs are rocklike underwater structures that provide homes and food for fish and other forms of wildlife.

†*Preserves* are areas of land or water where animals and vegetation are protected from problems caused by human activity.

‡A *delta* is the broad, flat land area formed over the years at the mouth of a river; it is very rich in vegetation and animal life.

14   **Ethiopia.** For over one hundred years, the growing population of Ethiopia has cut more than 90% of the country's forests for firewood and farmland, allowing 1 billion tons of valuable earth to erode into the sea. As a result, some 8,000 acres of farmland can no longer produce food.

15   **Madagascar.** Madagascar is populated by at least 150,000 species of plants and animals found nowhere else in the world. However, 80% of the island's forests has been cut for farming and fuel. If this continues, Madagascar will have no forests in 35 years.

16   **Persian Gulf.** About 8 million barrels of oil have been dumped into the Gulf in recent years, in some cases completely covering areas where animals and birds live.

17   **India.** The $10 billion Namada Valley Development Plan will include more than 3,000 dams, displace as many as 100,000 people, submerge forests and farms, and increase the river's salt levels and mud content.

18   **Malaysia.** If the rate of logging continues, Malaysia's forests will disappear in about ten years.

19   **Indonesia.** Over 2.2 million acres of tropical forest are cut every year here for wood products. In Kallmantan province, fires, logging, and coal mining have destroyed so much forest that environmentalists say all is lost.

20   **Australia.** Miners, loggers, and tourists have damaged the Tasmanian Tarkine Wilderness area, adding to problems caused by years of overgrazing of cattle and sheep. At least half of the region's animals have become extinct, including the desert bandicoot and the lesser bilby.

21   **Johnston Atoll.** This tiny island 700 miles west of Hawaii is a U.S. national wildlife area. It is also the site of a $240 million toxic waste disposal system that threatens the health of the area.

22   **China.** A proposed dam on the Yangtze River will take 18 years to build and could provide China with 17,680 megawatts of power. However, the dam could cost $29 billion, and more than 1 million people will be displaced.

23   **Nepal.** Foreigners have long left trash along the trails that lead to the world's highest mountains. The government can do little to stop this, and several international environmental groups have begun a yearly effort to clean up the area.

Discussion/Composition

1. Why should people be concerned about the loss of forests in countries far from their own?

2. What would you say is the most serious cause of environmental problems? Support your answer with examples from your reading and your personal experience.

3. The brief reports describe a problem faced by both India and China. What is it? What are their choices? What would you recommend they do?

4. What do you think you and other individuals might do to help solve these problems? Choose an area of the world where you have experience, and give examples of things you might do.

Vocabulary from Context

Exercise 1

Both the vocabulary and the ideas in the exercise below are taken from "Summit to Save the Earth."
Use the context provided to decide on meanings for the italicized words. Write a definition, synonym, or
description in the space provided.

1. _____ It has been known for some time that *population* growth is a serious
problem. As the number of people in the world increases, the need for
food, water, and homes also increases.

2. _____ People from around the world recently met to discuss serious
environmental problems such as dirty air and water, overpopulation,
and the effect on nature of growing cities.

3. _____ *Summits,* meetings which bring together leaders from important
countries, are often the only way to solve such complex problems.

4. _____ When *industrialization* first began in the early 1900s, few people
questioned the value of using machines to do the work commonly
done by humans.

5. _____
6. _____ The growing *economies* that provided jobs and produced goods for
people to buy also *polluted* the air and the water supplies near the
cities. Factories filled the air with smoke while at the same time they
sent waste products into the rivers and streams.

7. _____ Many of the chemical by-products of modern farm and factory
processes are *toxic*. Because they kill animals and plants, it is
important to dispose of them properly so that they do not harm forests,
rivers, or farmland.

8. _____ Factories and farms produce *chemical waste*. Because the chemicals
cannot be used, they are often just washed into open fields and rivers,
creating toxic conditions for plants and animals.

9. _____ When power and water was needed by the growing cities, people
dammed the rivers around the world. The lakes that resulted often
destroyed land used for crops and forced people to move from their
farms.

10. _____ When *lumber* was needed to build houses, people cut down trees. The
11. _____ population increased and more *timber* was needed to build houses.
Serious problems began to develop. Very often the lumber companies
12. _____ *clear-cut* the forests, removing all the trees and leaving the land bare.
13. _____ When the rains came, the earth was washed away. This *erosion* of rich
earth left land where no food could grow.

14. _____

15. _____

16. _____

Unfortunately, most of us did not realize the damage that our growing cities were causing. The *rate* of growth was so fast, and the needs of industrialized countries so great, that we did not stop to ask ourselves what was being *threatened* by these efforts. In fact, our behavior endangered forests and animals. We often chose to ignore the fact that our growing cities *displaced* birds and animals, who had to move away from humans.

17. _____

Humans have developed many ways to hurt the environment. *Damage* can be caused by farming, by industrial development, and by hunting and fishing.

18. _____
19. _____

Another serious environmental problem comes from *trash.* Hikers and tourists often throw cans and paper away instead of *disposing* of the trash in trash cans.

20. _____

There is a *balance* in nature that can be hurt by the smallest change in living conditions. For example, in a healthy environment, the amount of plant food is just right for the number of fish in a river; however, when the river is dammed, the balance changes. Too many fish or too much plant life can make the river unliveable.

Many countries have passed laws to protect the environment; these include such things as requiring factories and automobiles to reduce pollution and limiting the numbers of animals that can be killed by *hunters.*

21. _____

22. _____

In their efforts to protect the environment, governments are often forced to choose between farm animals and *wild* animals. This is because land which has been cleared for farm animals is unhealthy for animals living outside human control.

23. _____

Increasingly, people are cutting down forests in *tropical* areas of the world, where the hot temperatures and large amounts of rainfall produce fast-growing timber.

24. _____

25. _____
26. _____

27. _____

Some types of animals (the jaguar, for example) have been killed off to the point that very few still exist. A number of these *rare* animals live in areas where new dams are planned. In many cases, they could become *extinct.* It would be sad if we lost these animals forever. For this reason, environmentalists work to *protect* animals so that they can reproduce until their numbers increase to a safe level. One solution is to create *preserves,* large areas of land or water where animals and fish are protected.

28. _____

Most people would want to protect their *quality of life,* for example, good jobs and comfortable homes in clean cities. But environmentalists point out that the first step in protecting our quality of life is protecting our environment.

Exercise 2

This exercise gives you additional clues to the meaning of unfamiliar vocabulary in context. In the brief report indicated in parentheses, find the word or phrase that best fits the meaning given. Your teacher may want to read these aloud as you quickly scan the text to find the answer.

1. (United States) What phrase means *a safe place for sea animals and plants?*

2. (Belize)   What word means *delicate; easily damaged?*

3. (The Alps)   What word means *damaged; hurt?*

4. (Australia)   What word means *to eat the grass down to the roots; to hurt the land by overeating?*

Nonprose Reading

College Application and Tuition Chart

Part 1: College Application

On pages 125 and 126 is an application for admission to Washtenaw Community College (WCC). It is similar to application forms used by many colleges and universities.

Getting Oriented

It is often useful to get a quick overview of an application before you work on it. Skim the two pages quickly, and answer the following questions.

1. Note that the application is composed of four parts. What kinds of information will you need to give? (Circle all that you notice.)

Health information	Address	Military experience
Previous education	Income	Employment history
Educational goals	Marital status	Physical appearance

2. How long do you think it will take you to complete the application form? _____

Comprehension

Complete the application form now. The pages facing the application give information and ask questions about the form. Refer to them *as* you complete the application. Notice that they refer to specific questions or sections of the form. True/False items are indicated by a T / F before a statement. Some questions may have more than one correct answer. Others require an opinion. Choose the answer you like best; be prepared to defend your choices. Your teacher may want you to work individually, in pairs, or in small groups.

1. (Re: Attention New Students)

   a. How much does it cost to apply to WCC? _____

   b. Do you think if you apply now, but decide not to take classes immediately, you will have to pay

      the application fee when you do decide to attend? _____

2. (Re: item 1) Note: The word *former* refers to any family name you have used before.

3. (Re: item 5)

   a. If your local address and phone are the same as your permanent address, just put "same."

   b. Why do you think the school wants both local and permanent addresses?

   _____

4. (Re: item 8)

   a. Why does the school want to know if you are a resident of Washtenaw County? _____

   _____

   b. What do you think the school will take as "proof of residency"? _____

5. (Re: item 9)

   a. Why does the school want an emergency contact person? _____

   b. Who might you put in this blank—family, friends, employers? _____

6. (Re: items 10–19)

   a. (Re: section heading) The phrase *admission status* means whether or not you are admitted as a
           student.

   b. T / F   If you do not answer the questions in this section, you may not be admitted to WCC.

   c. (Re: item 10) The word *veteran* refers to one who has served in the army, navy, air force, etc.,
           of a country.

   d. If the answers to the questions in this section do not affect whether or not you will be admitted,
      why do you think they are here? Put a check (✓) next to all possible answers.

      ___ (1) because the school keeps a detailed file on all students

      ___ (2) because the school uses the information in reports to the legislature, to request money,
            etc.

      ___ (3) for researchers who study education

      ___ (4) to make sure that the school does not get problem students

Application For Admission

Washtenaw Community College
Admissions Office
4800 East Huron River Drive - P.O. Box D-1
Ann Arbor, MI 48106 - (313) 973-3543

ATTENTION NEW STUDENTS

This application cannot be processed unless accompanied by a $15 application fee. This fee is non-refundable and is assessed one time only.

Application for : Fall 19 ____ Winter 19 ____ Sp/Su 19 ____

1. **Name** _____
   (Please print)   Last   First   Middle   Former

2. **Social Security Number:** [ ][ ][ ][ ][ ][ ][ ][ ][ ]   PLEASE BE ACCURATE. THIS BECOMES YOUR STUDENT I.D. NUMBER

3. **Please check One:** ☐ New Student ☐ Former Student at WCC   Last semester in attendance at WCC _____

4. **Permanent Address** _____
   Number and Street   City   State   Zip Code   County

5. **Local Address** _____
   Number and Street   City   State   Zip Code   County

6. **Permanent Phone** (____) _____ 7. **Local Phone** (____) _____

8. **Are you a resident of Washtenaw County?** ☐ Yes ☐ No   If yes, how long? _____
   (Proof of residency is required – contact the Admissions Office for details)

9. **In case of emergency, whom may we contact?**
   Name _____ Telephone Number (____) _____

YOUR ANSWERS TO THE FOLLOWING QUESTIONS WILL NOT AFFECT YOUR ADMISSION STATUS

10. **Are you a U.S. Military Veteran?** ☐ Yes ☐ No   11. **Is English your first language?** ☐ Yes ☐ No

12. **I am a** (check one): ☐ U.S. Citizen ☐ Visa Holder _____ F1 Student? ☐ Yes ☐ No
    TYPE OF VISA (for foreign nationals only)

    ☐ Permanent Resident-Alien Registration # _____ Date _____
    (Green Card)

13. **Gender:** ☐ Male ☐ Female 14. **Birthdate:** ___/___/___ 15. **Country of Citizenship:** _____
    (Optional)   (Optional) MONTH DAY YEAR   (Optional)

16. **Ethnic Group:** ☐ American Indian/Alaskan Native ☐ African-American, Non-Hispanic ☐ White, Non-Hispanic
    (Optional)   ☐ Hispanic ☐ Asian/Pacific Islander ☐ Non-Resident Alien ☐ Other (describe) _____

17. **Give name of last high school attended below**

    _____
    Name of School   City/State

    Did you graduate? ☐ Yes ☐ No Graduation Date: _____
                                                         Month/Year

18. **Are you a GED recipient?** ☐ Yes ☐ No (If yes, please provide a copy of the GED certificate.)

19. **List all colleges you have attended**✶✶ (beginning with the college most recently attended)

    Name of College   City/State   Dates of Attendance   Graduation Date

    _____

    _____

✶✶If you plan to receive a certificate or degree from Washtenaw Community College or are receiving Veteran's benefits, please request an official transcript from all colleges attended.
An Evaluation of Transfer Credit must be _requested_ – contact the Student Records Office for details at (313)973-3548.

I certify that the information given on this form is correct and complete to the best of my knowledge. It is understood that tuition charges are subject to adjustment should it be determined that the information set forth is incorrect.

Signature _____ Date _____

It is the policy of Washtenaw Community College not to discriminate on the basis of sex, race, age, or handicap in admissions, employment or in the operation of any educational program or activity.

Washtenaw Community College.

Residency	
I	S
O	C

County	

Citizenship		
C	P	F

Survey		
I	H	A	X
W	N	O	B

High School	
2	
3	

Grad	
01	
06	

College	
0	
0	

College	
0	
0	

Orientation		
O	E	A
G	P	L

Term of App	
01	
05	
09	

Student Type	
HSG	CGD
TCC	GED
T4Y	NHS
CHS	GST

Program	

Intent		
AS	AT	AE
CE	TR	JS
NJ	AP	PI
GS	PH	OT

Source		
AR	NP	CE
AO	FR	JS
HC	ST	BI
EM	FL	RC
TV	TS	OT

K.P.	
A.L.	
UPDATE:	
FT	PT
D	E
E/W	P.C.
D.H.	

Application For Admission

20. Current Employment Status: ❑ Full-Time (F) ❑ Part-Time (P) ❑ Not Employed (N)

_____
Place of Employment   City/State   Telephone Number   Type of Work

21. Are the courses you are taking related to your current employment? ❑ Yes ❑ No

22. How did you first learn about WCC? (Check only <u>one</u> answer)

❑ Admissions Representative (AR)
❑ Admissions Office (AO)
❑ High School Counselor (HC)
❑ Employer (EM)
❑ Radio / Television (TV)

❑ Newspaper (NP)
❑ Relative / Friend (FR)
❑ Another Student (ST)
❑ Flyer (FL)
❑ Time Schedule (TS)

❑ Continuing Education (CE)
❑ Job Skills Center (JS)
❑ Business / Industry Program Guide (BI)
❑ Regional Center (RC)
❑ Other (OT) (please specify) _____

_____

23. How long do you intend to pursue your studies at Washtenaw Community College?

❑ On a continuous basis until I reach my goal. (C) ❑ On an occasional basis. (S) ❑ Only one semester. (O)

24. Do you plan to attend: (answer both A and B)

A. ❑ Full-Time (F) ❑ Part-Time (P)   **B.** ❑ Day (D) ❑ Evening (E) ❑ Evening/Weekend (W)

YOUR ANSWERS TO THE FOLLOWING QUESTIONS WILL NOT AFFECT YOUR ADMISSIONS STATUS

25. What most influenced your decision to attend WCC?

❑ Cost (1)   ❑ Counselor (2)   ❑ Program Availability (3)   ❑ Class Sizes (4)   ❑ Time of Class Offerings (5)
❑ Reputation (6)   ❑ Location (7)   ❑ Financial Aid (8)   ❑ Accessibility (9)   ❑ Other (10) (please specify)

26. Your highest level of education attained:
_____

❑ 8th grade (8)   ❑ 9th grade (9)   ❑ 10th grade (10)   ❑ 11th grade (11)
❑ High school graduate (12) ❑ GED recipient (13)   ❑ Trade or technical (14) ❑ Some college (15)
❑ Associate's Degree (16)   ❑ Bachelor's Degree (17) ❑ Master's Degree (18)   ❑ Doctorate (19)

27. Are you a single parent? ❑ Yes ❑ No

28. Will you need help because of a physical disability? ❑ Yes ❑ No

29. Will you need help because of a learning disability? ❑ Yes ❑ No

30. Educational attainment of parents (check highest level):

Mother: ❑ No College (N) ❑ Some College (S) ❑ 2-Year Degree (2) ❑ 4-Year Degree (4)
Father: ❑ No College (N) ❑ Some College (S) ❑ 2-Year Degree (2) ❑ 4-Year Degree (4)

31. Household income:

❑ 0-4,999 (04)   ❑ 10,000-14,999 (10) ❑ 20,000-29,999 (20) ❑ 40,000-49,999 (40)
❑ 5,000-9,999 (05) ❑ 15,000-19,999 (15) ❑ 30,000-39,999 (30) ❑ 50,000+ (50)

32. Marital Status ❑ Single (S)   ❑ Married (M)
                        ❑ Divorced (D) ❑ Widowed (W)

7. (Re: item 23) T / F   It is possible to take only one or two courses at WCC.

8. (Re: item 24) T / F   WCC offers classes days, nights, and weekends.

9. (Re: item 25) What reasons can you think of for item 25? How might the school use the information?

_____

_____

10. (Re: items 28 and 29) T / F   WCC offers special services to students who are blind or need special help learning.

11. (Re: item 30) T / F   WCC has found that students who have educated parents are better students.

12. (Re: item 31) T / F   WCC charges according to income—the more you make, the more you pay.

Part 2: Tuition Chart

On page 128 is a chart showing the tuition of Bellevue Community College (BCC) in Washington State. Study the chart to find out how much it would cost you to attend.

The cost for tuition is based on the number of credits you take (usually, one hour a week of class equals one credit) and who you are (definitions of these terms can be found beneath the chart). Notice that the far left column lists the number of credits you might take and that the other columns show how much you would pay depending on who you are.

Answer the following questions according to your understanding of the chart. Your teacher may want you to work individually, in pairs, or in small groups. Some questions may have more than one correct answer. Others require an opinion. Choose the answer you like best; be prepared to defend your choices.

1. How much would a resident pay for a three-hour course? _____

2. How much would a refugee pay for the same course? _____

3. Who pays the least for a three-credit class? _____

4. Why do you think veterans pay less than other groups for classes at the community college?

_____

5. If you were to take a class at BCC, how much would *you* pay for a three-credit course? _____

6. If you needed to take four three-credit courses, would you take all four classes in one term, or would you spread them out over several terms? What would the difference in cost be if you took all in one term or if you took only one course a term?

_____

_____

Bellevue Community College
Fall-Winter-Spring

Credits	Tuition				
	Resident	Nonresident	SEA Veteran	Persian Gulf Veteran	Refugee
1 or 2	$68.80	$ 324.00	$19.20	$60.80	$106.10
3	133.20	513.00	28.80	91.20	159.15
4	177.60	684.00	38.40	121.60	212.20
5	222.00	855.00	48.00	152.00	265.25
6	266.40	1,026.00	57.60	182.40	318.30
7	310.80	1,197.00	67.20	212.80	371.35
8	355.20	1,368.00	76.80	243.20	424.20
9	399.60	1,539.00	86.40	273.60	477.45
10–18	444.00	1,710.00	96.00	304.00	530.50
19 & over	*	**			***

* Residents will pay $444.00 plus $38.85 per additional credit.

** Nonresidents will pay $1,710.00 plus $165.45 per additional credit.

*** Refugees will pay $530.50 plus $48.50 per additional credit.

Resident: a person who lives in the area (city, county, state) of the school; for most schools, international students are not considered residents for purposes of tuition.

Veteran: one who has served in the army, navy, air force, etc. of a country (SEA = South East Asian).

Refugee: a person who has been forced to leave his or her country, usually because of war.

Bellevue Community College, Fall-Winter-Spring, 1994–1995.

Word Study

Context Clues

These exercises give you practice using context clues from a reading passage. Use your general knowledge, your knowledge of stems and affixes, and information from the entire text below to write a definition, synonym, or description of the italicized word on the line provided. Note that some of the words appear more than once. Read through the entire passage before deciding on a definition of each term. By the end of the passage, you should have a good idea of the meaning. You do not need an exact definition; with only a general idea of the meaning, you will often be able to understand the meaning of a written text.

Passage 1: Fixing Broken Bones with Sound

If you break your arm, you may find your doctor using sound to help you. Doctors are excited about a new way they have found to help broken bones *heal*. This new *technique* uses sound waves. Sound waves seem to make *fractured* bones *heal* faster. How does this work? A machine sends out sound waves toward the broken bone. These waves make the bone cells *vibrate*. This movement of the cells seems to cause them to give off chemicals that help the bone *mend*. Using sound waves can greatly *reduce* the time that it takes for a broken leg to *heal;* it may take only six weeks instead of 12 weeks for the bone to *mend*.

1. heal: _____

2. technique: _____

3. fractured: _____

4. vibrate: _____

5. mend: _____

6. reduce: _____

Adapted from "Mending Bones with Sound," by Peter D. A. Warwick, *Reader's Digest,* January, 1991, 168.

Passage 2: World Population Continues to Rise

The next 10 years will be a critical *decade.* The choices made will decide the speed of population growth for much of the 21st century; they will decide whether world population triples or merely doubles before it finally stops growing; they will decide whether the *pace* of damage to the environment speeds up or slows down.

The world's population, now 5.3 billion, is increasing by three people every second—about a quarter of a million every day. Between 90 and 100 million people—*roughly equivalent* to the population of Eastern Europe or Central America—will be added every year during the next *decade;* a billion people—a whole extra China—over the next 10 years.

No less than 95% of the *global* population growth over the next 35 years will be in the developing countries of Africa, Asia, and Latin America.

It has been more than 30 years since the population growth rate of the developing countries reached its *peak.* But it will be only in the next five years that the additions to total numbers in developing countries will reach their maximum. It's difficult to move fast enough to meet the needs caused by this growth.

Racing to provide services to fast-growing populations is like running up the down escalator. You have to run very fast indeed to keep going up. So far, all the effort put into social programs has not been quite enough to meet growing needs.

1. decade: _____

2. pace: _____

3. roughly: _____

4. equivalent: _____

5. global: _____

6. peak: _____

7. racing: _____

Adapted from "World Population Continues to Rise," by Nafis Sadik, *Futurist,* March–April, 1991, 9.

Word Study

Stems and Affixes

Below is a chart showing some commonly occurring stems and affixes.* Study their meanings; then do the exercises that follow. Your teacher may ask you to give examples of other words you know that are derived from these stems and affixes.

Prefixes

anti-	against	anti-American
in-, im-, il-, ir-	not	inactive, impossible
micro-	small	microphone
peri-	around	perimeter
sub-	under	subway
super-	above, greater	superior, superpower, superstar
syn-, sym-, syl-	with, together, same, alike	symphony synonym

Stems

-anthropo-	human	anthropology
-aqua-	water	aquarium
-bio-	life	biology
-chron-	time	chronology, chronological
-geo-	earth	geology
-hydr-, -hydro-	water, liquid	hydrothermal
-log-, -logy	speech, word, study	biology
-path-, -pathy	feeling, disease	sympathy, sympathetic
-phon-	sound	telephone
-psych-	mind	psychology
-son-	sound	sound, sonic
-therm-, -thermo-	heat	thermal

Suffixes

-ate (verb)	to make	activate
-ic, -al (adj.)	relating to, having the characteristics of	comic, musical
-ist (noun)	one who	biologist, dentist
-meter (noun)	measuring instrument, measure	thermometer
-scope (noun)	instrument for looking	telescope

*For a list of all stems and affixes taught in *Choice Readings,* see the Appendix.

Exercise 1

Use your knowledge of stems and affixes to answer the following questions.

1. What do you think each of these scientific instruments measures?

   speedometer _____

   chronometer _____

   thermometer _____

   micrometer _____

   telemeter _____

   hydrometer _____

2. What do you think these scientific instruments are used for?

   telescope _____

   microscope _____

   periscope _____
   (Hint: a submarine uses a periscope above the water.)

3. Many scientific fields of study end with *-ology*. Match the names of the fields to the descriptions.

   ___ phonology   a. the study of the culture and behavior of humans

   ___ anthropology   b. the study of mental processes and behaviors

   ___ pathology   c. the study of the physical structure and history of the Earth

   ___ psychology   d. the study of speech sounds

   ___ hydrology   e. the study of life and life processes

   ___ biology   f. the study of relationships between mental and physical processes

   ___ microbiology   g. the study of the causes and consequences of disease

   ___ psychobiology   h. the study of life forms too small to be seen by the naked eye

   ___ geology   i. the study of water

4. *Onym* (or *nomen*) is a word part that means *name.*

   Which word below is a synonym for *weak*?
   a. not strong   b. strong   c. week

   Which word below is an antonym for *weak*?
   a. not strong   b. strong   c. week

   Which word below is a homonym (or homophone) for *weak*? (Hint: *homo-* means *same.*)
   a. not strong   b. strong   c. week

5. What source of power is used to make electricity at a *hydroelectric* power plant? _____

6. What do you think hydrothermal energy is? _____

   _____

7. Cars use *hydraulic* brakes to stop; buses and planes use air brakes. What is in the braking system of cars that is not in the braking system of buses and planes?

   _____

8. Which choice below shows a *superscript?* _____   Which shows a *subscript?* _____

   a. 5^3 b. 5_3 c. 53   d. 53

9. Many common English words begin with one of the spellings of the prefix *in-, im-, il-, ir-* with the meaning *no, not,* or *without.* List four words like this. (Can you think of one for each of the four different spellings of the prefix?)

   _____

10. Which of these words is the *superlative* form of the word *good?*

    a. good   b. better   c. best

Exercise 2

Word analysis can help you to guess the meaning of unfamiliar words. Using context clues and what you know about word parts, write a definition, synonym, or description of the italicized words.

1. _____   The *perimeter* of a square is four times the length of one of its sides.

2. _____   Not all sailors feel comfortable in *submarines;* many prefer to be above water all the time.

3. _____   Submarines use *sonar* instruments to give them information about the location and size of underwater objects.

4. _____   The Concorde flies from Paris to New York at *supersonic* speed.

5. _____   The police said the killer is a *psychopath.*

6. _____   Make sure you drink a lot of water when you exercise on a hot day; you don't want to get *dehydrated.*

7. _____   Elizabeth is studying *biochemistry* as an undergraduate at the university and hopes to go to medical school when she graduates.

8. _____   Don has an appointment with a *psychologist* once a week to talk about the problems he has making friends.

9. _____   The doctor told me to take the *antibiotic* for seven days.

10. _____   If we spill oil in our oceans, we will endanger *aquatic* life.

11. _____   The insect that is eating my flowers is so small that it is almost *invisible.*

12. _____   If your lips move when you are reading silently, you are *subvocalizing.*

13. _____   Ms. Smith's class had an average score of 80% on the test. Ms. Jones's class had an average of 79%. This does not mean that Smith's class is smarter than Jones's class because the difference in scores is statistically *insignificant.*

14. _____   It does not cost a lot to travel in London. You can use the *inexpensive*
15. _____   *subway* system that Londoners call the tube.

16. _____   Many children's books and movies *anthropomorphize* animals. Children enjoy that bears "talk" and rabbits "cry."

17. _____   I *sympathize* with Debbie because I had the same problem last year as she has now.

18. _____   It can be very expensive to heat your home in the winter in parts of the U.S. To save money—and energy—lower the *thermostat* to 55° F when you go to bed at night.

19. _____   The rock band needs a new *vocalist;* the old lead singer left them to form his own band.

20. _____   There is a lot of *antipathy* toward politicians who promise they will do something for this country and then do not do what they promised.

21. _____   During the late 1960s and early 1970s, there were many *antiwar* protests at U.S. colleges and universities.

22. _____   Everyone gets a cough sometimes, but many smokers develop a *chronic* cough.

23. _____   When the teacher asked the students to return at 1:30, he told them all to *synchronize* their watches.

Sentence Study

Restatement and Inference

Each sentence below is followed by five statements.* The statements are of four types:

1. Some of the statements are restatements of ideas in the original sentence. They give the same information in a different way.

2. Some of the statements are inferences (conclusions) that can be drawn from the information given in the sentence.

3. Some of the statements are not true based on the information given.

4. Some of the statements cannot be proved true or false based on the information given.

Put a check (✓) next to all restatements and inferences (types 1 and 2). Note: do not check a statement that is true of itself but cannot be inferred from the paragraph. There is not always a single correct set of answers. Be prepared to discuss your choices with your classmates.

Example   Nine out of ten doctors responding to a questionnaire said they recommend our product to their patients if they recommend anything.

        ___ a. Nine out of ten doctors recommend the product.

        ___ b. Of the doctors who responded to a questionnaire, nine out of ten doctors recommend the product.

        ___ c. If they recommend anything, nine out of ten doctors responding to a survey recommend the product.

        ___ d. Most doctors recommend the product.

        ___ e. We don't know how many doctors recommend the product.

Explanation   ___ a. This is not true. We don't have information about all doctors; we only have information about doctors who responded to a questionnaire.

        ___ b. This is not true. Nine out of ten doctors responding recommend the product if they recommend anything. We can assume that some doctors don't recommend anything.

---

*For an introduction to sentence study, see Unit 1.

✓ c. This is a restatement of the original sentence.

d. We cannot know this from the information given.

✓ e. This is an inference. From the information given, we don't know how many doctors recommend the product.

---

1. Only a few modern artists are as internationally successful as the sculptor Carl Andre.

___ a. Only a few modern artists are successful.
___ b. Carl Andre is an artist.
___ c. Carl Andre is known around the world.
___ d. Carl Andre is more internationally successful than most modern artists.
___ e. Many modern artists are more successful than Carl Andre.

2. Unlike women's clothes, menswear styles don't usually undergo dramatic changes.

___ a. Women's clothing styles often change dramatically.
___ b. Men's clothing styles often change dramatically.
___ c. Men who style women's clothes dislike women.
___ d. Men's underwear, unlike women's clothes, is likely to undergo dramatic changes.
___ e. Men's clothes don't change as much as women's styles.

3. Apart from the fact that women everywhere give birth and care for children, there is surprisingly little evidence to support the idea that women are better parents than men.

___ a. Women are better parents than men.
___ b. There is surprisingly little evidence that women everywhere care for children.
___ c. Women are naturally better parents than men.
___ d. The fact that women everywhere give birth and care for children supports the idea that nature makes women better parents.
___ e. There is not very much evidence that women are better parents than men.

4. It is not an overstatement to say that most people in the U.S. are close to being obsessed with their physical appearance.

___ a. Most people in the U.S. are very concerned with how they look.
___ b. It is too strong to say that most people in the U.S. are very concerned with their physical appearance.
___ c. Most people in the U.S. are obsessed with their physical appearance.
___ d. It is overstating it to say that most people in the U.S. are close to being obsessed with their appearance.
___ e. Apparently, *obsessed* means much too concerned.

5. Despite what many people believe, writing is not only a matter of putting one's ideas into words.

___ a. Writing is only a matter of putting one's ideas into words.
___ b. Writing requires putting one's ideas into words.
___ c. Many people believe that writing is only a matter of putting one's ideas into words.
___ d. Many people believe that writing is not only a matter of putting one's ideas into words.
___ e. Writing is more than just putting one's ideas into words.

6. It is often said of poets, but in Tsvetayeva's case it appears true: she must have been impossible to live with.

___ a. Poets are often said to be difficult to live with.
___ b. It seems that Tsvetayeva was very difficult to live with.
___ c. Because she was a poet, Tsvetayeva was impossible to live with.
___ d. Poets are often impossible to live with.
___ e. Many people seem to believe that poets are impossible to live with.

7. It's a wonderful world that we live in—a world filled with rainbows and rockets, with echoes and electricity, with atomic particles and planets, with invisible forces that affect us without our even knowing they exist.

___ a. We live in a wonderful world.
___ b. Most of the time, we don't know that the world exists.
___ c. Apparently, *invisible* means not visible, not able to be seen.
___ d. Electricity affects us without our knowing it exists.
___ e. This sentence is probably taken from a research journal.

8. An interesting fact about technology is that it can both hurt the environment and be our best hope for preventing or repairing such damage.

___ a. Apparently, the meaning of *damage* is similar to *hurt.*
___ b. Technology can hurt the environment.
___ c. Technology can help the environment.
___ d. Technology can cause environmental damage.
___ e. Technology is the only way to repair environmental damage.

9. It was almost 40 years ago that the sun began to set on the day of the large ocean liners, the great ships that carried travelers across the Atlantic Ocean—and to every corner of the world where there were bands that played welcoming music.

___ a. Large ocean liners have been popular for 40 years.
___ b. 40 years ago, ocean liners were more popular than they are today.
___ c. Apparently, liners are ships.
___ d. True ocean liners only traveled across the Atlantic Ocean.
___ e. Ocean liners brought their own musical bands with them.

10. As anyone who has ever visited Paris will know, the difference between a traveler and a tourist lies not in the place visited but in the way it is visited, not in where you go but how.

___ a. For this author, the terms *traveler* and *tourist* are synonyms.
___ b. Tourists visit different places than do travelers.
___ c. Only a tourist would visit Paris.
___ d. You can see both travelers and tourists in Paris.
___ e. Travelers and tourists go to the same places but, once there, they visit them differently.

Paragraph Reading

Main Idea

Before You Begin   Fables are a type of story told around the world. They are short, easy-to-remember tales that teach lessons about how people behave or about how they should behave. Read the fable below. What is the *moral,* that is, lesson about human behavior, of this fable?

Example: The Child Who Cried Wolf

Once there was a child whose job was to watch the sheep of the town. It was a lonely and often boring job. One day, the child thought it would be fun to cry "Wolf!" and watch the people working in nearby fields come running to help save the sheep. The child did this several times. Each time, the townspeople left their work, ran to help, and found the child laughing. Finally, the people got tired of the joke and decided not to listen to the child any longer.

Soon afterward, a wolf really came. The child shouted for help: "Wolf, wolf!" But the townspeople ignored the shouts, and all the sheep were killed.

Moral: _____

Have you heard this fable before? In "The Child Who Cried Wolf," the characters are people. In many other fables, the characters are animals, but they are animals who act just like people. What are some fables that you have heard? Your teacher may want you to work in small groups to make a list of fables you know before you read the fables in this section.

Read the fables that follow and, after each one, write the moral. You may find that some fables have more than one moral or that two individuals see different morals in the same fable. You also may notice that different fables have the same moral.

Fable 1: The Lion and the Four Bulls

Lion used to walk about a field in which four bulls lived. Many times he tried to attack them, but whenever he came near they turned their tails toward one another so that whichever way Lion tried to attack, he would have to face the horns of one of them.

At last, however, the bulls started arguing with each other, and each went off to a different part of the field by himself. Then Lion attacked them one by one and soon had killed all four.

Moral: _____

_____

Example fable adapted from "The Boy Who Cried Wolf," in *Tales from Aesop,* edited by Harold Jones (New York: Franklin Watts, 1981).

Fable 1 adapted from "The Four Oxen and the Lion," in *The Fables of Aesop,* retold by Joseph Jacobs (New York: Macmillan, 1966), 74.

Fable 2: The Goose That Laid Golden Eggs

A man once owned a goose that laid eggs made of gold. Every day, the man took a golden egg from the goose's nest, sold it at the market, and used the money to buy the things that he needed for the day. Then one day, the man got tired of waiting patiently for each golden egg to be laid. He wanted all his treasure at once, and so he killed the goose, thinking that inside her he would find solid gold. Sadly, after cutting open the goose, he found only the inside of a goose.

Moral: _____

_____

Fable 3: The North Wind and the Sun

The North Wind and the Sun were arguing about which of them was the stronger when they saw a man walking along a country road. They agreed that whichever one of them could make the man take off his coat was the stronger. The North Wind tried first, blowing hard at the man. The man buttoned his coat. Then the North Wind blew even more violently, but that made the man hold his coat more closely to him. The Sun's turn came next. Gently, the Sun shone on the man. After a while, the man became warm, so he unbuttoned his coat. Soon, he took it off. Thus the Sun was the winner.

Moral: _____

_____

Fable 2 adapted from "Much Wants More," in *Tales From Aesop,* edited by Harold Jones (New York: Franklin Watts, 1981).
Fable 3 adapted from "The North Wind and the Sun," in *Tales from Aesop,* edited by Harold Jones (New York: Franklin Watts, 1981).

Fable 4: The Fox in the Well

One day an unlucky fox who was trying to get a drink of water fell into a deep well and could not get out. Along came a thirsty goat and asked Fox if the water was good. "Oh yes," said Fox, "the water is excellent." And Fox told the goat to jump in and have a drink. Without stopping to think, Goat jumped into the well and took a long drink. Then both animals began to wonder how they would get out of the well. "I have an idea," said Fox. "Put your feet against the wall, and I will climb on top of you to get out. After I am out, I'll pull you up too." The goat gladly agreed, so the fox climbed onto Goat's shoulders and out over the edge of the well. Then Fox started to leave. Goat cried out, "What about me? Aren't you going to help me out?" "You have more hairs on your chin than brains in your head," answered Fox. "If you were smart, you never would have jumped in without first thinking how you would get out."

Moral: _____

_____

Fable 5: The Tortoise and the Hare

A rabbit and a turtle were looking for something to do one afternoon and decided to have a race. "You are the slowest fellow I've ever met," said the rabbit to the turtle. "Really?" answered the turtle. "I'll race you any time you choose, and I'll win." "Impossible," cried the rabbit.

The rabbit, with his long legs, started to run down the path so fast he seemed to be flying. But the turtle, with his short legs and his heavy shell, had a hard time moving at all. Soon the rabbit was so far ahead that he decided to stop for a rest. The rabbit said to himself, "I'll sleep a little while before I run any farther. It still will be easy to beat that slow, old turtle."

Before long, the rabbit fell asleep in the warm sun. The turtle, although far behind, just kept walking. When the rabbit woke up, the stars were shining in the night sky. He jumped up and ran as fast as he could to the finish line of the race. He arrived just in time to see the turtle cross the finish line ahead of him.

Moral: _____

_____

Fable 4 adapted from "Look Before You Leap," in *Tales from Aesop,* edited by Harold Jones (New York: Franklin Watts, 1981).

Fable 5 adapted from "The Rabbit and the Turtle," in *Twelve Tales from Aesop,* retold by Eric Carle (New York: Putnam Publishing Group, 1980), 10 and from "The Hare and the Tortoise," in *Aesop's Fables,* by Heidi Holder, illustrator (New York: Viking Penguin, 1981), 23.

Fable 6: The Milkmaid

Patty the milkmaid was going to market carrying her milk in a pail on her head. As she walked, she began to think of what she would do with the money she would get from selling the milk.

"I'll buy some chickens from Farmer Brown," she said, "and they will lay eggs each morning. I'll sell the eggs to the school teacher. With the money that I get from selling the eggs, I'll buy myself a new hat. Then when I go to market, I will look more beautiful than all the other milkmaids! I will turn to the left and turn to the right to make sure that everyone sees how lovely I look in that hat."

As she spoke, she turned her head to the left and then to the right. The pail of milk fell off it, and all the milk spilled.

Moral: _____

_____

Fable 7: The Bird and the Ant

A thirsty ant, which had crawled near a stream, was carried away by the rushing water. A bird, seeing that the ant might drown, threw a big leaf into the water. The ant climbed onto it and was saved. A short time later, a hunter tried to shoot the bird. But just as he was about to fire his gun, the ant crawled up the back of his leg and bit him. He dropped his gun, and the bird flew away to safety.

Moral: _____

_____

Fable 8: The Donkey and the Horse

A horse and a donkey were traveling together with their master. The horse carried nothing while the donkey carried many heavy bundles. Stumbling under her heavy load, the poor donkey cried out to the proud horse, "Please, good Sir, I beg of you to help me carry these heavy packages. If you don't, I fear that I shall die." But the horse refused to share the heavy load.

Soon, the little donkey was so completely tired that she fell. No matter how bravely she tried, she could not stand up again. Seeing this, their master lifted the many packages from the donkey and put them all on the back of the horse, who immediately cried out, "Oh, poor me! Look what trouble I have caused myself! I would not share the load, and now I must carry everything alone."

Moral: _____

_____

Fable 6 adapted from "The Milkmaid and Her Pail," in *The Fables of Aesop,* retold by Joseph Jacobs (New York: Macmillan, 1966), 84.

Fable 7 adapted from "The Dove and the Ant," in *Tales from Aesop,* edited by Harold Jones (New York: Franklin Watts, 1981).

Fable 8 adapted from "A Laden Ass and a Horse," in *Aesop's Fables,* by Heidi Holder, illustrator (New York: Viking Penguin, 1981), 10–11.

Fable 9: The Mice and the Cat

Long ago, the mice held a meeting to discuss what they could do about the problems they had with their enemy the cat. Some said this, and some said that; but at last a young mouse got up and said he had an idea of what should be done.

"You will all agree," he said, "that the greatest danger from the cat is that she comes up behind us so silently. Now, if we could hear her coming, we could easily escape her. I suggest, therefore, that a small bell be tied around her neck on a string. Then we would always know when she was nearby, and we could easily hide until she went away."

Most of the mice cheered this idea until an old mouse stood up and said, "That idea sounds very good, but who will tie the bell around the cat's neck?"

The mice looked at each other, and nobody spoke.

Moral: _____

_____

Vocabulary Study: Idiomatic Expressions

Here is a list of some commonly used sayings in English. People use these sayings when they are giving advice or talking about another person's behavior. These sayings come from some of the fables you have read in this unit. Next to each saying, write the number of the fable that the saying comes from. When you have finished, your teacher may ask you to describe a situation in which you might use each of the sayings.

___ 1. Slow and steady wins the race.

___ 2. Don't cry wolf!

___ 3. Don't count your chickens before they hatch.

___ 4. He killed the goose that laid the golden eggs.

___ 5. Look before you leap.

___ 6. But who will bell the cat?

Fable 9 adapted from "Belling the Cat," in *The Fables of Aesop,* retold by Joseph Jacobs (New York: Macmillan, 1966), 39.

Discourse Focus

Careful Reading / Drawing Inferences

This exercise is similar to the one you did in Unit 3. Read each mystery carefully, and then answer the question that follows it. Your teacher may want you to work with your classmates to answer the question. Be prepared to defend your answers with details from the story. (If you're having trouble solving a mystery, additional clues can be found on page 146.)

Mystery 1: The Case of the Telltale Clock

Police found the body of Buffalo Fenn in his apartment. The electric cord of his clock was tied around his neck. The clock had stopped at 7:00.

Police Inspector Winters had Pete Skones, Buffalo's long-time enemy, arrested for questioning.

Pete claimed that on the morning of Buffalo's murder, he had been playing cards with friends. The friends said he never left the hotel room where they had been playing all night.

A week passed with no new clues to the murder. Then Nick the Nose went to see Inspector Winters, who had Dr. Haledjian in his office.

Nick grinned. "I know something," he said. "I know someone who saw Buffalo's murder. Broadway Ben."

"Ben," said Nick, "had a room down the hall from Buffalo. He was passing Buffalo's room when he saw Buffalo's door was open a little. He didn't hear anything at first except the ticking of Buffalo's clock. And suddenly the ticking stopped.

"Then Ben heard a man scream. He hid in a doorway at the end of the hall. Two minutes later he saw Pete Skones run out of Buffalo's room and race downstairs.

"Ben was so scared after he read what happened to Buffalo that he hasn't looked at a clock for a week. He's hiding, but I can take you to him if you pay me $5,000."

"Don't pay, Inspector Winters," said Dr. Haledjian. "Nick is lying."

How did Dr. Haledjian know Nick was lying?

Mysteries adapted from *Two-Minute Mysteries,* by Donald J. Sobol (New York: Scholastic Book Services, 1967): "The Case of the Telltale Clock," 149–50; "The Case of the Murdered Wife" (here "The Case of the Murdered Brother"), 103–4; "The Case of the Suicide Room," 147–48; "The Case of Willie the Wisp," 157–58; "The Case of the Locked Room," 83–84.

Mystery 2: The Case of the Murdered Brother

Dr. Haledjian finished examining the body of Mike Page, which lay on the red carpet of his fashionable home.

"Mr. Page was beaten to death with the handle of that gun," the famous detective said.

The gun had been found near the body. Sheriff Monahan was carefully examining it for fingerprints.

"I've telephoned his brother at his office," the sheriff said. "I only told him he'd better hurry home. I hate the job of telling him that his brother has been killed. Will you do it?"

"All right," Haledjian agreed as he watched the body being carried to an ambulance. Then he sat down to wait for John Page.

The ambulance had driven off to the hospital when John Page rushed through the front door. "What happened? Where's Mike?"

"I'm sorry to have to tell you this. He was murdered about two hours ago," said Haledjian. "Your cook found the body in the living room and telephoned the police."

"I can't find fingerprints on the gun that was used to murder him," interrupted the sheriff, holding the gun wrapped in a cloth. "I'll have the laboratory examine it thoroughly."

Page stared at the outline of the gun through the cloth. Suddenly he grabbed the sheriff's arm. "Find the monster who beat Mike to death. I'll offer a $50,000 reward!"

"Save your money," said Haledjian. "The murderer won't be hard to find!"

Why not?

Mystery 3: The Case of the Suicide Room

Sir Cecil Brookfield pulled back a large, heavy door at the end of one of the long halls in his 600-year-old castle in England.

Dr. Haledjian, a weekend guest, looked down into the darkness.

"A room with four walls—and no floor," said Sir Cecil. "Or rather, with a floor 100 feet below the level of the door.

"The room was built as a way to secretly kill the first owner's enemies," explained Sir Cecil. "Later, when the beautiful wife of the first Lord Brookfield died suddenly, her young lover threw himself to his death here.

"His suicide was not the last one in this room either. Ever since then, a young man has jumped to his death in the lifetime of every fourth owner. I am the fourth since the last time a young man killed himself in this room."

Sir Cecil pushed the heavy door shut. "I've ordered a worker from the village to come tomorrow to seal off the door. Then no one will ever be able to open it again."

Haledjian's bedroom was three doors away from the "suicide room." As he was getting ready for bed, he heard a dull thud, like the sound of something heavy falling. It could mean only one thing. He rushed into the hallway.

Sir Cecil was running toward the "suicide room." Together the two men pulled open the heavy door. Sir Cecil shined a flashlight down into the darkness below.

There, at the bottom of the hole, was the body of a young man.

"It's Ritchie, my wife's lawyer!" gasped Sir Cecil. "Why would he kill himself?"

"He didn't," corrected Haledjian. "He was pushed!"

How did Haledjian know?

Mystery 4: The Case of Willie the Wisp

Dr. Haledjian was vacationing in a small country in Europe when General Schwinn, head of the border guards in the country, asked for help on a "puzzling problem of possible smuggling."

Schwinn went to see Haledjian in his hotel room and asked him if he had heard of a man named Eugene W. McNally.

"Ah, yes, Willie the Wisp!" answered Haledjian. "He smuggled diamonds from the U.S. into Canada for years, and the border guards never caught him. He's a very clever criminal."

"That's the man," replied Schwinn. "He's tricking us again, but I don't understand how. Six months ago he appeared at the border of our country driving a new black Fiorta, a foreign sports car that costs $60,000. We've heard all about Willie, so of course we looked everywhere in that car. Nothing. But each of his three suitcases had a false bottom like smugglers use to hide things.

"Under the false bottoms were three bottles—one filled with bits of colored glass, one with sugar, and one with sea shells. Naturally, we couldn't arrest him for hiding those things. So we let him cross the border into our country.

"Now, twice a month we see a shining black Fiorta driving up to our border crossing. It's always Willie, of course! And he always has those three suitcases with the three bottles filled with the same strange things—colored glass, sugar, and sea shells.

"That thief just sits and laughs at the border guards. They're forced to let him in!" said Schwinn.

"Colored glass, sugar, and sea shells," said Haledjian to himself.

"What do they mean?" cried Schwinn. "What is he smuggling into our country?"

Haledjian lit a pipe and smoked it quietly for a few minutes. Then he grinned. "What a clever fellow that Willie is!"

What was Willie smuggling?

Mystery 5: The Case of the Locked Room

"I think I've been tricked, but I don't know how it was done," said Archer Skeat, the blind violinist, to Dr. Haledjian, as the two friends sat in the musician's library.

"Last night Marty Scopes came to visit," continued Skeat. "He told me he was tired of hearing me talk about how good my hearing is, and he convinced me to make a crazy $10,000 bet.

"Marty then went to the bar over there, filled a glass with six cubes of ice, and gave it to me. He took a bottle of cola and left the room.

"I locked the door and the windows from the inside, felt Marty's glass to make sure it held only ice, and put it on the table next to the bar. Then I turned off the lights and sat down to wait.

"The bet was that in less than an hour, Marty could enter the dark, locked room, walk over to the table, pick up the glass, remove the ice, pour in half a glass of soda, put the glass back on the table, and leave the room, locking it behind him—all without my hearing him!

"I heard nothing during the hour I waited in the locked room. At the end of the hour, I unlocked the door. Marty waited in the hall while I walked back to the table. The glass was exactly where I had left it. And it was half full of soda—and only soda. I tasted it! How did he do it?"

After a moment's thought, Haledjian said, "There is nothing wrong with your hearing; no one could have heard . . . . "

Heard what?

Additional Clues

If you had trouble solving any of the mysteries, here are additional clues. True/False items are indicated by a T / F before a statement.

Mystery 1: Here's a timely clue: What kind of clock did Buffalo have?

Mystery 2: Are you still puzzled?

a. When was Mike's body taken away from the house?
b. What did John Page offer a reward for?
c. How did John Page learn of his brother's death?
d. Who killed Mike Page?

Mystery 3: Before you jump to conclusions, do you want some more clues?

a. What did Sir Cecil and Haledjian have to do before they shined the flashlight down into the "suicide room"?
b. Could you close a heavy door behind you if you were falling?
c. Who do you think pushed Ritchie?

Mystery 4: Has Willie confused you, too? Maybe answering these questions will help.

a. Is Willie worried when the border guards find the suitcases with the false bottoms and the three jars? Why or why not?
b. What else besides the jars and the suitcases is Willie taking into the country each time he crosses the border?

Mystery 5: If you're not sure, perhaps answering this question will improve your powers of detection:

a. T / F   Skeat saw the ice cubes Marty put in the glass.
b. T / F   Ice cubes are always made only of water.

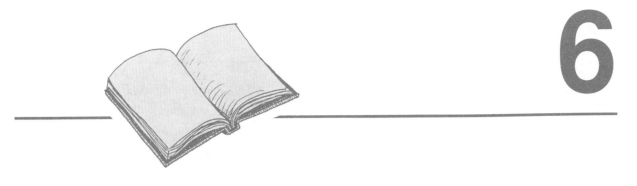

Reading Selection 1

Advice Column

In many countries, newspapers publish letters written to advisers, such as Ann Landers. The letters usually ask for advice concerning personal problems, and they are of general interest. The following letter is from a smoker who is angry at being told by family and friends to quit smoking.

Before You Begin

1. Do you smoke? Do you have friends who smoke?

2. Have you ever tried to stop smoking? Or do you know anyone who is trying to quit?

3. What do you think is the most effective way to stop smoking? How do you get someone else to stop smoking?

Read the letter, and answer the questions that follow. As you read, put yourself in the place of the smoker or in the place of the family and friends. Think of advice you would give to help solve this problem. Your teacher may want you to do Vocabulary from Context exercise 1 on page 151 before you begin.

Adamant Smoker Says Stop Nagging

Dear Ann Landers:

1   Please print an open letter to all my friends and relatives who want me to stop smoking. Here it is:

2   I am not a child. I will soon be celebrating my 30th birthday. I appreciate your concern for my health, but please keep it to yourself. I have not been living in a cave for the past ten years. I know about the dangers of smoking. The fact that I still smoke does not mean that I am ignorant of the health hazards. I know more than I want to about the dangers of smoking.

3   Bullying and begging have no effect on me. When you get children to leave me notes saying, "Please stop smoking. We love you and want you to live," it makes me angry. And, Mother, offering money to anyone who can get me to quit makes me feel like a hunted animal.

4   Let's make a deal. I promise to keep my mouth shut when I see you putting a third chunk of butter on your baked potato and adding a dollop of sour cream. I will remain silent when you order pecan pie for dessert and ask for a scoop of vanilla ice cream on top. I would appreciate the same consideration from you when I light up. I know you are concerned about my health, but I am not ready to quit. When I decide to quit smoking, you will be the first to know.

Sincerely,

Chicago Tribune Reader in Wheaton, Illinois

Adapted from the *Denver Post,* June 18, 1990.

Discussion/Composition

Give a brief answer to this person with your opinion of the problem and a solution. Then read Ann Landers's answer.

Ann Landers's Response

Dear Friend in Wheaton:

5   My theory is that nagging never works. It only irritates the person you want to help and often makes him or her more defensive and determined not to change.

6   People don't stop smoking, drinking, eating too much, popping pills, or doing other kinds of self-destructive behaviors until they are ready. The best approach is to let them know there is plenty of help available, if and when it is wanted, and then leave them alone.

Sincerely,

Ann Landers

Comprehension

Answer the following questions according to your understanding of the passage. Your teacher may want you to work individually, in small groups, or in pairs. True/False items are indicated by a T / F before a statement. Some questions may not have one correct answer. Others require an opinion. Choose the one you like best; be prepared to defend your choices.

1. T / F   Friend in Wheaton is a child.

2. How old is Friend in Wheaton? _____

3. Is Friend in Wheaton male or female? _____

4. How long has s/he been smoking? _____

5. What are the ways that family and friends have attempted to get him/her to stop smoking?

    a. _____

    b. _____

    c. _____

6. What is the deal that Friend proposes? In your opinion is this an equal agreement? Are the risks equal in both cases? Are the problems associated with both types of behaviors the same?

_____

_____

7. What is Ann Landers's advice to Friend in Wheaton? What is her advice to readers? _____

_____

8. T / F   Ann Landers does not think that smoking is harmful to one's health.

9. What examples does Ms. Landers give of self-destructive behaviors? _____

_____

Discussion

1. Following are some ways of getting people to stop smoking. Indicate if you think they are effective or not effective by circling the appropriate number. Make notes about the problems involved with each one.

Effective ↔ Not effective
1   2   3   4   5

a) Holding your nose and fanning the air with your hand every time smokers light a cigarette.

Problems: _____

1   2   3   4   5

b) Talking with them every chance you get about the dangers of smoking.

Problems: _____

1   2   3   4   5

c) Cutting articles from newspapers about the dangers of smoking and leaving them around for your smoker friends to see.

Problems: _____

1   2   3   4   5

d) Asking other friends and family to talk to them.

Problems: _____

1   2   3   4   5

e) Making doctor appointments for them so that they can get their health checkups.

Problems: _____

1   2   3   4   5

f) Informing them that they cannot smoke in your house and that you would prefer that they not smoke near you.

Problems: _____

1   2   3   4   5

g) Giving them your opinion and then not mentioning it again.

Problems: _____

2. T / F   Friend in Wheaton solved his/her problem by writing to Ann Landers.

Composition: Letter Writing

1. Write a letter to Ann Landers asking for help with a problem. You will need to describe the problem in enough detail for Ms. Landers to respond.

   a. List several problems that you think Ann Landers might be able to give you advice on.

   b. With a classmate, briefly discuss the problems you have identified. Take notes as you talk, so that you can use the ideas in your letter to Ann Landers.

Following are some points you may want to mention:

- What is the problem?
- Who is involved?
- How long have the problems existed?
- Who are the people involved in the problem?
- Who will have to change?

Composition: Understanding Cultural Differences

Following is an outline of a letter to Ann Landers about cultural differences between your community/culture and another community/culture. Using the suggestions provided, develop your own questions and write your own letter. Your teacher may want you to work in pairs or small groups as you begin thinking about the topic.

Street address
City, State Zip
Date

Dear Ann Landers:

Paragraph 1: Introduce yourself.

Paragraph 2: Ask for information or advice about a custom or behavior that you do not understand.
(Here is a list of examples.)

- Alcohol: What if I don't drink? What if I drink and my hosts do not?
- Smoking: What if I don't smoke? What if I smoke and they do not?
- Shopping: When is it okay to bargain for a lower price? Do I tip the clerks who help me? How do I know when it is my turn to be waited on by a clerk?
- Dating: Who asks whom? Who pays? Should we go out in groups or alone? Do we need to take chaperons?
- Meals: At what times do people eat? What should I say if my hosts eat something I do not eat? North Americans seem to eat a lot of salty foods, and meat, and dairy products; I am not used to this kind of food.

- Invitations: When should guests show up for dinner? For parties? What should I wear? Should I bring gifts for my hosts?
- Other: From your own experience, choose a cultural difference that has caused you some confusion or difficulty.

Paragraph 3: Tell a brief story illustrating the problem you are asking advice about.

Paragraph 4: Describe the customs you follow with regard to the story you have told above.

I look forward to hearing from you.

Sincerely,

(Your name)

Vocabulary from Context

Exercise 1

Both the ideas and the vocabulary in the exercise below are taken from the advice column. Use the context provided to decide on meanings for the italicized words. Write a definition, synonym, or description in the space provided.

1. _____   The family has been trying to get Herbie to stop smoking for several years now, but he is *adamant*. He refuses to change his habits.

2. _____   The *hazards* of smoking are well known: cancer, lung disease, and heart disease, among others.

3. _____   Herbie says that although he understands his family's concern for his health, he is *irritated* by their constant attempts to get him to stop smoking. He finds that he feels slightly angry and upset with them all the time because of their efforts.

4. _____   He realizes that he is very sensitive to criticism. He is quick to argue; his *defensiveness* makes him unpleasant to be around, but he thinks that this is as much their fault as his.

Exercise 2

This exercise gives you additional clues to the meaning of unfamiliar vocabulary in context. In the paragraph of the advice column indicated by the number in parentheses, find the word that best fits the meaning given. Your teacher may want to read these aloud as you quickly scan the paragraph to find the answer.

1. (2) What phrase means *do not give advice?*

2. (3) What word means *using one's position over someone else to make them do what you want; mistreating someone who is weaker or smaller than you?*

3. (4) Find *chunk, dollop,* and *scoop.*

   a. All have one meaning in common. What is it? _____

   _____

   b. What makes each one different? _____

   _____

4. (5) What word means *bothering; complaining; talking constantly to someone about something you think they should do?*

5. (6) What phrase means *taking drugs?*

Reading Selection 2

Newspaper Article

In "Reading for Different Goals," in Unit 1, you learned that there are different reasons for reading and that for different reading tasks, you must use different strategies. This exercise is designed to show you that you can understand the main ideas in a reading selection without understanding every detail and without knowing the meaning of all of the vocabulary.

Overview

In most cases, when you read a newspaper article, you do not need to comprehend everything in order to understand what the story is about. Look at the headline, the subtitle, and the photograph on page 154 to answer the following questions.

1. What do you guess the article will be about?

2. What does "Midwest" refer to?

Now read "Bugs Make Skin Crawl in Midwest" quickly, without stopping to look up unfamiliar words. Then answer the Comprehension questions.

Comprehension

Answer the following questions using short answers. In some cases you can mark your answer on the story itself. True/False items are indicated by a T / F before a statement.

1. What is a cicada? _____

2. Where was the story written? _____ Will readers in Los Angeles and New York be having problems with cicadas?

   _____

3. T / F   The cicada is a yearly problem in the Midwest.

4. T / F   The cicadas arrive every 17 years from South America.

5. How long does the problem last? _____ Why do the cicadas come out of the ground?

   _____

Bugs Make Skin Crawl in Midwest
Region worked up about cicada invasion

By The Associated Press

1   CHICAGO — The Windy City is going bonkers over bugs.

2   There are nightly updates on the TV news, recipes in the newspaper, even a special hot line heralding not the coming of the apocalypse, but the emergence of inch-long critters called cicadas.

3   The noisy devils unearth themselves every 17 years to mate, shriek incessantly, and drive homeowners crazy.

4   Millions of the winged creatures are expected to emerge in parts of Illinois, Iowa, Indiana and Wisconsin during the next few days, covering backyards and forests with their brownish, crunchy bodies.

5   After mating and laying eggs that will remain underground for another 17 years, the cicadas will die. The orgy should be over by early July, and experts say the creatures are harmless.

6   But that hasn't calmed the hysteria.

7   "It's completely unfounded," said Field Museum entomologist Phil Parrillo. "People are going out and getting insecticide to spray on them, but they're only going to be here for a few weeks. Gee whiz, don't worry about it."

8   The males produce a large shrill sound; the females are mute.

9   "They may be a nuisance in terms of the sound that they make," he said yesterday. And they can damage young trees where they lay their eggs.

10   "Other than that, they're really not going to cause a problem," he said.

11   Midwesterners might get a different impression from reading the newspaper or watching the news lately.

12   "The cicadas have reached Elmhurst," a broadcaster announced in a teaser for a recent television newscast.

13   WLS-TV news has run five or six reports "saying that they're on their way, and also a story on what people

INVADER EMERGES: Robby Graves, 3, of Elmhurst, Ill., watches a cicada shed its shell yesterday.

can do to protect their young trees," said Jim Lichtenstein, assignment editor.

14   The cover of a recent Chicago Tribune Sunday magazine featured the warning: "Get Ready! The 17-year itch of the cicada is about to begin."

15   The Chicago Sun-Times last week set up a hot line, which has received at least 60 calls a day from curious or horrified homeowners with questions about the bugs.

16   Michael Kendall, a Chicago attorney, tested one of the recipes with some cicadas he found Monday night in his brother's suburban backyard.

17   "We parboiled them and then sauteed them in butter and garlic and ate them sort of like shrimp," Kendall said. "They taste like sort of a starchy potato. They had a sort of scalloplike consistency."

Reprinted from the *Denver Post*, May 30, 1990, 2A.

6. What is the problem? Check (✓) all answers that you think are correct. Be prepared to defend your choices.

___ a. They are noisy.

___ b. They bite.

___ c. They harm young trees.

___ d. They eat clothing.

___ e. They make you itch.

___ f. They get in your food, especially shrimp dishes.

7. T / F   The best way to solve the problem is to spray insecticide on them.

8. You should be able to guess the general meanings of the following words from the context of the story. The numbers in parentheses indicate the paragraph in which each word can be found.

a. (3) What is the meaning of *shriek?* _____

b. (8) Which word means *silent?* _____

c. (9) What is the meaning of *nuisance?* _____

d. (15) What is the meaning of *hot line?* _____

9. What is the effect of the newspaper and television stories? Check (✓) all answers that you think are correct. Be prepared to defend your choices.

___ a. They are helping people deal with a serious problem.

___ b. They provide entertainment.

___ c. They are causing problems.

___ d. They provide important information.

___ e. They make money for themselves by selling newspapers and attracting viewers.

___ f. They will help scientists in efforts to get rid of the problem.

10. If Michael Kendall invites you to dinner soon, will you go? _____

_____

11. In the headline: What is the meaning of *make skin crawl?* Check (✓) all answers that you think are correct. Be prepared to defend your choices.

    ___ a. cause your skin to itch

    ___ b. horrify

    ___ c. make nervous

    ___ d. make curious

    ___ e. cause hunger

    Does your skin crawl at the thought of bugs like this? _____

12. The following words are used to describe the cicada. The number in parentheses indicates the paragraph in which each word can be found. Using the descriptions, draw a picture that expresses your impression of the cicada.

    a. (1) bugs
    b. (2) inch-long critters
    c. (3) noisy devils
    d. (4) winged creatures
    e. (4) brownish, crunchy bodies
    f. (9) nuisance

Reading Selections 3A–3C

Popular Science

In recent years, science and technology have become more and more a part of peoples' everyday lives, both at home and at work. Does this mean that most people today are well informed about general science? Do they understand the science behind everyday events? The three reading selections that follow address these questions.

Selection 3A   **Survey**

How much does the average person today understand about science and technology? To answer this question, researchers recently asked people a number of questions about "basic ideas of science." The results of their survey, which are reported on page 158, may surprise you. Don't turn to that page yet, though!

Before You Begin   Before you read about what the researchers discovered, test your own knowledge of general science by answering the questions below. True/False items are indicated by a T / F preceding a statement.

1. T / F   Lasers work by focusing sound waves.

2. T / F   Electrons are smaller than atoms.

3. T / F   The earliest humans lived at the same time as the dinosaurs.

4. Which travels faster—light or sound? _____

5. Does the Earth go around the Sun, or the Sun around the Earth? _____

   _____

6. How long does it take the Earth to go around the Sun? _____

Here are the answers: 1-F, 2-T, 3-F, 4-light, 5-The Earth goes around the Sun, 6-365 days.

How did you and your classmates do?

Do you think most people in the United States would get these questions right? What about people in other countries? After you make your predictions, read on to see what the researchers found in their survey.

What We Don't Know

A study of general scientific knowledge among adults in the United States and Great Britain found that many people are misinformed about very basic scientific information. Here is a sampling of several questions and the percentages in each country who answered correctly. Look at the table, then answer the questions that follow.

Question	Correct Answer	Percentage Answering Correctly	
		U.S.	Britain
1. Lasers work by focusing sound waves.	False (Lasers focus light waves.)	36.0	41.8
2. Electrons are smaller than atoms.	True	42.7	30.9
3. The earliest humans lived at the same time as the dinosaurs.	False (Humans appeared nearly 65 million years after dinosaurs vanished.)	36.8	46.2
4. Which travels faster—light or sound?	Light	76.1	74.7
5. Does the Earth go around the Sun or the Sun around the Earth?	The Earth goes around the Sun	72.5	62.8
6. How long does it take the Earth to go around the Sun?	One year	44.9	34.1

Source: Jon D. Miller, Northern Illinois University.

Comprehension

Answer the following questions based on the information in the table. For statements preceded by T / F / N, circle T if the statement is true, F if the statement is false, and N if there is not enough information given in the chart to tell whether the statement is true or false.

1. T / F / N   The questionnaire was given to high school students.

2. T / F / N   The questionnaire was answered by people in the U.S. and Great Britain.

3. T / F / N   The questionnaire had more than six questions.

From "Basic Science, Technology Leave Americans in Dark," by Richard Saltus, *Boston Globe,* February 26, 1989, 1.

4. T / F / N   Several thousand people answered the questionnaire.

5. T / F / N   The people in Great Britain who answered the questionnaire had the same number of years of education as the people in the U.S. who answered the questionnaire.

6. Which question in the chart was easiest for people in the U.S. and Britain to answer correctly? _____

7. Which of the following statements are inferences or conclusions that can be drawn from this chart? Check (✓) all the correct inferences.

___ a. Many people in the U.S. and Great Britain don't understand some basic ideas about science.

___ b. In general, people in Great Britain did better on these six questions than did people in the U.S.

___ c. In general, people in the U.S. and Great Britain know less about science than people in many other countries.

___ d. This research study was well designed.

Discussion/Composition

1. Is it important that nonscientists understand basic ideas of science? Give reasons and examples from your reading and personal experience to support your opinion.

2. If you were making up a quiz about basic ideas of science, what questions would you include? Make up a quiz like this and test your classmates.

Selections 3B–3C   **Popular Science Articles**

The questions in the survey in Selection 3A are about basic ideas of science, but they aren't really about the science of everyday life. For example, do you know why your voice sounds so good when you sing in the shower, or why mountains look more blue the farther away you are from them, or why a rainbow is always curved? Recently, there have been several popular books written that answer questions like these, books about the science of everyday life. The two readings that follow are taken from one of these books.

    The author, Ira Flatow, is an engineer who writes about science for nonscientists; he believes that "the real fun in life is uncovering its secrets." In the following articles, Flatow explains the secrets of two everyday events—letting water out of the bathtub and washing things that are dirty. Before you read each article, see how much you already know (or don't know) about these topics by answering the questions in the Before You Begin sections. Your teacher may want to save the second article for a later time.

Selection 3B   **Popular Science Article**

Before You Begin   Check (✓) all the statements below that you think are true.

1. When you let water out of the bathroom sink or bathtub, it . . .

    ___ a. always circles to the right as it goes down the drain.

    ___ b. sometimes circles to the right and sometimes circles to the left as it goes down the drain.

    ___ c. sometimes goes straight down the drain.

2. What makes water circle as it goes down the drain in a sink or bathtub?

Read the following article to learn the answers. Your teacher may want you to do the Vocabulary from Context exercise on page 163 before you begin.

Tornado in the Drain

1   There is something that happens in the bathroom sink and bathtub that has kept scientists wondering for many years. It is nothing very important, but it is something that scientists are continually trying to explain to themselves: Why does water circle as it goes down the drain and in what direction does it go—clockwise or counterclockwise. Why doesn't the water go straight down?

2   For years the simple answer has been the *Coriolis force.* The Coriolis force (or Coriolis effect) is responsible for the circular winds of hurricanes and tornados. And some scientists believe it is the force that makes water swirl down the drain.

3   How does it work?

4   The Coriolis force is due to the eastward rotation of the earth. The rotation affects any moving body of air or water and causes it to be deflected to the right in the Northern Hemisphere of Earth and to the left in the Southern Hemisphere.

5   If a rocket ship were sent from the equator toward the North Pole, the rocket would also be moving eastward. At the equator, the earth is rotating eastward over a thousand miles per hour, and the speed is passed on to the rocket. But north of the equator, the speed of the Earth's rotation decreases as the distance around the Earth gets smaller. (It's like a phonograph record spinning faster on the outside than near the middle.) At 30 degrees north latitude—for example, in New Delhi, India—the speed of the earth is only about 935 miles per hour. But because our rocket ship is still moving independently at its original higher speed, it will be moving slightly faster than the part of the earth's surface below it. So, to someone

---

Adapted from "Tornado in the Drain," in *Rainbows, Curve Balls, and Other Wonders of the Natural World Explained,* by Ira Flatow (New York: Harper and Row, 1989), 151–55.

standing in India, the rocket will appear to be moving eastward. This is the Coriolis effect.

6   If the rocket had been aimed at New York City's Statue of Liberty without correcting for the Coriolis effect, it would have gone far to the right of that statue as its path curved eastward because of the Coriolis effect. Rocket ships and even airplanes have to aim slightly left in order to reach their destinations.

7   A rocket ship fired from the North Pole toward the equator would experience the same effect. It would seem to curve toward the right, this time westward. It is just as impossible to hit Paris by aiming at it directly from the north as it is by aiming at it directly from the equator.

8   In the Southern Hemisphere, the situation is exactly the opposite: the Coriolis effect makes the path of objects curve toward the left.

9   Now consider moving air (the wind) or moving water (ocean currents) instead of our flying rocket. The right-turning effect of the Coriolis force (in the Northern Hemisphere) makes any wind or water want to flow to the right. Major ocean currents (such as the Gulf Stream) and large movements of winds (such as weather patterns) are deflected to the right. The Coriolis effect explains why high pressure weather fronts spin clockwise—the winds are deflected to the right.

10   The counterclockwise spin of low pressure fronts is also due to the Coriolis effect. Areas of low pressure act like holes, like drains that suck in high-pressure winds. As the winds are pulled toward the areas of low pressure, their straight-line direction of travel is deflected to the right by the Coriolis effect. The combination of both forces results in the circular, counterclockwise swirl of areas of low pressure such as hurricanes and tornados.

11   What does all this have to do with water running down the drain? We can think of the drain—a hole—as an area of low pressure. So, in theory, water in the tubs in the Northern Hemisphere should swirl down the drain like a small tornado—counterclockwise. But this doesn't always happen. Open your drain a few hundred times and, if your drain is like mine, the water will sometimes go in one direction and at other times go in the opposite direction.

12   Does this mean that the Coriolis effect is not working? This is what scientists do not agree on. Many scientists believe the effect can be seen only on large bodies of water. But others believe it can be observed even in a small bathtub, but only under controlled circumstances.

13   These true believers are so convinced that they went to all the trouble of building special research bathtubs. Their bathtubs were perfectly round and the sides and bottoms perfectly square (unlike the sides and bottoms of most tubs) so the tubs do not give the water any movement before the drain is opened. After filling the bathtubs, the researchers waited hours, even days, for the water to become perfectly still. They controlled for any wind disturbances in the room and any other outside influences they could think of; even the drain was specially built.

14   Then they took their tubs to locations north and south of the equator, filled them with water, and opened the drains. And sure enough, through many fillings and drainings, the tubs in the north drained counterclockwise; those in the south drained clockwise—or so say the researchers.

15   What about on the equator? A group of scientists were staying in an African hotel on the equator. In a totally unscientific experiment, they filled the tub and opened the drain. They report that the water went straight down the drain without swirling in either direction.

16   Despite the research, many scientists still do not believe that the Coriolis effect has any noticeable influence on small bodies of water such as a bathtub full of water. So, next time you're washing your face or draining the tub, conduct your own experiment in full knowledge that serious scientists are conducting theirs in bathtubs around the world.

Comprehension

Answer the following questions. For statements preceded by T / F / D, circle T if the statement is true, F if the statement is false, and D if experts disagree about whether the statement is true or false. Your teacher may want you to answer the questions orally, in writing, or by underlining appropriate parts of the text.

1. T / F / D   The Coriolis force affects how ocean currents move.

2. T / F / D   The Coriolis force affects how rockets move.

3. T / F / D   The Coriolis force affects how bathwater goes down the drain.

4. T / F / D   The Coriolis force moves large bodies of moving water in the same direction everywhere on the Earth.

5. T / F / D   The Coriolis force is caused by the direction of winds in the Earth's atmosphere.

6. T / F / D   The Coriolis force is caused by the spinning of the Earth.

7. T / F / D   A point on the Earth's equator spins slower than a point near Tokyo.

8. T / F / D   A point on the Earth's equator spins faster than a point in Australia.

9. T / F / D   In theory, the Coriolis force has no effect at the equator.

10. T / F / D   Airlines need to consider the Coriolis force when they plan their flights.

11. T / F / D   To get a rocket from the equator to New York City, it should be aimed to the west of New York City.

12. T / F / D   To get a rocket from the North Pole to a certain point on the equator, it should be aimed to the east of that point.

13. Check (✓) all of the following that may affect the direction water swirls as it goes down a bathtub drain.

___ a. the shape of the tub

___ b. the Coriolis force

___ c. the shape of the drain

___ d. wind in the bathroom

___ e. movement of the water in the tub before the drain is opened

___ f. the temperature of the water

___ g. whether the tub is in the Northern or Southern Hemisphere

___ h. the types of chemicals in the water

Vocabulary from Context

Both the ideas and the vocabulary in the exercise below are taken from "Tornado in the Drain." Use the context provided to decide on meanings for the italicized words. Write a definition, synonym, or description in the space provided.

1. _____
2. _____

Two of nature's most dangerous types of storms are *tornados* and *hurricanes.* Both are windstorms, but tornados begin over land and hurricanes form over water. In both, the winds do not travel in a straight direction.

3. _____

4. _____
5. _____

Instead, the winds *rotate,* circling faster and faster as the storm grows. In the center of the storm is an area of low air pressure. Winds are pulled into this area the way water is *sucked* into the *drain* at the bottom of a bathtub.

6. _____
7. _____
8. _____
9. _____
10. _____

The winds in these storms rotate in opposite directions in the northern half of the Earth from those in the southern half. In the Northern *Hemisphere,* the winds in a low pressure area (like a tornado or hurricane) *swirl* to the left, in a *counterclockwise* direction. South of the equator, the situation is the opposite—the winds *spin* in a *clockwise* direction. This difference in the direction that winds turn in the two hemispheres is caused by the Coriolis force.

11. _____
12. _____

The Coriolis force also affects the direction of the wind in areas where air pressure is high. Winds in high pressure weather patterns are turned slightly to the right in the Northern Hemisphere. In contrast, winds in high-pressure weather *fronts* are *deflected* slightly to the left in the Southern Hemisphere.

Selection 3C   **Popular Science Article**

Before You Begin   Indicate whether you think the following statements are true (T) or false (F).

1. T / F   Washing dishes in water alone will get them clean.

2. T / F   Soap and water cleans better than water alone.

3. T / F   Soap works better in some water than in other water.

4. T / F   Soap that makes a lot of bubbles is always better than soap that makes fewer bubbles.

5. T / F   The soap you use to wash your hands works the same way as the detergent you use to wash your clothes.

6. T / F   Detergent is just another name for soap.

Now, read Flatow's explanation of how soap works. Your teacher may want you to do Vocabulary from Context exercise 1 on page 168 before you begin.

Making Water Wetter

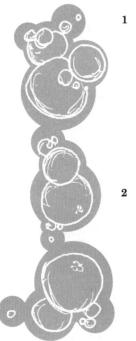

1 Some years ago, a TV commercial for a new laundry detergent proudly said that it worked because it made water "wetter." The commercial went on to explain that while we all think of water as being naturally wet, what we really mean when we say water is "wet" is its ability to attach itself to anything it touches: dishes, skin, or clothing. In the kitchen, bathroom, or laundry room, this can be translated as the ability of water to stick to grease and dirt and carry it away. As anyone who has tried to wash a greasy face or a dirty dish knows, water alone does not work. It does not stick to the soil and wash it away; it just forms little beads and rolls off. What soap and detergent do to make water wetter—to increase its stickiness—is a fascinating bit of chemistry with a long and interesting history.

2 Soap was used for hundreds of years without anyone really knowing why it worked. Soap was (and still is) produced by combining animal fat with other substances to form a compound that was later discovered to be sodium stearate. Sodium stearate belongs to a family of chemicals that can overcome the incompatibility of oil and water. It's no secret that oil and water do not mix. Thrown together, each one naturally wants to avoid the other; the oil forms into a big drop. But if you're going to get clothes, dishes, or skin clean, you've got to find a way to make water "wet" enough so it will stick to oil and wash it away. And that's what soaps and detergents can do.

Adapted from "A Real Soap Opera: Making Water Wetter," in *Rainbows, Curve Balls, and Other Wonders of the Natural World Explained,* by Ira Flatow (New York: Harper and Row, 1988), 141–45.

3   How? First, it is important to understand how electrical charges are distributed in a water molecule (H_2O). One end (hydrogen) is positively charged (a positive pole); the other end (oxygen) is negatively charged (a negative pole). Oil, on the other hand, has an electrical distribution that is quite uniform—it has no positive or negative pole—explaining why oil and water don't mix. To bring the two together, you need a substance that is like both oil and water, a substance that is partly polar and partly nonpolar. Soap is just such a substance.

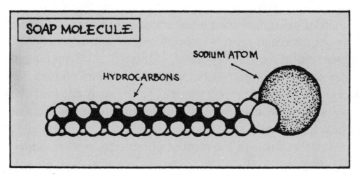

Illustration 1: Soap Molecule, with Head and Tail

4   The soap molecule looks like a long snake (see Illustration 1). It helps to visualize the soap molecule as having a sodium "head" and a fatty "tail." When soap is added to water, it does not dissolve. The fatty tails push the water away. The soap molecules rush to the surface of the water and gather into small round bodies, with their tails pointed toward the center and heads pointed outward.

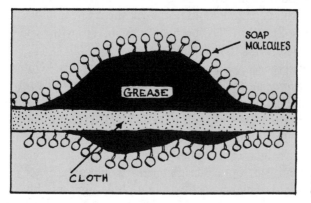

Illustration 2: Detergent Circling Grease with Heads and Tails Shown

5   When greasy or soiled cloth is added to the soapy water, or if soapy water is put on your dirty hands and face, the soap molecules rush to the newcomer (see Illustration 2). Soil usually has an oily film that holds it on cloth or skin so the fatty tails of the soap find a substance similar to themselves in the greasy mess. They rush to the oil and push their tails into it, trying to bond with the oil. They break away pieces of the large oil and dirt particles and separate them from the cloth. Freed from the cloth, the grease forms into small oil droplets that are again attacked by soap molecules that push their tails into the oil. With their heads sticking into the water and their tails surrounding the dirt and grease, the soil-soaked soap follows the water down the drain. The soap around each piece of grease stops the dirt from getting back into the cloth.

6   After World War II, as more and more people stopped washing their clothes by hand and began using a washing machine, they wanted better washing products, ones that would make clothes clean in "hard water" (water containing large amounts of calcium). Chemists worked to invent products that would make

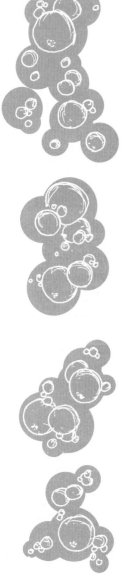

hard water soft and that would work better in washing machines. They realized that they could keep the soap molecule as a model—with a head that dissolves in water and a fatty tail that does not—but they added ingredients to it to create a whole new family of washing substances that were better than plain soap: detergents.

7   Read the ingredients on a box of today's laundry detergent and you'll find a long list of additives. Topping the list are water softeners. Softeners are necessary because detergents and soaps do not easily make bubbles in hard water. The large amount of calcium in hard water attracts soap before it starts to clean. The soap does not foam and get to work cleaning the dirt until after it takes all of the calcium out of the water—that is, if there is any soap remaining to do the job. Water softeners in detergents replace the calcium with sodium. Sodium doesn't interfere with the cleansing process, so the soap can start cleaning the dirt right away. Detergents became very popular mostly due to the water softeners that made them work so well.

8   Water softeners in the form of phosphates were so widely used that in the 1960s they became a danger to the environment. The phosphates in washing machine and dishwasher water, as it poured into lakes, caused too much algae to grow in the lakes and caused many fish to die. On many of today's detergents you will find the words "contains no phosphorus" written in large letters. Less harmful water softeners are used instead.

9   A second environmental danger that resulted from increased use of detergents was that rivers became full of suds. When early types of detergents left the washing machine, nature could not break them down into harmless chemicals so they continued to foam. The problem was solved by the use of "biodegradable" detergents, detergents that *do* break down.

10   Some detergents are advertised as making whites "whiter." If white is white, what does *whiter* mean? Many times white clothes will yellow a little with age, and while the clothes are still perfectly usable, soap companies have convinced us that yellowing is bad. So to sell more soap, detergent manufacturers first added "whiteners." The whiteners are usually simply a blue coloring. This blue dye absorbs yellow light, causing the yellowed garment to appear white. Later, chemists found that "optical brighteners" would do a better job than coloring agents. Optical brighteners act by adding blue light, not blue dye. They absorb ultraviolet light, change its wavelength, and send it out as blue light. Blue light mixes with the yellow and adds up to white. Brighteners do the job so well that sometimes it seems that the bright shirts and towels have a little blue in them— which they do.

Comprehension

Answer the following questions. Your teacher may want you to answer the questions orally, in writing, or by underlining appropriate parts of the text. True/False items are indicated by a T / F preceding a statement.

1. T / F   Soap is made of sodium stearate.

2. T / F   Soap is something like water and something like oil.

3. T / F   Soap cleans by allowing water and oil molecules to mix.

4. T / F   Soap cleans by making water stick to oil.

5. T / F   Soap is the same as detergent.

6. T / F   Detergent molecules have basically the same structure as soap molecules.

7. T / F   A detergent that makes more suds always cleans better than a detergent that foams less.

8. a. What is hard water? _____

   b. What is soft water? _____

   c. Why does hard water make it difficult to wash clothes? _____

   _____

9. What are two environmental hazards that resulted from the use of detergents? _____

   _____

   _____

10. T / F   If we are concerned about our environment, we should not use detergents to wash our clothes.

11. T / F   The additive that is most responsible for making detergents popular is whitening.

12. T / F   White clothes that look a little yellow after you wash them are still dirty.

13. T / F   Some detergents contain an additive that makes clothes washed in them send out more blue light.

14. T / F   Biodegradable detergents do not make suds.

Discussion/Composition

1. Explain to your classmates how to do something that they do not know how to do. For example, you might describe the steps in a process such as changing an automobile tire, or deciding which computer to buy, or cooking one of your family's favorite meals.

2. Explain some natural event. For example, Why is the sky blue? Why does your voice sound better when you sing in the shower than when you sing in the living room? Why does popcorn pop?

Vocabulary from Context

Exercise 1

Both the ideas and the vocabulary in the exercise below are taken from "Making Water Wetter." Use the context provided to decide on meanings for the italicized words. Write a definition, synonym, or description in the space provided.

1. _____
2. _____

It is not easy to get dirty clothes clean. The *soil* in clothes contains a lot of *grease* from our skin. This oily dirt is especially hard to wash away since oil and water do not mix.

3. _____
4. _____

5. _____

6. _____
7. _____

As you can see by pouring oil into water, oil will not *dissolve* in water the way sugar would. It just makes *droplets* of oil that float in the water. Similarly, if you pour water onto grease, the water will form into little round *beads* that roll around on the surface of the grease. The grease and the water will not mix; oil and water are as *incompatible* as fire and water. To *overcome* this problem, it is important to use a good detergent.

8. _____

9. _____
10. _____

Detergents used to wash clothes are different from detergents used to wash dishes. Detergents for *laundry* contain substances that make clothes look whiter. These laundry detergents also have substances added to them so they do not make too many soap bubbles. In contrast, many detergents for dishes have *additives* that make lots of soap *suds*.

11. _____
12. _____

Unfortunately, some types of detergents are harmful to the environment. For example, detergents that make a lot of bubbles can cause rivers to fill with mountains of white *foam*. Some detergents cause large amounts of *algae* to grow in rivers and lakes. In some lakes, these plants caused fish to die.

Exercise 2

This exercise gives you additional clues to the meaning of unfamiliar vocabulary in context. In the paragraph indicated by the number in parentheses, find the word or phrase that best fits the meaning given. Your teacher may want to read these aloud as you quickly scan the paragraph to find the answer.

1. (1) Which phrase means *attach itself to?*

2. (3) Which word means *arranged; organized?*

3. (3) Which word means *smallest piece of a chemical compound that is still that compound?*

4. (5) Which phrase means *to connect to; to attach to?*

5. (5) Which word means *forming a circle around?*

6. (5) Which word means *the hole through which dirty water is carried from a kitchen or bathroom sink?*

7. (6) Which word means *a pattern or example used for making something?*

8. (10) Which word means *a coloring?*

9. (10) Which word means *takes in?*

Dictionary Study

Many words have more than one meaning. When you use the dictionary to discover the meaning of an unfamiliar word or phrase, you need to use the context to determine which definition is appropriate. Use the portions of the dictionary provided to select the best definition for each of the italicized words in the following sentences. Write the number of the definition in the space provided.

___ 1. Soap was (and still is) produced by combining animal fat with other substances to form a *compound* that was later discovered to be sodium stearate.

> **com·pound¹** (käm pound′, kəm-; *for adj. usually, and for n. always,* käm′pound) *vt.* [ME. *compounen* < OFr. *compon-(d)re,* to arrange, direct < L. *componere,* to put together < *com-,* together + *ponere,* to put, place] **1.** to mix or combine **2.** to make by combining parts or elements **3.** to settle by mutual agreement; specif., to settle (a debt) by a compromise payment of less than the total claim **4.** to compute (interest) on the sum of the principal and the accumulated interest which has accrued at regular intervals [interest *compounded* semiannually] **5.** to increase or intensify by adding new elements [to *compound* a problem] —*vi.* **1.** to agree **2.** to compromise with a creditor **3.** to combine and form a compound —*adj.* made up of two or more separate parts or elements —*n.* **1.** a thing formed by the mixture or combination of two or more parts or elements **2.** a substance containing two or more elements chemically combined in fixed proportions: distinguished from MIXTURE in that the constituents of a compound lose their individual characteristics and the compound has new characteristics **3.** a word composed of two or more base morphemes, whether hyphenated or not: English compounds are usually distinguished from phrases by reduced stress on one of the elements and by changes in meaning (Ex.: *black′bird′, black′ bird′; grand′-aunt′, grand′ aunt′*) —**compound a felony** (or **crime**) [< *vt.,* 3] to agree, for a bribe or repayment, not to inform about or prosecute for a felony (or crime): it is an illegal act
> **com·pound²** (käm′pound) *n.* [Anglo-Ind. < Malay *kampong,* enclosure] **1.** in the Orient, an enclosed space with a building or group of buildings in it, esp. if occupied by foreigners **2.** any similar enclosed space

---

Entries from *Webster's New World Dictionary,* Second College Edition, 1984.

___ 2. Oil, on the other hand, has an electrical distribution that is quite *uniform*—it has no positive or negative pole.

u·ni·form (yōō′nə fôrm′) *adj.* [MFr. *uniforme* < L. *uniformis* < *unus,* ONE + *-formis,* -FORM] **1.** *a*) always the same; not varying or changing in form, rate, degree, manner, etc.; constant *[a uniform speed] b*) identical throughout a state, country, etc. *[a uniform minimum wage]* **2.** *a*) having the same form, appearance, manner, etc. as others of the same class; conforming to a given standard *[a row of uniform houses] b*) being or looking the same in all parts; undiversified *[a uniform surface]* **3.** consistent in action, intention, effect, etc. *[a uniform policy]* —*n.* the official or distinctive clothes or outfit worn by the members of a particular group, as policemen or soldiers, esp. when on duty —*vt.* ☆**1.** to clothe or supply with a uniform **2.** to make uniform —*SYN.* see STEADY —**uniform with** having the same form, appearance, etc. as —**u′ni·form′ly** *adv.*

Vocabulary Review

Three of the words in each line below are similar in meaning. Circle the word that does not belong.

1. foam   models   suds   bubbles

2. greasy   oily   laundry   fatty

3. dye   coloring   whitener   molecule

4. bond   dissolve   stick   attach

5. droplets   drops   drains   beads

Reading Selection 4

Children's Literature

You can find out a lot about a culture by reading its literature for children. The selection that follows is the first chapter of a book called *The Rescuers*. In it, mice rescue prisoners from jails around the world.

Before You Begin   Why do you think the author chose mice to rescue prisoners? What things are universal about prisons and prisoners?

Read the passage, then do the exercises that follow. You may want to do Vocabulary from Context exercise 1 on pages 178–79 before you begin reading.

The Meeting

I

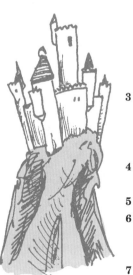

1   "Ladies and gentlemen," cried Madam Chairwoman Mouse, "we now come to the most important topic of our meeting! Silence for the Secretary!"

2   It was a full meeting of the Prisoners' Aid Society. Everyone knows that the mice are the prisoner's friends—sharing dry bread crumbs even when they are not hungry in order to cheer the lonely hours. What is less well-known is how remarkably they are organized. All prisons in every land have their own national branch of a wonderful, world-wide system. Long, long ago a French mouse took a ship all the way to Turkey, to join a French sailor-boy locked up in Constantinople! The Jean Fromage Medal was created in his honor.

3   The Secretary rose. Madam Chairwoman sat back in her seat and fixed her clever eyes on his graying back. How she would have liked to introduce the matter to the meeting herself! A job so difficult and dangerous! Dear, faithful old comrade as the Secretary was, had he the necessary eloquence? But rules are rules.

4   She looked anxiously over the assembly, wondering which members would support her; there were at least a hundred mice present.

5   "Well, it's like this," began the Secretary. "You all know the Black Castle . . ."

6   Every mouse in the hall shuddered. The country they lived in was not very civilized. Even in its few towns, even here in the Capital, its prisons were awful enough. But the Black Castle!

7   It sat on a cliff, the Black Castle, above the angriest river of all. Its dungeons were cut in the cliff itself—windowless. Even the bravest mouse, assigned to the Black Castle, trembled in fear at the sight of it.

8   From a front seat spoke a mouse almost as old as the Secretary himself. But he wore the Jean Fromage Medal.

9   "I know the Black Castle. Didn't I spend six weeks there?"

10   Around him cries of "Yes, yes!" "Splendid fellow!" and other encouragements.

Adapted from *The Rescuers,* by Margery Sharp (New York: Dell Yearling/Bantam Doubleday Dell, 1959), 1–13.

11   "And did no good there," continued the old hero seriously. "I say nothing of the personal danger—though what a cat that is of the Head Jailer!—twice natural size, and four times as dangerous—I say only that not even a mouse can aid a prisoner in the Black Castle, a prisoner down in the dungeons. Call me defeatist if you will—"

12   "No, no!" cried the mice behind.

"—but I speak from sad experience. I couldn't do anything for my prisoner at all. I couldn't even reach him. One can't cheer a prisoner in the Black Castle."

13   But one can get him out," said Madam Chairwoman.

II

14   There was stunned silence. In the first place, Madam Chairwoman shouldn't have interrupted; in the second, her proposal was so astounding, so revolutionary, no mouse could do more than gape.

15   "Mr. Secretary, forgive me," apologized Madam Chairwoman. "I was carried away by your eloquence."

16   "As we seem not to be following the rules, you may as well take over," said the Secretary unhappily.

17   Madam Chairwoman did so.

18   "It's rather an unusual case," said Madam Chairwoman. "The prisoner is a poet. You will all, I know, remember the many poets who have written favorably of our race. Thus do not poets deserve specially well of us?"

19   "If he's a poet, why's he in jail?" demanded one of the mice.

"Perhaps he writes free verse," Madam Chairwoman suggested cleverly.

20   Everyone agreed. Mice are all for people being free, so that they too can be freed from their eternal task of cheering prisoners—so that they can stay at home, eating the family cheese, instead of sleeping on a wet floor and eating old bread.

21   "I see you follow me," said Madam Chairwoman. "It is a special case. Therefore we will rescue him. I should tell you also that the prisoner is a Norwegian—Don't ask me how he got here, really no one can answer for a poet! But obviously the first thing to do is to find a mouse from his country and bring him here, so that he may communicate with the prisoner in their common tongue.

22   One hundred mice listened intelligently. All mice speak their own universal language, also that of the country they live in, but prisoners as a rule spoke only one.

23   "We therefore bring a Norwegian mouse here," said Madam Chairwoman, "send him to the Black Castle—"

"Stop a bit," said the Secretary.

Madam Chairwoman had to.

24   "No one more than I," said the Secretary, "admires Madam Chairwoman. But has she, in her enthusiasm, considered the difficulties? Bring a mouse from Norway—in the first place!—How long will that take, even if possible?"

25   "Remember Jean Fromage!" pleaded Madam Chairwoman.

"I do remember Jean Fromage. No mouse could ever forget him," agreed the Secretary. "But he had to be located first; and traveling isn't as easy as it used to be."

26   How quickly a public meeting can change! Now all Madam Chairwoman's eloquence was forgotten; there was general agreement.

27   "In the old days," continued the Secretary, "when every vehicle was horse-drawn, a mouse could cross half Europe really in luxury. How delightful it was, to

get up into a rich coach, make a little nest among the cushions, go out regularly to eat—Farm carts were even better; there one had room to stretch one's legs, and meals were simply continuous! Even railroad cars, of the old wooden sort, weren't too uncomfortable—"

28   "Now they make them of metal," put in a mouse at the back. "Has anyone here ever tried eating steel?"

29   "And at least trains were speedy," went on the Secretary, "Now, as our friend points out, they are practically impossible to get a seat in. As for automobiles, apart from the fact that they often carry dogs, in a car, there is no place to hide. A ship, you say? We are a hundred miles from the nearest port!"

30   "As a matter of fact," said Madam Chairwoman, "I was thinking of an airplane."

Every mouse in the hall gasped. An airplane! To travel by air was the dream of each one; but if trains were now difficult to board, an airplane was believed impossible!

31   "I was thinking," added Madam Chairwoman, "of Miss Bianca."

The mice gasped again.

III

32   Everyone knew who Miss Bianca was, but none had ever seen her.

What was known was that she was a white mouse belonging to the Ambassador's son, and lived in the schoolroom at the Embassy. Apart from that, there were the most fantastic rumors about her: for instance, that she lived in a Glass Castle; that she ate only cream cheese from a silver dish; that she wore a silver chain around her neck, and on Sundays a gold one. She was also said to be extremely beautiful, but self-centered.

33   "It has come to my knowledge," continued Madam Chairwoman, rather enjoying the excitement she had caused, "that the Ambassador has been transferred, and that in two days' time he will leave for Norway by air! The Boy of course travels with him, and with the Boy travels Miss Bianca—to be precise, in the Diplomatic Bag. No one on the plane is going to examine that; she has diplomatic immunity. She is thus the very person for this job."

34   By this time the mice had had time to think. Several of them spoke at once.

"Yes, but—" they began.

"But what?" asked Madam Chairwoman sharply.

35   "You say, 'the very person,'" pronounced the Secretary, speaking for all. "But is that true? From all one hears, Miss Bianca has grown up with complete luxury and laziness. Will she have the necessary courage? This Norwegian, whoever he is, won't know to get in touch with her, she will have to get in touch with him. Has she even the necessary wits? Brilliant as your plan is, I for one have the strongest doubts that it is possible.

36   "That remains to be seen," said Madam Chairwoman. She had indeed some doubts herself; but she also had great faith in her own sex. In any case, she wasn't going to be led into argument. "Is there anyone," she called, "from the Embassy here with us now?"

37   For a moment all waited; finally a short, strong young mouse came towards the front. He looked rough but clean; no one was surprised to learn (in answer to Madam Chairwoman's questioning) that he worked in the kitchen.

38   "I suppose you, Bernard, have never seen Miss Bianca either?" said Madam Chairwoman kindly.

"Not me," mumbled Bernard.

"But could you reach her?"

"I guess so," admitted Bernard slowly.

39   "Then reach her you must, and without delay," said Madam Chairwoman. "Present our greetings, explain the situation, and ask her immediately to find the bravest mouse in Norway, and send him back here."

40   Bernard looked uncomfortable.

"Suppose she doesn't want to ma'am?"

"Then you must persuade her, my dear boy," said Madam Chairwoman. "What's that you have on your chest?"

41   Bernard looked down self-consciously. His fur was so thick and rough, the medal scarcely showed.

"The Tybalt Star, ma'am . . ."

42   "For Bravery in the Face of Cats," nodded Madam Chairwoman. "I believe I remember. You let a cat bite your tail, didn't you, thus permitting a nursing mother of six to return to her hole?"

43   "She was my sister-in-law," said Bernard, embarrassed.

"Then I know that you can persuade Bianca!" cried Madam Chairwoman.

IV

44   With that, the meeting broke up; and Bernard, feeling important but uneasy, set off back to the Embassy.

45   At least his route to the Boy's schoolroom presented no difficulties: there was a small elevator running directly up from the kitchen itself, used to carry such light refreshments as glasses of milk, chocolate cookies, and tea for the Boy's tutor. Bernard waited till half-past eight, when the last glass of milk went up (hot), and went up with it by holding on to one of the elevator ropes. When he reached the upstairs, he slipped into the nearest shadow to wait again. He waited a long, long time; he heard the Boy put to bed in a nearby room as the Boy's mother came to kiss him good night. (Bernard was of course waiting with his eyes shut; nothing draws attention to a mouse like the gleam of his eyes.) Then at last all was quiet, and he came out for a good look round.

46   In one respect at least the rumors had been true; there in the corner of the great room, on a low table, stood a Glass Castle.

Comprehension

Answer the following questions according to your understanding of the passage. Your teacher may want you to answer orally, in writing, or by underlining parts of the text. True/False items are indicated by a T / F before a statement.

1. T / F   "The meeting" is of the Prisoners' Aid Society.

2. T / F   The leader of this organization is the Secretary.

3. T / F   The Black Castle is in Norway.

4. What was surprising about the Chairwoman's suggestion to aid a prisoner in the Black Castle?

5. T / F   To carry out Madam Chairwoman's plan, the mice would have to travel by car.

6. T / F   Miss Bianca often attends these meetings.

7. T / F   Miss Bianca is a pet mouse.

8. If Miss Bianca agrees to help, what will she need to do in Norway? _____

_____

9. T / F   Bernard works in the embassy.

10. How do we know that Bernard is brave? _____

_____

_____

11. T / F   Bernard walked up the stairs to find Miss Bianca.

Restatement and Inference

The sentence(s) below are adapted from "The Meeting." Each is followed by four statements.* The statements are of four types:

1. Some of the statements are restatements of ideas in the original paragraph. They give the same information in a different way.

2. Some of the statements are inferences (conclusions) that can be drawn from the information given in the paragraph.

3. Some of the statements are not true based on the information given.

4. Some of the statements cannot be judged true or false based on the information given.

Put a check (✓) next to all restatements and inferences (types 1 and 2). Note: do not check a statement that is true of itself but cannot be inferred from the sentence(s) or your knowledge of the reading selection.

1. Madam Chairwoman sat back in her seat and fixed her clever eyes on the Secretary's graying back.

___ a. The Secretary is old.
___ b. Madam Chairwoman is clever.
___ c. Madam Chairwoman is more clever than the Secretary.
___ d. Madam Chairwoman is old.

_____

*For introductions to restatement and inference, see Units 3 and 5.

2. Madam Chairwoman thought, "Dear, faithful old comrade as the Secretary was, had he the necessary eloquence? But rules are rules."

    ___ a. Madam Chairwoman believes in following rules.
    ___ b. The Secretary is too old for his job.
    ___ c. Madam Chairwoman is worried that the Secretary is not eloquent enough.
    ___ d. Madam Chairwoman believes that the Secretary must speak because of the rules.

3. The country they lived in was not very civilized. Even in its few towns, even here in the Capital, its prisons were awful enough. But the Black Castle!

    ___ a. The country they lived in was not modern.
    ___ b. The Black Castle is worse than the other prisons in their country.
    ___ c. The prisons in their country are worse than the Black Castle.
    ___ d. The Black Castle is in the Capital.

4. "I say nothing of the personal danger—though what a cat that is of the Head Jailer!—twice natural size, and four times as dangerous—I say only that not even a mouse can aid a prisoner in the Black Castle, a prisoner down in the dungeons."

    ___ a. The mouse who is speaking is afraid of cats.
    ___ b. Because the cat is dangerous, the speaker doesn't think that mice should try to help prisoners in the Black Castle.
    ___ c. The mouse believes that no one can help a prisoner in the Black Castle.
    ___ d. The cat is named Head Jailer.

5. Madam Chairwoman's proposal was so astounding, so revolutionary, no mouse could do more than gape.

    ___ a. All the mice were surprised.
    ___ b. It was revolutionary that the Chairwoman made a proposal.
    ___ c. The mice stared at the Chairwoman.
    ___ d. The mice did not like the proposal.

6. "The prisoner is a poet. You will all, I know, remember the many poets who have written favorably of our race. Thus do not poets deserve specially well of us?"

    ___ a. Poets have written about mouse races.
    ___ b. Many poets have written nice things about mice.
    ___ c. Many poets like mice.
    ___ d. Poets deserve help from mice.

7. All mice speak their own universal language, also that of the country they live in, but prisoners as a rule spoke only one.

    ___ a. All mice speak the same language.
    ___ b. Prisoners generally speak only the language of their native country.
    ___ c. Mice speak two languages.
    ___ d. Prisoners speak two languages.

8. There were the most fantastic rumors about Miss Bianca: for instance, that she lived in a Glass Castle; that she ate only cream cheese from a silver dish; that she wore a silver chain around her neck, and on Sundays a gold one. She was also said to be extremely beautiful, but self-centered.

___ a. Miss Bianca lived like other mice.
___ b. Miss Bianca was friendly.
___ c. Miss Bianca was liked by other mice.
___ d. Miss Bianca had a comfortable life.

9. Bernard wore a medal called the Tybalt Star. "For Bravery in the Face of Cats," nodded Madam Chairwoman. "I believe I remember. . . . You let a cat bite your tail, didn't you, thus permitting a nursing mother of six to return to her hole?" "She was my sister-in-law," muttered Bernard.

___ a. Bernard was brave.
___ b. The cat was Bernard's sister-in-law.
___ c. The cat bit Bernard because she was nursing.
___ d. The nursing mother was a mouse.

10. Bernard was of course waiting with his eyes shut; nothing draws attention to a mouse like the gleam of his eyes.

___ a. Bernard was asleep.
___ b. Bernard did not want to see.
___ c. Bernard did not want to be seen.
___ d. It is easier to see mice in the dark if their eyes are open.

Discussion

The Rescuers was first published in the United States in 1959. The author tries to describe a universal, international situation. In what ways does it seem universal? In what ways not?

Discussion/Composition

1. What do you think will happen next? Will Miss Bianca agree to help? Will the prisoner be freed? Write a section to follow this one in the story of the rescuers.

2. Why do you think all nations have prisoners?

Vocabulary from Context

Exercise 1

Both the ideas and the vocabulary in the exercise below are taken from "The Meeting." Use the context provided to decide on meanings for the italicized words. Write a definition, synonym, or description in the space provided.

1. _____
2. _____
3. _____
4. _____
5. _____

Sometimes people need help. If people are in a dangerous situation and can't save themselves, they need to be *rescued.* One group of people who might need *aid* are those in jail. *Prisoners* sometimes have very little to eat. They are fed like birds, given only bread *crumbs* to eat. In this unhappy situation, it is difficult to help people feel happy. However, sometimes one must try to *cheer* prisoners.

6. _____
7. _____

8. _____

9. _____

The Rescuers is about mice who are part of the Prisoners' Aid Society. Their meetings, or *assemblies,* discuss how to help people in jail. The leaders of this group, the Chairwoman and the *Secretary,* introduce important topics. Sometimes the Secretary must speak with great *eloquence* in order to convince the group that a certain plan is correct. If the Secretary speaks beautifully and convincingly, the group will follow the plan. No one *interrupts* to say something else while the Secretary is speaking.

10. _____
11. _____
12. _____
13. _____
14. _____
15. _____

16. _____

Sometimes the mice must do something dangerous. They will not stop until they are finished, although they might feel a little *anxious* or even so frightened that their whole body *trembles* and *shudders.* Sometimes they must help prisoners in small, dark, underground prisons. These *dungeons* are particularly frightening. But mice are brave. The bravest mice even wear a special *medal* on their coats the way that soldiers do. They have earned the respect of the other mice and *deserve* to have their actions recognized and appreciated. These brave mice never believe that they will be unsuccessful. That is, they are never *defeatist;* but they are sometimes surprised.

17. _____
18. _____
19. _____

At one meeting, the Chairwoman made a suggestion so surprising that the other mice could only sit and stare with their mouths open. After they finished *gaping* they let out a sound of complete surprise. With each new surprising suggestion, the mice *gasped* but did not speak in words. Finally some of the mice began to speak very low, *mumbling* to themselves.

20. _____
21. _____

22. _____

The plan required cleverness and intelligence. Only a special mouse would have the *wits* to carry it out. The Society needed to move a mouse to another country. The ambassador was being *transferred* from one country to another. The Prisoner's Aid Society hoped that a mouse could travel in the *diplomatic bag.* Diplomats like ambassadors can

23. _____

24. _____

travel from one country to another without having their bags examined. They can go from the city where the government is in one country to the *capital* of another without ever having anyone look in their bag. Some people tell stories about what travels in these bags, but others say that these are only *rumors* and that we will never know the truth.

Exercise 2

This exercise should be done after you have finished reading "The Meeting." The exercise will give you practice deciding on the meaning of unfamiliar words and phrases. Give a definition, synonym, or description of each of the words or phrases below. The number in parentheses indicates the paragraph in which the word or phrase can be found. Your teacher may want you to do these orally or in writing.

1. (2) branch: _____

2. (11) Head: _____

3. (14) astounding: _____

4. (18) case: _____

5. (19) free verse: _____

6. (21) tongue: _____

7. (35) get in touch with: _____

8. (45) gleam: _____

7

Nonprose Reading

Maps

On December 26, 1991, the Union of Soviet Socialist Republics (USSR) came to an end, and suddenly mapmakers and school children were hurrying to learn the names of countries and facts that for more than fifty years had been lost behind the initials U-S-S-R. The map on page 182 shows the borders of the new countries. Pages 183–85 give additional information about the countries and the area.

Getting Oriented

Look quickly at pages 182–85 to see what kinds of information are provided.

1. Which country in the former USSR appears to be the largest? _____

   The smallest? _____

2. What is the capital of Belarus? _____ What is the population of this capital

   city? _____

3. What is the population of Belarus? _____

Comprehension

Answer the following questions according to your understanding of the maps and pie charts. Your teacher may want you to work individually, in pairs, or small groups. True/False items are indicated by a T / F before a statement. Some questions may have more than one correct answer. Others require an opinion. Choose the answer you like best; be prepared to defend your choices.

1. The former USSR has been divided into two categories of countries.

   a. What are they? _____

   _____

b. Why were they grouped together? _____

_____

_____

2. How is the weather in this part of the world? Look at the area around the Yana river in the northeast corner of the large map. Now find the same area on the weather map. What is the normal January temperature for that area?

_____

3. Look at the Population map.

a. In what area do most people in the former USSR live? _____

b. Which city has the largest population? _____

c. How many people live in Tashkent? _____

4. Find Vladivostok in southeast Russia. What do we know about the population of Vladivostok? (Use information from all the maps.) _____

5. a. How many ethnic groups live in the former USSR? _____

b. Which of the Baltic Republics has the highest percentage of Russians? _____

c. Which has the lowest? _____

6. Which republic has the highest percentage of Russians outside of Russia? _____

7. Where is the highest percentage of Armenians outside of Armenia? _____

8. Which Republic has the most ethnically uniform population? _____

9. What country appears to have the most forest? _____

10. Which country appears to have the most oil? _____

11. Where would you choose to live if you were moving to this part of the world? Why?

_____

12. Where would you open a business? What kind of business? Why? _____

_____

_____

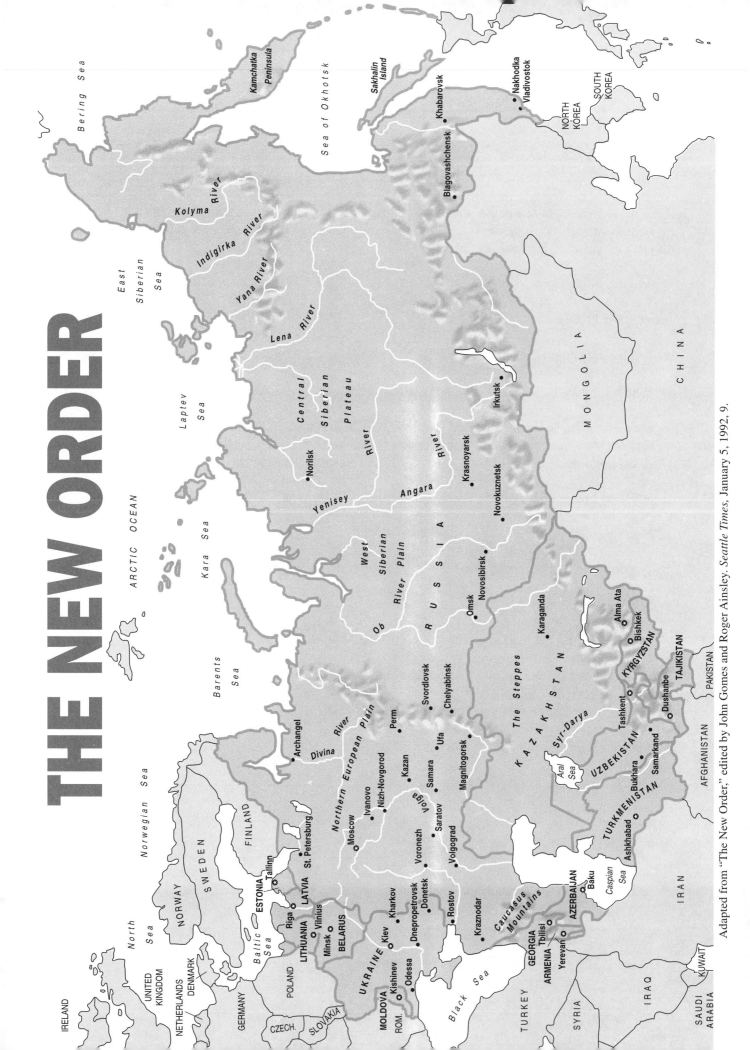

THE NEW ORDER

Adapted from "The New Order," edited by John Gomes and Roger Ainsley. *Seattle Times*, January 5, 1992, 9.

Population

The former Soviet Union takes up one-sixth of the world's land area and has the third largest population: 291 million (behind China and India). More than 200 ethnic groups, 112 recognized languages, five alphabets; main religious groups: Russian Orthodox, Muslims, Buddhists, Evangelical Christians - Baptists, Jews, Lutherans, Roman Catholics.

■ **Major cities and surrounding areas**

□ **Densely populated**

□ **Sparse or no population**

Minsk: 1.5 million
Kiev: 2.5 million
St. Petersburg: 4.9 million
Moscow: 8.5 million
Kharkov: 2.1 million
Baku: 1.7 million
Tashkent: 2.1 million

Severe Winters

It is cold six months out of the year in Moscow, where 8.5 million live. First frost: September; last freeze: late May; most snow: mid-November to early April. Siberia: Thick layer of snow covers northern Siberia more than half the year.

Normal January temperatures

■ **−50° F**

■ **−30° to −50°**

□ **−10° to −30°**

□ **−10° to 10°**

□ **10° to 30°**

Farm and Forest

■ **Mainly forest**

□ **Crops and livestock**

Barley, Corn, Cotton, Flax, Fruit, Oats, Potatoes, Rye, Sugar beets, Tea, Wheat, Vegetables

□ **Mainly livestock**

Beef cattle, Dairy cattle, Fur, Hogs, Sheep, Reindeer

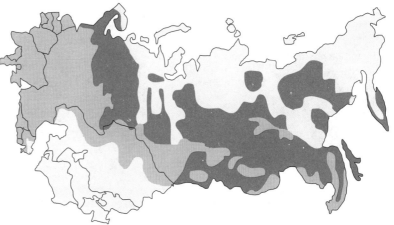

Fuel

The former Soviet Union is the world's leading oil and natural gas producer. Oil and gas regions are widely scattered and mostly distant from the country's population centers. The coal industry employs more than 1 million workers and provides nearly 40 percent of fuel used to generate electricity. Coal reserves are widely dispersed.

▨ **Oil and gas regions**

▨ **Coal reserves**

The Commonwealth of Independent States

December 26, 1991 was like any other day around the world, but in Moscow, history was made in a brief speech by Anuarbek Alimzhanov, the leader of the Supreme Soviet. With the words, "Until we meet again, wherever that may be," he announced the end of the USSR, a country made up of 15 republics and one-sixth of the earth's land. Twelve republics, led by Russia, have joined in a loose organization known as the Commonwealth of Independent States.

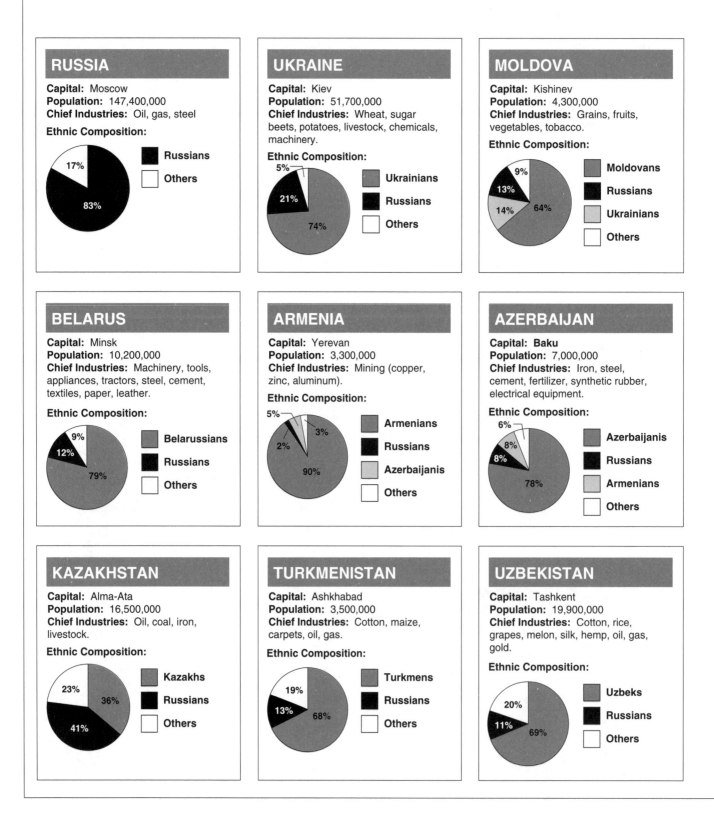

RUSSIA

Capital: Moscow
Population: 147,400,000
Chief Industries: Oil, gas, steel

Ethnic Composition:

17% — Others
83% — Russians
Russians
Others

UKRAINE

Capital: Kiev
Population: 51,700,000
Chief Industries: Wheat, sugar beets, potatoes, livestock, chemicals, machinery.

Ethnic Composition:

5%
21%
74%
Ukrainians
Russians
Others

MOLDOVA

Capital: Kishinev
Population: 4,300,000
Chief Industries: Grains, fruits, vegetables, tobacco.

Ethnic Composition:

9%
13%
14%
64%
Moldovans
Russians
Ukrainians
Others

BELARUS

Capital: Minsk
Population: 10,200,000
Chief Industries: Machinery, tools, appliances, tractors, steel, cement, textiles, paper, leather.

Ethnic Composition:

9%
12%
79%
Belarussians
Russians
Others

ARMENIA

Capital: Yerevan
Population: 3,300,000
Chief Industries: Mining (copper, zinc, aluminum).

Ethnic Composition:

5%
3%
2%
90%
Armenians
Russians
Azerbaijanis
Others

AZERBAIJAN

Capital: Baku
Population: 7,000,000
Chief Industries: Iron, steel, cement, fertilizer, synthetic rubber, electrical equipment.

Ethnic Composition:

6%
8%
8%
78%
Azerbaijanis
Russians
Armenians
Others

KAZAKHSTAN

Capital: Alma-Ata
Population: 16,500,000
Chief Industries: Oil, coal, iron, livestock.

Ethnic Composition:

23%
36%
41%
Kazakhs
Russians
Others

TURKMENISTAN

Capital: Ashkhabad
Population: 3,500,000
Chief Industries: Cotton, maize, carpets, oil, gas.

Ethnic Composition:

19%
13%
68%
Turkmens
Russians
Others

UZBEKISTAN

Capital: Tashkent
Population: 19,900,000
Chief Industries: Cotton, rice, grapes, melon, silk, hemp, oil, gas, gold.

Ethnic Composition:

20%
11%
69%
Uzbeks
Russians
Others

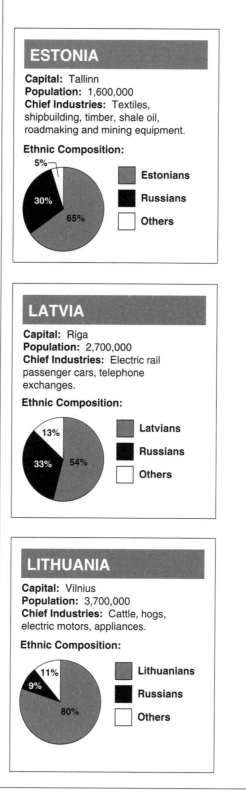

TAJIKISTAN

Capital: Dushanbe
Population: 5,100,000
Chief Industries: Oil, gas, gold, cotton.

Ethnic Composition:

8%
10%
23%
59%

Tajiks

Uzbeks

Russians & Ukrainians

Others

KYRGYZSTAN

Capital: Bishkek
Population: 4,300,000
Chief Industries: Cattle, horse breeding, cotton.

Ethnic Composition:

14%
12%
26%
48%

Kyrgyz

Russians

Uzbeks

Others

GEORGIA

Capital: Tbilisi
Population: 5,400,000
Chief Industries: Textiles, iron, steel, grain, tea, tobacco, fruits.

Ethnic Composition:

15%
7%
9%
69%

Georgians

Russians

Armenians

Others

The Baltic Republics

Lithuania, Estonia, and Latvia announced their independence before the official fall of the Soviet Union. In the March of 1990 Lithuania declared its independence, and the other two soon followed. They are known as the Baltic Republics.

ESTONIA

Capital: Tallinn
Population: 1,600,000
Chief Industries: Textiles, shipbuilding, timber, shale oil, roadmaking and mining equipment.

Ethnic Composition:

5%
30%
65%

Estonians

Russians

Others

LATVIA

Capital: Riga
Population: 2,700,000
Chief Industries: Electric rail passenger cars, telephone exchanges.

Ethnic Composition:

13%
33%
54%

Latvians

Russians

Others

LITHUANIA

Capital: Vilnius
Population: 3,700,000
Chief Industries: Cattle, hogs, electric motors, appliances.

Ethnic Composition:

11%
9%
80%

Lithuanians

Russians

Others

Word Study

Context Clues

This exercise gives you practice using context clues from a reading passage. Use your general knowledge, your knowledge of stems and affixes, and information from the entire text below to write a definition, synonym, or description of the italicized word on the line provided. Note that some of the words appear more than once. Read through the entire passage before deciding on a definition of each term. By the end of the passage, you should have a good idea of the meaning. You do not need an exact definition; with only a general idea of the meaning, you will often be able to understand the meaning of a written text.

Passage 1: Think Positive!

If you are an *optimist,* you probably look at life a little differently than many other people.

Partly cloudy to you means mostly sunny. If you lose your map and don't know where you are, you think of it as a chance to enjoy some *sightseeing.* When you lose your job, you think of it as a chance to change careers.

You have probably taken a few *digs* from *pessimists:* They call you "unrealistic"; they say you see the world "through rose-colored glasses" instead of "the way it really is." They say you're a dreamer.

Pessimism is often *portrayed* as the sign of the intellectual, and optimism as the philosophy of the fool. Voltaire said optimists *maintain* "that all is well when things are going badly." Novelist James Branch Cabell said, "The optimist *proclaims* that we live in the best of all possible worlds. The pessimist fears this is true."

But new scientific research suggests that optimists may know something we can all learn from. The research *links* optimism to health and well-being; optimists tend to be healthier and happier.

1. optimist: _____

2. sightseeing: _____

3. digs: _____

4. pessimists: _____

5. portrayed: _____

6. maintain: _____

7. proclaims: _____

8. links: _____

Adapted from "Think Positive!" by Pat Roessle Materka, *Michigan Alumnus,* March/April, 1992, 31.

Passage 2: Dumping Health Risks on Developing Nations

In May 1992 the International Heart Health Conference issued the Victoria Declaration, a 44-page world-wide plan for reducing health problems. It included several recommendations. First, governments should *adopt* laws that would end advertising and other types of *promotion* of tobacco products. Governments should work for a multinational *ban* on tobacco exports; tobacco exporting should be stopped. Finally, a tobacco *fund* would be created in each country that would be *funded* by a tobacco sales *tax*. Every time people bought tobacco, they would be contributing to the *fund*. This money would be used for creation of a smoke-free society.

"While smoking has slowly but surely *declined* in the United States since 1964, the World Health Organization (WHO) notes that smoking in developing countries has increased steadily," says John W. Farquhar, professor of medicine and director of the Stanford University Center for Research in Disease Prevention. WHO estimates that 550,000 of the 5,500,000,000 people in the world will die *prematurely* of smoking and its effects.

Farquhar says that politically, morally, and educationally, the *thrust* of future programs must be to help developing countries. These countries must receive the support they need to create programs that *strive* toward the same results that are finally being reached in the developed world. According to Farquhar, we should ensure that the developed world not look at *emerging* nations as a *dumping ground* for products, such as tobacco, that they no longer want, that is, products that are becoming less *marketable* in the developed world. To Farquhar, pushing dangerous products onto other countries just because they cannot be sold in the developed world is unjust.

1. adopt: _____

2. promotion: _____

3. ban: _____

4. fund/funded: _____

5. tax: _____

6. declined: _____

7. prematurely: _____

8. thrust: _____

9. strive: _____

10. emerging: _____

11. dumping ground: _____

12. marketable: _____

Adapted from "Dumping Health Risks on Developing Nations," *USA Today* (Special Newsletter Edition), April, 1993, 12.

Word Study

Stems and Affixes

Below is a chart showing some commonly occurring stems and affixes.* Study their meanings; then do the exercises that follow. Your teacher may ask you to give examples of other words you know that are derived from these stems and affixes.

Prefixes

a-, an-	without, not	apolitical, atypical
ante-	before	anteroom, ante meridiem (A.M.)
com-, con-, col-, cor-, co-	together, with	coauthors, connect
extra-, extro-	outside, beyond	extraordinary
inter-	between	international
intro-, intra-	within, into	introduce
post-	after	postgame, postgraduate

Stems

-ced-	go, move, yield	precede
-cred-	believe	credible, creed
-duc-	lead	introduce, conduct
-mort-	death	mortal
-polis-	city, state	politics
-spir-	breathe	respiration, expire
-terra-	earth	territory
-theo-	god	theology
-vac-	empty	vacuum
-ven-, -vene-	come	convene
-ver-	truth	verify
-vita-, -viv-	life	vital, survive

Suffixes

-fy (verb)	to make	simplify
-ism (noun)	action or practice, theory or set of beliefs	communism
-ity (noun)	condition, quality, state of being	simplicity
-ous, -ious, -ose (adj.)	full of, having the qualities of	poisonous, anxious

*For a list of all stems and affixes taught in *Choice Readings,* see the Appendix.

Exercise 1

Use your knowledge of stems and affixes to answer the following questions.

1. Do you think the word *vacation* is related to the stem *-vac-*? Explain your answer. _____

_____

2. Explain how the meaning of *introduction* (for example, the introduction to a book) is related to the

   meanings of the word parts it is formed from. _____

_____

3. Explain how the meaning of *political* is related to the meanings of the word parts it is formed from.

_____

_____

4. Look at the following sentence: *Maia picked up the ball and threw it to Doug.* Which word in the

   sentence is the grammatical *antecedent* of the word *it?* _____

5. The words *anterior* and *posterior* are opposite in meaning. Which means *in, on,* or *toward the back*

   and which means *in, on,* or *toward the front?* _____

_____

6. Some people are *introverts* and others are *extroverts.* Which ones like to talk to a lot of people at a
   party? Which ones would prefer to be alone? (Hint: *-vert-* or *-vers-* is a stem that means to turn.)

_____

_____

Exercise 2

*Word analysis can help you to guess the meaning of unfamiliar words. Using context clues and what
you know about word parts, write a definition, synonym, or description of the italicized words.*

1. _____   In these *post–Cold War* years, there have been many changes in the
   political map of Eastern Europe.

2. _____   Mark, Barb, and Sandy have been *collaborating* on a new textbook for
   several years now.

3. _____ Throughout southern Europe and in parts of North Africa, you still can see the giant stone *aqueducts* built by the Romans.

4. _____ One reason the world's population is increasing is that the infant *mortality* rate is decreasing.

5. _____ There was a *subterranean* water supply for the city.

6. _____ Sarah's *vivacious* personality helps her in her job as a salesperson.

7. _____ The group will *reconvene* at 10 A.M. tomorrow.

8. _____ Bob is studying for a master's degree in *theology*.

9. _____ Barry was *incredulous* when he heard that I like our physics class; he said everyone else in the class hates it.

10. _____ Teenagers often do very dangerous things because they think they are *immortal*.

11. _____ Although the city of Detroit itself has only about one million residents, there are about four million people living in the Detroit *metropolitan* area.

12. _____ Judaism, Islam, and Christianity are all *monotheistic* religions that
13. _____ began in the Middle East. Earlier, *polytheism* was common in the area.

14. _____ A *postmortem* medical examination showed that the man had died of a heart attack.

15. _____ The city police department and a group of teachers *cooperated* in developing a program to educate school children about the dangers of drugs.

16. _____ Fortunately, the city was *evacuated* before flood waters from the Mississippi River covered its streets and many of its houses. It was
17. _____ almost a week before the water *receded* and the people could return to their homes.

18. _____ Sharon believes that no country should ever *intervene* in the politics of another country.

19. _____ Mary believes in one all-powerful god, but her best friend, Celia, is an *atheist*.

20. _____ In Sandy's English classes, there is a lot of student-student *interaction*.

21. _____ Today's meeting has been *postponed* until tomorrow at 2:30 because three people were not able to attend today.

22. _____ Matt questioned the *veracity* of the report in the newspaper.

23. _____   Some people believe that *extraterrestrial* beings have visited the Earth.

24. _____   Barbara's *co-workers* gave her a party for her birthday.

25. _____   We've heard people say that the president may leave the company, but the story can't be *verified*.

26. _____   The nurse checked my grandfather's heart rate, temperature, and
27. _____   *respiration* every hour. She told me that his *vital* signs are good.

28. _____   A certain amount of *introspection* is good, but don't spend so much time trying to understand yourself that you don't have time to actually do something.

29. _____   There were so many teachers attending the National Association of Educators' *convention* in Denver that the hotels in the city were completely filled.

30. _____   The students *vacated* the auditorium when they smelled smoke.

31. _____   The farmer decided not to buy that piece of land because the *terrain* was too rocky.

32. _____   The author wrote such a *vivid* description of the house where he was born that I felt I would recognize it if I saw it.

Sentence Study

Restatement and Inference

This exercise is similar to the one found in Unit 5. Each sentence below is followed by five statements.* The statements are of four types:

1. Some of the statements are restatements of ideas in the original sentence. They give the same information in a different way.

2. Some of the statements are inferences (conclusions) that can be drawn from the information given in the sentence.

3. Some of the statements are not true based on the information given.

4. Some of the statements cannot be proved true or false based on the information given.

Put a check (✓) next to all restatements and inferences (types 1 and 2). Note: do not check a statement that is true of itself but cannot be inferred from the sentence. There is not always a single correct set of answers. Be prepared to discuss your choices with your classmates.

1. By the time he was 19, in 1963, Li Huasheng knew without any doubt that he wanted to be a painter.

   ___ a. In 1963, Li Huasheng was a painter.
   ___ b. In 1963, Li Huasheng doubted that he wanted to be a painter.
   ___ c. Li Huasheng is probably a painter today.
   ___ d. Li Huasheng was born in 1944.
   ___ e. Li Huasheng had always wanted to be a painter.

2. Stephen Dobyn's mystery novels have two very interesting elements: their location, Saratoga Springs, and their detective, Charlie Bradshaw.

   ___ a. Stephen Dobyn is the author of mystery novels.
   ___ b. Saratoga Springs is a place.
   ___ c. Charlie Bradshaw is an author.
   ___ d. Stephen Dobyn has written more than one mystery novel.
   ___ e. The author of this sentence seems to like Saratoga Springs as a location for a mystery novel.

3. The Ba-Benjelie tribe of central Africa are the keepers of a very special music, which, according to Louis Sarno, "may well antedate the birth of agriculture," and which was a source of great interest to the ancient Egyptians.

   ___ a. The Ba-Benjelie play very special music.
   ___ b. Louis Sarno is a musician.
   ___ c. Louis Sarno seems to know a lot about the music of the Ba-Benjelie.
   ___ d. The Ba-Benjelie have had their music for a very long time.
   ___ e. The birth of agriculture came after the beginnings of Ba-Benjelie music.

*For an introduction to sentence study, see Unit 1.

4. There should be a special place on bookshelves for well-meaning lesson books like Norman Leach's "My Wicked Stepmother."

___ a. This is a well-meaning book.
___ b. The book tries to teach a lesson.
___ c. Norman Leach is the author of the book.
___ d. This is a successful lesson book.
___ e. The author of this sentence doesn't like this book.

5. Boiling is the easiest, simplest, and most basic form of cooking, and the most mysterious because anyone who has ever watched water boil knows that boiling is not an easy event to understand.

___ a. Because boiling water is easy to do, it is easy to understand.
___ b. Although it is easy to do, boiling is difficult to understand.
___ c. The author of this sentence finds boiling the most mysterious form of cooking.
___ d. Cooking is not an easy event to understand.
___ e. The author does not know how to cook.

6. Imagine the worst time with lack of sleep you've ever had—perhaps after staying up all night to study for a final exam; then imagine your worst-ever case of flu; that combination and then some is what chronic fatigue syndrome (CFS) feels like on a "normal" day.

___ a. CFS is apparently some kind of illness.
___ b. CFS is a kind of flu.
___ c. If you have CFS, you have days when you feel fine.
___ d. Having CFS is worse than having the flu.
___ e. Apparently, CFS makes you feel very tired.

7. A trio of serious mental disorders—schizophrenia, severe depression, and mania—are two to three times more common among men in jails than among men in the general population.

___ a. Most men in jails have mental disorders.
___ b. A trio of men in jails have serious mental disorders.
___ c. People in jails are more likely to have certain mental disorders than are people in the general population.
___ d. Men in jails are more likely to have certain mental disorders than are men in the general population.
___ e. There are more men in jails who have certain mental disorders than there are men in the general population with those disorders.

8. As stories of farmers burning forests to create farmland appeared in newspapers in the late 1980s, rock stars and movie actors joined the fight to save tropical woodlands, helping make the technical term *deforestation* into a household word.

___ a. The actions of famous people trying to save forests have helped make the issue of deforestation well known.
___ b. Apparently, *deforestation* means to burn or otherwise destroy forests.
___ c. Newspapers can help make difficult terms and ideas well known.
___ d. The article that this sentence is taken from will mainly discuss events in the 1980s.
___ e. Most of the people who have tried to save the forests have been rock stars and movie actors.

9. Some people claim that the poor economy explains homelessness. Professor Jones rejects that explanation: "A lot of people are using the economy as a convenient excuse for doing nothing."

— a. Professor Jones agrees with the explanation.
— b. Professor Jones does not agree that the economy is poor.
— c. Apparently a lot of people agree with the explanation.
— d. Professor Jones thinks the explanation is an excuse.
— e. Professor Jones believes that a lot of people are doing nothing about homelessness.

10. Beginners used to want a short definition of economics; and in response to this request, there was no shortage of suggestions.

— a. There is a good short definition of economics.
— b. Many people have suggested short definitions of economics.
— c. This author will provide a short definition of economics.
— d. This author will not provide a definition of economics.
— e. This sentence may have been taken from an economics textbook.

Paragraph Reading

Main Idea

This exercise is similar to the Main Idea exercises found in Unit 1 and Unit 5. As you did in Unit 1, you will read nonfiction paragraphs for the main idea. As you did in Unit 5, you will write the main idea yourself instead of selecting it from a list. Readers often need to do this when taking notes on a passage.

Read the following paragraphs quickly. Concentrate on discovering the main idea. Remember, don't worry about details in the paragraphs. You only want to determine the general message.

After each of the paragraphs, write a sentence that expresses the main idea in your own words. When you have finished, your teacher may want you to discuss your ideas in small groups.

Example

In many ways, the Sun is a very ordinary star. There are stars smaller than the Sun, dimmer, and cooler; and there are stars much larger than the Sun, brighter, hotter—more energetic in every way. But the Sun is very special to astronomers interested in stars. It is the only star near enough to us that we see it as a flat disk instead of just a point of light. Scientists can study this disk to learn not only about the Sun but also about the other more distant stars.

Write a sentence that expresses the main idea of the paragraph.

_____

_____

Explanation

Notice that there are two important ideas in this paragraph, two ideas that are developed throughout:

1. that the Sun is an ordinary star and

2. that the Sun is very important to those who study stars.

The main idea of the paragraph includes both of these points, so you might have written something like this: Although the sun is an ordinary star, it is very important to those who study stars.

Example adapted from *Black Holes, White Dwarfs, and Superstars,* by Franklyn M. Branley (New York: Thomas Y. Crowell Company, 1976), 4.

Paragraph 1

All things that live in the world's oceans are placed in one of three categories by oceanographers, scientists who study the ocean. The three categories are plankton, nekton, and benthos. When scientists talk about *plankton,* they are referring to those plants and animals of the sea that float on or near the surface of the water, having little or no ability to move themselves. When oceanographers use the word *nekton,* they are talking about animals that can swim about freely and easily in the water. The word *benthos* refers to plants and animals that live on the bottom of the sea. Some benthos walk or crawl about at the bottom of the sea, while others stay in one place on the ocean floor.

Write a sentence that expresses the main idea of the paragraph.

_____

_____

Paragraph 2

Did you ever wonder how your brain knows when you've hurt your foot? In the human body, such messages are carried by nerve cells called neurons. At first it was thought that these messages were carried through the nervous system by electricity, like messages traveling along telephone wires. However, as scientists learned more about individual neurons, they discovered that the body's message system is much more complicated. Electricity is indeed involved in the work of the neurons, but chemical reactions are also important. Chemical reactions in one part of the nerve produce electric charges, and these charges start a chemical reaction in the next part of the nerve. In this way, messages travel along a nerve fiber.

Write a sentence that expresses the main idea of the paragraph.

_____

_____

Paragraph 1 adapted from "The Advance Organizer: Its Nature and Use," by Robert W. Jerrolds, in Theodore L. Harris and Eric J. Cooper, eds., *Reading, Thinking, and Concept Development* (New York: The College Entrance Examination Board, 1985), 77.

Paragraph 2 adapted from *World of the Brain,* by Alvin and Virginia Silverstein (New York: William Morrow and Co., 1986), 15–16.

Paragraph 3

An animal species that has shown signs of high intelligence is the dolphin. In their ocean home, dolphins live together in large groups, called schools, and cooperate to protect weak and sick members of the group. They seem to communicate with one another through a variety of different types of sounds. Scientists studying dolphin communication discovered that these mammals are able to learn human language as well. They easily learn to understand spoken commands and to imitate many human words. Often dolphins also seem to understand some of the words they repeat. Studies of dolphins' speech and behavior are providing insights into a nonhuman intelligence that some scientists believe is second only to ours on planet Earth.

Write a sentence that expresses the main idea of the paragraph.

_____

_____

Paragraph 4

The nervous system of insects is very different from ours. Although much insect behavior is very complicated, insects are not capable of thought. They are like small, living computers that always react in the same way to the world around them. When we smell good food, we think to ourselves, "I'm hungry! I'd like to eat that." But when an insect smells its food, its nervous system makes its muscles move its body toward the food. Once it has arrived at the food, its brain makes its mouth open and begin to bite and chew. The insect doesn't think about what it is doing; it just does it.

Write a sentence that expresses the main idea of the paragraph.

_____

_____

Paragraph 3 adapted from *World of the Brain,* by Alvin and Virginia Silverstein (New York: William Morrow and Co., 1986), 35.
Paragraph 4 adapted from *How Insects Communicate,* by Dorothy Hinshaw Patent (New York: Holiday House, 1975), 15.

Paragraph 5

To most people looking at the night sky, the stars seem to be always the same. Their locations appear unchanging; so does their brightness. Also, there seems to be always the same number of stars—no new ones have appeared, and no old stars have disappeared. But none of these conditions is true; stars do move, old stars do go out of existence (and some young stars also). New stars appear, too, and stars that have not been seen because of their dimness suddenly become brighter.

Write a sentence that expresses the main idea of the paragraph.

_____

_____

Paragraph 5 adapted from *Black Holes, White Dwarfs, and Superstars,* by Franklyn M. Branley (New York: Thomas Y. Crowell Company, 1976), 62.

Paragraph Reading

Reading for Full Understanding

In other paragraph reading exercises in this book, you read only to determine the main idea of a passage. This exercise requires you to read passages much more carefully. Each passage in this section is followed by a number of questions. The questions are designed to give you practice in

1. determining the main idea,
2. understanding supporting details,
3. drawing inferences,
4. guessing vocabulary items from context, and
5. using grammatical and stylistic clues to understand selected parts of the passages.

Read each passage carefully. Try to determine the main idea while noticing important details. For each of the questions below, select the best answer. You may refer to the passage to answer the questions.

Example: *The Adventures of Robin Hood*

1   Every day at sundown this week, the Summer Film Festival will be showing a
2   film you should really see. A lot of adventure films were made in Hollywood
3   during the 1930s and 1940s, but even in that crowd, *The Adventures of Robin*
4   *Hood* stands out. *The Adventures of Robin Hood* is based on the fourteenth-
5   century English stories about this charming thief. And like so many early movies,
6   this film is filled with good acting. A youthful Errol Flynn is everything the star
7   of a film should be. Tall, athletic, and very good looking, he captures the ideal
8   Robin Hood. Olivia de Havilland makes a perfect Maid Marian. As the "bad
9   guys," Claude Rains and Basil Rathbone give wonderful performances of ugly
10 behavior.

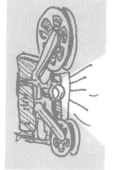

1. The person who wrote this movie review thinks that . . .

   ___ a. too many adventure films were made in the 1930s and 1940s.
   ___ b. a new Robin Hood movie should be made.
   ___ c. this movie is one of the best adventure films made in its time.
   ___ d. the Summer Festival will be crowded.

2. According to the reviewer, the story presented in *The Adventures of Robin Hood* . . .

   ___ a. is based on fourteen English stories.
   ___ b. is based on old stories about Robin Hood.
   ___ c. is totally new.
   ___ d. is like many other movie stories of that time.

Adapted from "The Adventures of Robin Hood," by Patrick McCarthy, *Ann Arbor Observer* (Special 15th Anniversary Edition), July, 1991, 43; questions adapted from "Examination for the Certificate of Competency in English, 1994" (Ann Arbor: English Language Institute, University of Michigan).

3. What does "he captures the ideal Robin Hood" (lines 7–8) mean?

___ a. He is perfect as a "bad guy."
___ b. He is more handsome than the real Robin Hood.
___ c. He follows and catches Robin Hood.
___ d. His acting as Robin Hood was very good.

4. In the opinion of the writer, Claude Rains and Basil Rathbone . . .

___ a. are not good-looking.
___ b. are good at acting like "bad guys."
___ c. are not as talented as Errol Flynn.
___ d. caused problems because they behaved badly.

5. What does the writer think of Errol Flynn as Robin Hood?

___ a. Flynn is too young for the part.
___ b. Flynn is the best actor in the movie.
___ c. Flynn is perfect for the part of Robin Hood.
___ d. Flynn's personality is like the real Robin Hood's.

Explanation

1. (c) The main idea of the passage is that this is a fine film. In line 2, the author says that people "should really see" the film, and, in line 4, that the movie "stands out" among the many adventure movies made in the 1930s and 1940s. The author says the film is "filled with good acting." From these and other details, we know that the author likes the movie and thinks that it is one of the best adventure films of its time.

2. (b) This tests your understanding of details. In lines 4–5, the author states that the movie is based on English stories about Robin Hood ("this charming thief") from the fourteenth century.

3. (d) This question checks whether you have a general understanding of the meaning of the word *captures* in this context—when actors "capture" their characters, they play them very well (they "catch" who the characters are).

4. (b) This is a restatement of the last sentence of the paragraph.

5. (c) This calls for your understanding of the author's point of view. In lines 7–8, the author tells us that Flynn is "the ideal Robin Hood." In lines 6–7, the author says, "Flynn is everything the star of a film should be."

Passage 1: Do Animals Sleep?

1   All animals must rest, but do they really sleep as we know it? The answer to
2   this question seems obvious. If an animal regularly stops its activities and stays
3   quiet and unmoving—if it looks as though it is sleeping—then why not simply
4   assume that it is in fact sleeping? But how can observers be sure that an animal is
5   sleeping?
6   They can watch the animal and notice whether its eyes are open or closed,
7   whether it is active or lying quietly, and whether it responds to light or sound.
8   These factors are important clues, but they often are not enough. Horses and cows,
9   for example, rarely close their eyes, and fish and snakes cannot close them. Yet
10 this does not necessarily mean that they do not sleep. Have you ever seen a cat
11 dozing with one eye partly open? Even humans have occasionally been observed
12 to sleep with one or both eyes partially open. Animals do not necessarily lie down
13 to sleep either. Elephants, for example, often sleep standing up, with their tusks
14 resting in the fork of a tree. Finally, while "sleeping" animals often seem unaware
15 of changes in the sounds and light and other stimuli around them, that does not
16 really prove they are sleeping either.
17   Observations of animal behavior alone cannot fully answer the question of
18 whether or not animals sleep. The answers come from doing experiments in "sleep
19 laboratories" using a machine called the electroencephalograph (EEG). The
20 machine is connected to animals and measures their brain signals, breathing,
21 heartbeat, and muscle activity. The measurements are different when the animals
22 appear to be sleeping than when they appear to be awake. Using the EEG,
23 scientists have confirmed that all birds and mammals studied in laboratories do
24 sleep. There is some evidence that reptiles, such as snakes and turtles, do not truly
25 sleep, although they do have periods of rest each day, in which they are quiet and
26 unmoving. They also have discovered that some animals, like chimpanzees, cats,
27 and moles (who live underground), are good sleepers while others, like sheep,
28 goats, and donkeys, are poor sleepers. Interestingly, the good sleepers are nearly
29 all hunters with resting places that are safe from their enemies. Nearly all the poor
30 sleepers are animals hunted by other animals; they must always be watching for
31 enemies, even when they are resting.

1. All animals . . .

___ a. sleep some time each day.
___ b. spend some time resting.
___ c. close their eyes to sleep.
___ d. react to sound while they are sleeping.

2. The authors use the elephant as an example of an animal that . . .

___ a. is a good sleeper.
___ b. wakes to dangerous sounds.
___ c. sleeps with its eyes open.
___ d. doesn't always sleep lying down.

Adapted from *Sleep and Dreams,* by Alvin and Virginia B. Silverstein (Philadelphia: J. B. Lippincott, 1974), 34–40.

3. The authors mention humans who sleep with one eye open to show that . . .

___ a. an animal's eyes don't have to be closed for it to be sleeping.
___ b. some humans are sensitive to light while they sleep.
___ c. human sleep is unlike animal sleep in some ways.
___ d. humans and cats have similar sleeping patterns.

4. The authors mention cows and horses in paragraph 2 in order to show that . . .

___ a. an animal does not have to close its eyes to sleep.
___ b. most mammals close their eyes to sleep.
___ c. all sleepers have something in common.
___ d. open eyes prove an animal is awake.

5. The best way to tell if an animal is sleeping is . . .

___ a. to see if its eyes are open.
___ b. to see if it is moving.
___ c. to use an EEG.
___ d. to see if it reacts to light and sound.

6. According to the passage, reptiles . . .

___ a. may not really sleep.
___ b. may not need to rest.
___ c. are not often studied in sleep laboratories.
___ d. cannot be studied with an EEG.

7. Scientists who study sleep think that some animals are better sleepers than other animals because the better sleepers . . .

___ a. are often tired from being hunted by other animals.
___ b. are often tired from hunting other animals.
___ c. have safe places to sleep.
___ d. awaken faster if an enemy finds them sleeping.

8. What does *dozing* (line 11) mean?

___ a. opening only one eye
___ b. sleeping
___ c. waking up
___ d. looking around

Passage 2: Temperature Patterns

1   Many processes within our bodies are timed to a cycle of about twenty-four
2 hours. If the body temperature is taken every hour or so throughout the day or
3 night, each person is found to have a certain pattern. The temperature rises and
4 falls about two degrees every twenty-four hours. Some people's temperatures rise
5 very rapidly after awakening and then begin to fall in the afternoon and evening.
6 For others their temperatures rise very slowly at first, reach a peak in the late
7 afternoon or evening, and do not begin to drop until quite late in the day. In all
8 cases, a person's temperature is at its lowest during the time of sleep. People tend
9 to feel most wide-awake and can work best at the high point of their temperature.
10 You may have noticed that some people jump out of bed bright and early and are
11 cheerful and active during the early part of the day, then grow tired in the evening
12 and go to bed quite early. Others find it difficult to get up in the morning and do
13 not seem able to get going very well until afternoon; during the evening, they are
14 wide-awake and hate to go to bed. People can usually adjust to a different
15 schedule if necessary, but it seems to be more difficult for some people than for
16 others.

1. The author says that people's body temperature . . .

___ a. rises two degrees when they first wake up.
___ b. falls two degrees when they first wake up.
___ c. rises and falls two degrees while they sleep.
___ d. rises and falls two degrees each day.

2. In general, people can get more done . . .

___ a. in the morning.
___ b. when their temperature is highest.
___ c. when their temperature is lowest.
___ d. in the middle of the day.

3. When people are sleeping . . .

___ a. their body temperature does not change.
___ b. their body temperature is lower than it is in the morning.
___ c. their body temperature is higher than it is in the morning.
___ d. their body temperature can change as much as two degrees.

4. According to the passage, people who have trouble waking up in the morning probably . . .

___ a. show a temperature pattern that is highest in the afternoon or evening.
___ b. show a temperature pattern that rises quickly in the morning.
___ c. should try to be more cheerful and active in the morning.
___ d. will all have difficulty changing to a different sleep schedule.

Adapted from *Sleep and Dreams,* by Alvin and Virginia B. Silverstein (Philadelphia: J. B. Lippincott, 1974), 21–22.

5. What does *peak* (line 6) mean?

___ a. change
___ b. low point
___ c. high point
___ d. temperature

Passage 3: Left-Handers in School

1   When children begin school in the United States, at the age of five or so, they
2   are usually clearly either right-handed or left-handed. In schools in the United
3   States, left-handed children are usually allowed to learn to write, cut with scissors,
4   and work with art supplies with their preferred hand. But in the past, it was often
5   the custom to force a left-handed child to learn to write and do other work with
6   the right hand. In some countries, this is done today. Researchers do not agree on
7   the effects of such a change. Some say that forcing a left-handed child to be right-
8   handed can cause emotional and physical problems and even learning difficulties.
9   They say such a child may start to confuse the directions left and right and reverse
10 letters and numbers accidentally, such as writing *36* instead of *63*. Other
11 specialists laugh at such findings and say that changing a child's handedness will
12 have no such effects. Perhaps part of the disagreement is due to the fact that
13 children differ in how strong their hand preference is. Some left-handers are so
14 strongly left-handed that they fight any change, and if they are forced, they may
15 indeed develop problems. Others are not so strongly left-handed and can make the
16 change without any great difficulty.

1. According to the passage, schools in the U.S. . . . .

___ a. want left-handed children to write with the right hand.
___ b. let left-handed children write with the left hand.
___ c. help left-handed children learn to write with both hands.
___ d. have found that left-handed children have more difficulty in learning than do right-handed
children.

2. Teaching a left-handed child to write with the right hand . . .

___ a. usually causes the child to have learning difficulties.
___ b. does not cause any problems.
___ c. usually causes the child to have emotional problems.
___ d. may or may not cause problems for the child.

Adapted from *The Left-hander's World,* by Alvin and Virginia B. Silverstein (Chicago: Follett, 1977), 28.

3. What is the "disagreement" (line 12) about?

___ a. whether left-handers are ill or not
___ b. the effects of teaching left-handers to write with the right hand
___ c. how strongly left-handed some people are
___ d. how often left-handers have fighting problems

4. How do the authors of this passage feel about teaching left-handers to use their right hands?

___ a. They think it should not be done to children who strongly prefer the left hand.
___ b. They think it prevents many serious problems.
___ c. We do not know what their opinion is.
___ d. They think it should never be done to any left-handers.

Passage 4: Headaches

1   Everyone has suffered from headaches, but until recently medical researchers
2   were not certain what caused them. New research is giving us more information
3   about two common types of headaches: tension headaches and migraine
4   headaches. The most painful ones are migraines, which occur about eight to ten
5   percent of the time and are experienced as a very sharp, throbbing pain. Most
6   headaches, however, are tension headaches. They are unpleasant, of course, but not
7   as painful as the migraine variety. Usually they are experienced as a dull ache on
8   both sides of the head or in the back or forehead. These headaches are caused by
9   the tightening of the muscles of the head and neck, which in turn causes the blood
10 vessels to narrow, making it difficult for the brain to receive the oxygen it needs.
11 This is what causes the pain. Migraines, on the other hand, result from the blood
12 vessels in the brain enlarging, causing swelling in the brain. This swelling results
13 in terrible pain. The headache may last for a day or two and leave the individual
14 sick and weak. Migraines are apparently inherited, because several individuals in
15 the same family usually have them. Doctors believe that the brains of these
16 individuals react in unusual ways to small problems, like failing a test or eating
17 unwisely. Sometimes there are warning signals before a migraine occurs, such as
18 spots appearing before the eyes or a sick feeling in the stomach. If the person
19 takes medicine or caffeine as soon as he or she begins to feel the headache coming
20 on, it can be avoided. Caffeine and the medicine, called ergot, cause the blood
21 vessels to narrow. Once the headache has started, sleep and a cool cloth on the
22 head may help. People who have migraines may also have tension headaches
23 following a migraine attack. Alcohol, which widens the blood vessels, can help
24 tension headaches, and warm cloths on the head can help the person relax and
25 thereby lessen the pain.

Adapted from *World of the Brain,* by Alvin and Virginia B. Silverstein (New York: William Morrow and Co., 1986), 170–71.

1. What will lessen the pain of a migraine headache?

    __ a. getting the blood vessels of the head to narrow
    __ b. getting the blood vessels of the head to enlarge
    __ c. relaxing the muscles of the head and neck
    __ d. putting a warm cloth on the head

2. What will lessen the pain of a tension headache?

    __ a. getting the blood vessels of the head to narrow
    __ b. getting the blood vessels of the head to enlarge
    __ c. sleeping
    __ d. tightening the muscles in the head

3. Tension headaches . . .

    __ a. are usually felt on one side of the head.
    __ b. often follow a feeling of being sick to one's stomach.
    __ c. are less painful than migraine headaches.
    __ d. seem to be more common in certain families.
    __ e. may be a reaction to eating unwisely.

4. T / F   Treatments for migraine headaches will also help tension headaches.

5. T / F   People who get tension headaches can also get migraine headaches.

Discourse Focus

Prediction

Reading is active. Meaning does not exist only on the page or in the mind of the reader. It is created by the *interaction* between reader and text. Good readers use their general knowledge and the information in a text to make predictions (remember, *dict* = say, *pre* = before), that is, to develop expectations about what they will read next; then they read to see if their predictions or expectations were correct. If readers are surprised, they reread, creating new predictions. Most often, however, readers are not greatly surprised; they continue reading. This exercise is designed to give you practice making and checking predictions. You will read part of an article, stopping several times to think about what you expect to read about next. Readers cannot always predict exactly what an author will talk about next, but you can practice using clues and your general knowledge to make good guesses.

The Fall of the Forest

Tropical Tree Losses Go from Bad to Worse

Recent studies of the burning and cutting throughout South America, Asia, and Africa show that trees in the world's tropical forests face greater danger than scientists had thought.

by Richard Monastersky

Example

1. Above are the title, subtitle, and editor's introduction from an article on tropical forests. On the basis of these, does the current situation for tropical forests seem good or bad? What words make you think so?

   _____

2. What aspects of these forests do you think the article will be about? List two possibilities:

   _____

   _____

Excerpt from "The Fall of the Forest," *Science News,* July 21, 1990, 40.

Explanation

1. The situation is not good. The main title tells us that the trees are *falling*. The subtitle reports that we are *losing* trees and that the situation is going *from bad to worse*. From the editor's introduction we learn that trees are being *burned* and *cut* and that this is a *danger* to the forests.

2. We know that the forests are in danger. Based on this information, you might predict that the article would be about such things as the problems facing tropical forests, the different situations worldwide, and why things are worse than previously thought.

3. Before you continue reading the article, decide how you expect it to begin. Remember, you cannot always predict exactly what an author will do, but you can use knowledge of the text and your general knowledge to make good guesses. Which of the following seems the most likely beginning?

__ a. The author will describe tropical forests.
__ b. The author will describe the dangers to tropical forests.
__ c. The author will describe increased danger to tropical forests.
__ d. The author will describe the locations of dangers to tropical forests.

Now read to see if your expectations were correct.

> The numbers tell a frightening story. Two new reports warn that the world's tropical forests are disappearing much faster than scientists thought, despite increasing efforts to save the forests.

4. The article begins by discussing the increased danger to forests. Is this what you expected?

5. What do you expect to read about next? What words or phrases give you this idea?

_____

_____

_____

Now read to see if your expectations are correct.

> Ten years ago, the United Nations calculated that the forests encircling the middle of the Earth were disappearing at a rate of 11.3 hectares per year, and until now that number has stood as the estimate of tropical forest loss. "For most of the past 10 years, that number has determined how people have analyzed the problem of deforestation," says Eric Rodenburg of the World Resources Institute (WRI) in Washington, DC.

6. The author gives the old number for how fast the forests are disappearing. Is this what you expected? If not, why not? Did you misunderstand something in the previous section? Even if you didn't guess exactly what the author was going to do, do you think your expectations were good ones anyway?

7. Now that the author has described what people have believed for the past 10 years, what do you think he will discuss next?

_____

_____

Discuss your choices with your classmates. Then read to see if your expectations are confirmed.

> But last month WRI released a new study based on more recent information that indicates tropical deforestation destroys 16.4 to 20.4 million hectares each year—an area almost the size of Tunisia. And new numbers released last month by the United Nations are similar. Cutting and burning of trees each year destroy about 1 percent of the tropical forests says Karna D. Singh, who coordinates Forest Resources Assessment for the Food and Agriculture Organization in Rome. His group will not complete their calculations for two years, so current numbers are not exact.
>
> Whatever the final estimates, they will be much greater than those of 10 years ago and deforestation experts say there are two possible reasons for this increase.

8. Were your expectations confirmed in this section of the text?

9. What do you think the author will discuss next? What aspects of the text and your general knowledge help you to make this prediction?

_____

_____

Read to see if your expectations are correct.

> For one, many countries are simply cutting down more trees today than they were 20 years ago. But this doesn't tell the whole story. Estimates in earlier studies didn't have available the satellites we do today. Earlier studies overestimated the amount of forest land left and underestimated the amount of deforestation.

10. Were your predictions confirmed?

11. What other topics do you think will be discussed in the rest of this article? Check (✓) all those issues below that *might* be discussed. Be prepared to defend your choices.*

___ a. Reasons for concern about the loss of tropical forests
___ b. The definition of tropical forests
___ c. Discussion of forests in different parts of the world
___ d. Worldwide efforts to save tropical forests
___ e. Differences in forests from place to place
___ f. Attempts to carry out better studies
___ g. Reasons for deforestation
___ h. Reasons not to worry about deforestation

_____

*The rest of the article is not reprinted here; however, a summary of the ideas can be found in the Answer Key.

8

Reading Selections 1A–1B

Popular Press

> *Tomorrow is often the busiest day of the year.*
> —Spanish proverb

> *Lost time is never found again.*
> —Benjamin Franklin, 1748

> *Never put off till tomorrow what you can do today.*
> —Lord Chesterfield, 1749

> *If once a man indulges himself in murder, very soon he comes to think little of robbing; and from robbing he comes next to drinking and Sabbath-breaking, and from that to incivility and procrastination.*
> —Thomas De Quincey, 1827

Should you be reading this now? Is there something else you should be doing? If you don't know what *procrastination* means and haven't yet looked it up in the dictionary, you may be a *procrastinator,* someone who puts off doing things that must be done. Read on to find out whether you are a procrastinator.

Selection 1A   **Questionnaire**

Are You a Procrastinator?

Everyone occasionally delays something that should be done now. A procrastinator, however, *habitually* postpones tasks. It's a way of life. To help you discover whether or not you're a procrastinator, Professor Loren Broadus included this "Procrastination Survey" in his book *How to Stop Procrastinating and Start Living.* The test requires only minutes, so why put it off?

		Yes	No
1.	Do you feel angry when someone reminds you of tasks you have left undone?	—	—
2.	Do you feel you have too much to do each day?	—	—
3.	Do you find yourself frequently making excuses for work unfinished?	—	—
4.	Do you spend time on unimportant things while letting important work go?	—	—
5.	Do you sometimes delay a task until it's so late you're embarrassed to do it?	—	—
6.	Do you use high-energy times to do unimportant tasks?	—	—
7.	Do you often have a hard time deciding what to do first?	—	—
8.	Do you often make promises (to yourself and others) and fail to keep them?	—	—
9.	Do you sometimes agree to do something and then regret it?	—	—
10.	Do you forget to write down what you agreed to do?	—	—
11.	Do you often fail to list tasks and then not know what to do?	—	—
12.	Do you think you work better under pressure?	—	—
13.	Do you almost always feel in a hurry?	—	—
14.	Do you continue to work on tasks even when they're as complete as necessary?	—	—
15.	Do you think that by waiting longer, some tasks won't need to be done?	—	—
16.	Do you have difficulty saying no to people?	—	—

Questionnaire adapted from "Procrastination," by James Braham, *Industry Week,* March 3, 1986, 40–41.

	Yes	**No**
17. Do you think more about the one negative comment than the many positive things people say?	—	—
18. Do you feel you should be doing something else when playing with your children or friends?	—	—

Scoring

Give yourself five points for each Yes answer and total your score. The lower the better. 0–20, Well-organized and Efficient; 21–40, Doing Well; 41–60, Need Improvement; 61–80, You Need Help; 81–90, True Procrastinator.

Discussion

1. How did you do? Are you a procrastinator or not? Do you believe the results of this questionnaire? If not, why not?

2. On this questionnaire, it's difficult to tell the difference between what the authors believe are "bad" behaviors and what we've been taught are "good" things to do. Following are two lists. On the left are "bad" behaviors from the questionnaire; on the right, are "good" behaviors. How do you think we can tell the difference?

   a. You have too much to do (because you procrastinate).

   a′ You are a busy person (because you do many things well).

   b. You spend too much time on unimportant things.

   b′ You do everything well.

   c. You still work on things even when they're as complete as necessary.

   c′ You believe that if something is worth doing, it's worth doing right.

   d. You do unimportant things first.

   d′ You don't put off until tomorrow what you can do today.

3. What do you think are causes and solutions for procrastination?

Selection 1B   **Magazine Articles**

Many popular magazines offer self-help for procrastinators. The discussion that follows contains information from several such articles. Read to find out the causes of procrastination and some solutions. Remember, you can't be helped if you put off reading this! Your teacher may want you to do Vocabulary from Context exercise 1 on pages 217–18 before you begin. (That's not procrastinating!)

Procrastination: What You Can Do about It. . . . When You Get around to It

By May B. Later*

1   People like to joke about procrastination: "I've been meaning to read a book on procrastination, but I never seem to get around to it." Sometimes procrastination can even be a positive process, because some things should be left until later. And some people work faster and more efficiently under pressure. Sometimes procrastinators become lucky. For example, the unmet problem solves itself; the files you can't find are no longer needed, the meeting you haven't prepared for gets canceled. But one cannot always be lucky.

2   "Very often procrastination becomes a serious problem, because it truly can make life unhappy," says Dr. Lenora M. Yuen, a Palo Alto, California, psychologist who coauthored the book *Procrastination*.

3   Most often, procrastination—generally defined as an "irrational" delay or postponement of a "relevant" activity—is anything but humorous. It can produce stress, anxiety, embarrassment, or conflict—sometimes leading to depression, guilt or anger, and illness, even to loss of friends, divorce, and overuse of alcohol and drugs. In the workplace, procrastination can result in loss of a job. And it costs U.S. businesses billions of dollars each year.

4   A recent survey based on interviews with vice presidents of 100 of the 1,000 largest companies in the United States found that the average employee procrastinates an estimated 18% of the time.

5   Procrastination—and we are talking here of *chronic* behavior, for we all put off things from time to time without serious consequences—is found in every profession. In his research, Professor Loren Broadus found that people from just about every vocation and profession admitted to being procrastinators. Even doctors. He found one physician who was afraid to go to the hospital because, although he was a very good doctor, he couldn't get around to writing on a patient's chart.

6   Why do so many of us procrastinate? Let's look at the reasons and some solutions.

---

*Text is a composite of excerpts from "After All, Tomorrow is Another Day," by Pat Roessle Materka, *Michigan Alumnus,* May/June 1990, 31–34; "Procrastination," by James Braham, *Industry Week,* March 3, 1986, 38–39, 40–41; and "Stop Procrastinating," by Diane Cole, *Working Mother,* December, 1990, 26, 28.

Perfectionism

7   A main cause of procrastination, perfectionism is caused by unrealistic attitudes. Perfectionist-procrastinators usually expect more of themselves than is realistic.

8   One psychologist tells of a patient who has been working on his doctoral dissertation for 10 years. Every new piece of information sends him back to the library for additional research and data. "He's got a roomful of notes, but it doesn't do him any good," says the psychologist. "It's too much, more than he needs."

9   The most effective executives are generally not perfectionists. Rather, Dr. Yuen says, "they know whether something is really important or not. They can make a distinction." But the perfectionist-procrastinators find it "really hard to distinguish between what is and what isn't important." That's when you get into trouble.

Fear of Failure

10   Procrastination often comes from fear, particularly fear of failure. Those who procrastinate for this reason tend to define failure very broadly, Dr. Yuen points out. They frequently equate performance and ability with self-worth. And procrastination breaks the equation for them. Because a complete effort has not been made, performance cannot be equated with ability.

11   Dr. Brian Kleiner, professor of management at California State University, Fullerton, says that these procrastinators "are fearful that their best efforts won't be good enough." By procrastinating, there can never be a true test of their abilities.

Low Tolerance for Frustration

12   This refers to not being able to do what is uncomfortable. People generally can understand the benefits of completing a certain task, but the thought of doing the work may be unbearable. The procrastinator avoids this anxiety.

Anger

13   Some people procrastinate when they're angry at a person or organization connected with the task. Also, when people are angry at having too much work to do, procrastinating is a way of saying, "This is too much."

Inability to Say No

14   Even executives have a difficult time refusing additional work when they already have too much to do, Professor Broadus discovered. When their boss (or subordinate) says, "We need this," they find it difficult to tell that person: "If I do this, then I'll have to let that go." Or "That will be done only 75% as well as it could be done."

Working Better under Pressure

15   This refers to the person who waits until the last minute to do something. "These people sometimes say they work better under pressure, or they like the excitement. This can work in certain areas of life," says Peter Turla, director of the

National Management Institute of Roanoke, Texas, "but it creates a lot of problems, affects the way you interact with people, and ultimately can kill you."

Not Having a Deadline

16   When we don't have a deadline, we can tell ourselves that we will do things when we get around to it. And we may never get around to it.

Having Too Little to Do

17   According to Professor Broadus, "too little to do causes more procrastination than too much." It's difficult to get going.

*   *   *

18   So, if it's time to stop putting things off, read on. There are a variety of ways to start getting things done. Here are some suggestions.

Identify the Problem

19   You may be a perfectionist or afraid of failure. As you examine the reasons for your delays, you will probably find a pattern. You may discover that you always delay jobs that require new skills out of fear of failure. Or you may always put off parts of the job you don't like out of anger at having to do them.

Make a Commitment

20   Make a commitment to change.

Set a Starting Time

21   While people who like to work under pressure usually only write deadlines on their calendars, a scheduled starting time is just as important. Mr. Turla backs up from the deadline, figuring the longest (rather than the shortest) probable time required, and adds a little time to that.

Set a Deadline

22   Make the length of time right for the task: six months to finish your doctoral dissertation; two minutes to leave your chair and start dinner.

Set a Schedule

23   Set a specific amount of time each day on the project. Write the appointment on your calendar and keep your date with yourself. Doing exactly what you said you would do will make you feel successful.

Break Big Jobs into Little Ones

24   If your goal is to write a book, don't think in terms of a 400-page manuscript, but a series of short paragraphs, one word at a time.

First Things First

25   If you have a number of important, as well as trivial, tasks to do, Mr. Turla advises, instead of doing the trivia first to get it out of the way, work on the important things and put the trivia aside. Save it for when you're tired, or the computer's down, or you're waiting for someone, or you've got nothing better to do.

Do the Worst First

26   Make your first task Monday morning the thing you hate to do. Then the rest of the week will seem easy.

Improve the Environment

27   Make a boring task easier by putting on music or inviting a friend to keep you company. Music and conversation can help a mindless task, but they'll slow down a difficult task. If you're writing a speech, go someplace quiet.

Give Yourself Rewards

28   Give yourself rewards along the way. Lawrence Sank, PhD, director of the Center for Cognitive Therapy in Bethesda, Maryland, confesses that the only way he got himself to finish writing his doctoral dissertation was to reward himself with his favorite food after he completed each paragraph.

Go Public and Get Support

29   Tell others what your goals are. This can create positive pressure and a group of people who can be of help.

Keep an Occasional Record of Your Time

30   Note how much time you spend procrastinating, telephoning, sitting in meetings. This way you can see how much time you spend on trivial things.

31   Make a game of winning against procrastinating. Give yourself points not just for the end result but for each success along the way. Here's a summary of things that can help you win:

1. State the goal.
2. Set a reasonable deadline.
3. Divide it into tasks with deadlines for each.
4. Find someone who can give you advice and encouragement.
5. Promise yourself a reward at each step along the way.

So when are you going to start??

Comprehension

Answer the following questions according to your understanding of the passage. Your teacher may want you to work individually, in small groups, or in pairs. True/False items are indicated by a T / F before a statement. Some questions may have more than one correct answer. Others require an opinion. Choose the answer you like best; be prepared to defend your choices.

1. T / F   Whenever you put off doing something, you are procrastinating.

2. T / F   Procrastination is usually harmless.

3. T / F   The average employee procrastinates 18% of the time.

4. T / F   Businesses lose billions of dollars a year because of procrastinators.

5. T / F   Doctors seem to procrastinate more than other people.

6. In paragraph 7, the author says that perfectionists "usually expect more of themselves than is

   realistic." What is meant by this? _____

   _____

7. According to the article, why do people who fear failure procrastinate? _____

   _____

8. T / F   Some people procrastinate because they believe they work better at the last minute.

9. T / F   People who have trouble saying no to their boss don't have trouble saying no to a
            subordinate.

10. T / F   Lawrence Sank weighs too much.

Discussion/Composition

1. Among the suggestions offered to help procrastinators, which two do you find the most helpful? The
    least helpful? Why?

2. In which situation do you work best: having too little to do or having too much to do? In paragraph
    17 Professor Broadus is quoted as saying, "too little to do causes more procrastination than too
    much." Do you agree? Why or why not?

3. Is it always better to get things done on time? Are there cultural differences in attitudes toward
    "procrastination"? Compare and contrast what you know of attitudes toward work in North America
    with other cultures. Give examples from your reading and your personal experience.

Vocabulary from Context

Exercise 1

*The vocabulary in the exercise below is taken from "Procrastination." Use the context provided to
decide on meanings for the italicized words. Write a definition, synonym, or description in the space
provided.*

1. _____   Saul was under a lot of *pressure*. He was told that he only had three
                          weeks to finish a task at work and that if it wasn't done well, he
2. _____   would lose his job. His *stress* was made worse by the fact that he is a
                          procrastinator and didn't feel like working.

3. _____

4. _____

5. _____

This *deadline* of three weeks caused a great deal of worry for Saul's brother Paul. Paul was worried that, in the end, he would have to do all of Saul's work. This *anxiety,* however, was *irrational;* Paul should have known that he wouldn't know how to do his brother's work.

6. _____

To make matters worse, Saul began experiencing *delays* in his work that were not his fault. For example, one day he was not able to use the printer for two hours, and the next day, his computer would not work until noon.

7. _____

At first Saul was quite *embarrassed* that he had gotten himself into this situation. He felt silly that he had trouble getting his work done on time, and he hoped that no one would find out.

8. _____

As time went by, however, Saul's embarrassment changed to feelings of *guilt.* He felt that he was responsible for making many people unhappy.

9. _____

10. _____

And then Saul and his brother began arguing. This *conflict* between Saul and Paul left them both feeling deeply unhappy. Their friends became worried about how *depressed* the two brothers seemed. They never went out, they were silent and were having trouble eating and sleeping.

11. _____

Just when the situation seemed *unbearable,* when Saul felt he couldn't stand it another minute, he realized he needed to look for a new job— one with less stress.

12. _____

13. _____

One Monday morning, Saul applied for a job with a new company. On Tuesday he had an *interview* with a vice president of the company. The meeting went well, and the next day he met with another vice president and other *executives.*

14. _____

Then, on Wednesday, Saul's deadline was *canceled.* He no longer had to work under pressure; he could take as much time as he wanted. Of course Saul was quite happy, but he decided to go work for the new company anyway.

15. _____

And that is not the only change Saul will make. He has decided never again to procrastinate. First, he must learn to *distinguish* between important and unimportant things. Once he can clearly see the difference, he will spend time first on important tasks. He has promised never again to waste time on things that are not related to the task he is working on. From now on his work time will be spent

16. _____

on *relevant* activities.

17. _____

18. _____

"I know this will be hard," Saul said to his brother, "but I can see the *benefit* in learning not to procrastinate. It will put me under less stress, and it will help our relationship. I have made a *commitment* to change, and I intend to keep my promise."

Exercise 2

This exercise gives you additional clues to the meaning of unfamiliar vocabulary in context. In the paragraph of "Procrastination" on page 213, indicated by the number in parentheses, find the word that best fits the meaning given. Your teacher may want to read these aloud as you quickly scan the paragraph to find the answer.

1. (5) What word means *habitual; constant; lasting a long time?*

2. (5) What word means *medical record; place where information is written?*

3. (14) What word means *person working under another person; person of lower rank?*

4. (25) What word means *unimportant?*

5. (27) What word means *requiring no thought or intelligence?*

Dictionary Study

Many words have more than one meaning. When you use the dictionary to discover the meaning of an unfamiliar word or phrase, you need to use the context to find the right definition. Use the dictionary entries provided to find the best definition for each of the italicized words in the following sentences. Write the number of the definition in the space provided.

___ 1. Mr. Turla backs up from the deadline, *figuring* the longest (rather than the shortest) probable time required, and adds a little time to that.

___ 2. He's got a roomful of notes, but it doesn't do him any *good.*

___ 3. This can *work* in certain areas of life, but it creates a lot of problems.

> **fig·ure** (fig-yŭr) *n.* 1. the written symbol of a number. 2. a diagram. 3. a decorative pattern, a pattern traced in dancing or skating. 4. a representation of a person or animal in drawing, painting, sculpture, etc. 5. a person as seen or studied, *saw a figure leaning against the door; the most terrible figure in our history.* 6. external form or shape, bodily shape, *has a good figure.* 7. a geometrical shape enclosed by lines or surfaces. 8. *figures,* arithmetic, calculating, *she is good at figures.* **figure** *v.* (**fig·ured, fig·ur·ing**) 1. to represent in a diagram or picture. 2. to picture mentally, to imagine. 3. to form part of a plan etc., to appear or be mentioned, *he figures in all books on the subject.* □**figure of fun,** a person who looks ridiculous. **figure of speech,** a word or phrase used for vivid or dramatic effect and not literally. **figure on,** *(informal)* to count on, to expect. **figure out,** *(informal)* to work out by arithmetic; to interpret, to understand.

From the *Oxford American Dictionary* (New York: Oxford University Press, 1980), *figure; good; and work.*

good (guud) *adj.* **(bet·ter, best)** 1. having the right or desirable properties, satisfactory, *good food.* 2. right, proper, expedient. 3. morally correct, virtuous, kindly. 4. (of a child) well-behaved. 5. gratifying, enjoyable, beneficial, *have a good time; good morning, good evening,* forms of greeting or farewell. 6. efficient, suitable, competent, *a good driver; good at chess.* 7. thorough, considerable, *a good beating.* 8. not less than, full, *walked a good ten miles.* 9. used in exclamations, *good God!* **good** *adv.* *(informal)* entirely; *good and angry,* very angry. **good** *n.* 1. that which is morally right; *up to no good,* doing something mischievous or criminal. 2. profit, benefit, *it will do him good; five dollars to the good,* having made this profit. □**as good as,** practically, almost, *the war is as good as over.* **for good,** permanently. **good behavior,** conduct that is legally correct. **Good Book,** the Bible. **good cheer,** hope and trust; having a very good time. **Good Conduct Medal,** a U.S. army medal given to enlisted men who have served with merit. **good for,** beneficial to; able to pay or undertake; *he is good for one hundred dollars, for a ten-mile walk; good for you!,* well done! **Good Friday,** the Friday before Easter, commemorating the Crucifixion. **good humor,** a cheerful mood or disposition, amiability. **good nature,** a kindly disposition, willingness to humor others. **good night!,** an exclamation of surprise or exasperation. **good offices,** influence deriving from one's position or power to reconcile; mediation. **Good Samaritan,** a genuinely charitable person who goes out of his way to help others. **in good time,** with no risk of being late; *all in good time,* in due course but without haste. **make good,** *see* **make. to the good,** as a balance on the right side; something extra.

▷It is incorrect to say *the machine works good* or *I am doing pretty good.* It is also incorrect to say *I feel good* when speaking of one's health. Say *I feel well.*

work (wurk) *n.* 1. use of bodily or mental power in order to do or make something, especially as contrasted with play or recreation. 2. something to be undertaken, the materials for this. 3. a thing done or produced by work, the result of action. 4. a piece of literary or musical composition, *one of Mozart's later works.* 5. what a person does to earn a living, employment. 6. doings or experiences of a certain kind, *nice work!* 7. ornamentation of a certain kind, articles having this, things or parts made of certain materials or with certain tools, *fine filigree work.* 8. *works,* operations in building etc.; the operative parts of a machine; a place where industrial or manufacturing processes are carried on. **work** *v.* 1. to perform work, to be engaged in bodily or mental activity. 2. to make efforts, *work for peace.* 3. to be employed, to have a job, *she works in a bank.* 4. to operate, to do this effectively, *it works by electricity; a can opener that really works; that method won't work.* 5. to operate (a thing) so as to obtain material or benefit from it, *the mine is still being worked; my partner works the Dallas area,* covers it in his work. 6. to purchase with one's labor, *work one's passage.* 7. to cause to work or function, *he works his staff very hard; can you work the elevator?* 8. to bring about, to accomplish, *work miracles.* 9. to shape or knead or hammer etc. into a desired form or consistency, *work the mixture into a paste.* 10. to do or make by needlework or fretwork etc., *work your initials on it.* 11. to excite progressively, *worked them into a frenzy; the candidate worked the crowd,* sought enthusiastic support for himself. 12. to make (a way) or pass or cause to pass slowly or by effort, *the grub works its way into timber; work the stick into the hole.* 13. to become through repeated stress or pressure, *the screw had worked loose.* 14. to be in motion, *his face worked violently.* 15. to ferment, *the yeast began to work.* 16. to solve by calculation, *work the problem.*

Reading Selections 2A–2D

Feature Articles

Newspapers and magazines often present articles that feature special topics. These "feature articles" are often on social and cultural topics.

Selection 2A   **Magazine Questionnaire**

at · tract \ə-trakt\ vb: to draw someone to you, to appeal to someone, to excite interest *syn:* fascinate, charm

What attracts you to someone else?

What's the Attraction?

Recently, a magazine published in the United States asked readers what attracts them to "that someone special." Following is the list of characteristics that readers mentioned.

a. On the list below, indicate which three characteristics are most important for people you are attracted to (M) and which three are least important (L).
b. Then guess what you think were the results of this survey: What are the three characteristics most often mentioned by the people questioned (M)? Least often mentioned (L)?
c. After you have made your decisions, discuss your responses with your classmates, then compare your results with those printed on page 222.

The person should . . .

	For me	For survey		For me	For survey
be caring and kind	____	____	have an attractive body	____	____
be charming	____	____	have an attractive face	____	____
be a good conversationalist	____	____	have a good sense of humor	____	____
be intelligent	____	____	have a lot of money	____	____
be a good sexual partner	____	____	have power and influence	____	____
be romantic	____	____	have similar interests	____	____
be widely respected	____	____	have similar religious beliefs	____	____

Adapted from "What's the Attraction?" by Ingrid Groller, *Parents,* February, 1990, 36.

The list below shows the percentage of magazine readers in the United States who mentioned each characteristic.

78%	Be caring and kind	44%	Be widely respected
68%	Have a good sense of humor	33%	Have similar religious beliefs
58%	Have similar interests	33%	Be charming
57%	Be a good conversationalist	15%	Have an attractive body
55%	Be intelligent	11%	Have an attractive face
50%	Be a good sexual partner	4%	Have a lot of money
49%	Be romantic	4%	Have power and influence

Discussion

1. Did any of the magazine results surprise you? Which were these, and why did you find them surprising?

2. Were there important ways in which your feelings differed from those of the people who answered the magazine survey? Why do you think this is?

3. Are there cultural differences in what attracts people to their partners? Do you think there are cultural differences between what men and women find attractive?

4. Do you think there are important differences between what attracts us to people at first and what should attract us to people if we are looking for a life partner?

Selection 2B   **Newspaper Article**

Before You Begin   Have you heard of advertising for a life partner in the newspaper? Do you think this is a good way to find someone to share your life with? Do you think you might try advertising in the newspaper?

In the newspaper article that follows, a professor from the United States describes learning the customs of newspaper advertising while he was in India. Read how Joseph and Punit meet through the Indian matrimonial ads. Your teacher may want you to do Vocabulary from Context exercise 1 on pages 226–27 before you begin.

Looking for a Mate in India

By Joseph Di Bona

1   If you have ever thought of advertising for a husband or a wife, you must consult the Indian matrimonial ads, where people have been finding mates for as long as anyone remembers.

2   The first part is easy. Include your profession; height is important; education a must; for men, how much you earn must be very clearly stated; and of course, "community," that category which includes caste, race, religion, region, and anything else you want it to mean.

3   But today many young people don't like this system whereby parents place ads for their children. They say the only ones who are advertised are the ones whose parents have tried everything else—marriage brokers, family friends, the local astrologer, work mates, and anyone else they can find. Their new way is to advertise for themselves in magazines for younger people.

4   This is a new and exciting development in Indian arranged marriages, and recently I responded to one such ad. It was placed by Anita K. described as a 40-year-old divorcee. I wrote:

Dear Miss K.,

5   *You will no doubt be surprised to have this late reply to your matrimonial ad of some time ago, but the truth is a friend of mine showed it to me just yesterday. I am an active 61-year-old divorced professor from the United States working in India temporarily and looking for someone special. I would like to meet you sometime soon in Delhi in order to become better acquainted.*

Joseph Di Bona is a Duke University professor of education working in India.
Adapted from "Brides and Grooms Wanted: Looking for a Wife in India—Not for the Faint of Heart," by Joseph Di Bona, *Christian Science Monitor,* July 19, 1981, 19.

In about a week I received this reply.

Dear Mr. Joseph,

6   *Thanks for your letter dated 1 March in response to my matrimonial ad. I was glad to read the particulars written by you and am attracted toward you. I am looking for someone who is mature, understanding, and maybe you are the right man. Incidentally, I have obtained the U.S. visa, and as my plans go, I ought to be leaving for America by the end of March. Your plan to visit Delhi at that time would not be of much help if we want to meet. However, I have another suggestion.*

7   *Do you think you can make it to Delhi earlier than that? If so, that would be lovely, and if not, I could visit your place and meet you, and we can talk things over. If we happen to like each other, then I could postpone my departure for the U.S.*

8   *But now let me give you some information about myself. I have divorced my husband, have one son who is 17 years old and is living with his father. I have had no contact with my son for eight years. I am single and lonely. I would like to settle with someone who is kind, affectionate, and broad-minded enough to help me to live my life and not rule my life. I am very straightforward. I hate hypocrisy, and unfaithfulness. I had a very bad experience with my first marriage. In my ad I gave a false name for obvious reasons. My name is Punit, and my height is 5 ft 7 in and not 170 cm which was wrongly printed. I am attractive, smart, and am cheerful. One of my hobbies is to laugh. Do I sound crazy? I am enclosing a photo; you may kindly send me yours.*

Much love, Punit

9   What to do next? I decided to ask my neighbor who originally showed me the ad. He has been searching for a spouse for several years but has not yet found the right woman.

"Shambhu," I asked, "what should I do about Punit?"

10   "She looks like the right one for you. She doesn't care about your caste, nationality, or religion, and she seems very smart. I would visit her if I were you or invite her to come here. Talk to her on the telephone just to hear her voice. I find that's a wonderful way to get to know someone."

11   I was surprised at how fast things seemed to be moving. I had a much slower schedule in mind, but I was quickly learning a new way to think about this.

"If I invite her to come here," I asked, "where would she stay, etc.?" The answers were all well-established customs, worked out over many, many years of experience.

12   "She will take care of the overnight travel and you pay for the hotel and meals. No, she will not share a room with you. You will get her a room in a nice nearby hotel."

"I think I am learning how this works. Your advice is to go for it?"

"Of course, my friend!" said Shambhu enthusiastically.

13   "I am now getting my photos ready. I have changed my opinion about long-distance phone calls and travel to unheard-of places. I am still not ready to agree to marriage after moments of introduction, but I'm working on that, too."

"Good," said Shambhu, "that's progress."

Comprehension

Answer the following questions according to your understanding of the article. Your teacher may want you to work individually, in small groups, or in pairs. True/False items are indicated by a T / F before a statement. Some questions may have more than one correct answer. Others require an opinion. Choose the answer you like best; be prepared to defend your choice.

1. T / F   Advertising for a marriage partner is a relatively new custom in India.

2. Which of the following is *not* mentioned as important to include in a matrimonial ad?

    a. height   b. weight   c. salary   d. education   e. religion

3. T / F   In India today, young people no longer like to advertise for partners.

4. T / F   Neither Joseph nor Punit has ever been married before.

5. T / F   Joseph and Punit are about the same age.

6. T / F   Punit will go to the U.S. in March, then try to visit Joseph when she returns.

7. Why do you think Punit gave a false name in her advertisement? _____

    _____

8. T / F   When responding to a matrimonial ad, it is unusual for the woman to travel to visit the man.

9. T / F   If Punit visits, she will probably be ready to share a room with Joseph.

10. Why do you think Joseph Di Bono is getting his photos ready?

    _____

    _____

11. Do you think Joseph and Punit will meet? If they do, does this mean they will marry? _____

    _____

Discussion/Composition

1. When people advertise in the newspaper, we have only their written words from which to form a picture of them. Based on your reading of Punit's letters, check (✓) all of the following that *you* think describe Punit. Be prepared to defend your opinion as you compare your answers with your classmates'.

__ crazy	__ old	__ lonely
__ interesting	__ brave	__ smart
__ straightforward	__ a good mother	__ fun to be with
__ tall	__ a good wife	__ traditional
__ attractive	__ religious	__ wise
__ stubborn	__ shy	__ independent

2. What do you think will happen next? Does Punit seem like the right person for Joseph? It seems that the two will meet. Write a description of what you think will happen next. You may write from either Joseph's or Punit's point of view.

3. Find personal ads in an English-language newspaper. Are these ads only for marriage or are other relationships suggested? What kind of information is provided? Why might this be a dangerous way to meet people?

Vocabulary from Context

Exercise 1

Both the ideas and the vocabulary in the exercise below are taken from "Looking for a Mate in India." Use the context provided to decide on meanings for the italicized words. Write a definition, synonym, or description in the space provided.

1. _____ Tom hopes some day to get married, but his *matrimonial* plans will have to wait until he finds someone to marry.

Because Tom was having trouble meeting someone to marry, he was going to try having someone arrange a marriage for him. However,
2. _____ when he found out how much a *marriage broker* would cost him, he
3. _____ decided that he would have to find a *mate* another way.

4. _____ Tom's next plan was to put an *ad* in the newspaper. He had heard that matrimonial *advertisements* were a good way to meet other people who were trying to find a mate.

5. _____   In his ad, Tom said that he was *mature* and was looking for someone like himself, not an inexperienced young person.

6. _____
7. _____   Tom soon received a letter from Betsy. She said that she, too, was looking for someone mature. She added that she hated *hypocrisy* and *unfaithfulness.* Tom thought this might be the person for him. He wrote back that he also hated people who say one thing and do something else; he added that he would never have a relationship with someone else when he was married.

8. _____   Betsy answered Tom's letter *enthusiastically.* Tom was excited, too, and the next week Tom and Betsy met.

Exercise 2

This exercise gives you additional clues to the meaning of unfamiliar vocabulary in context. In the paragraph of "Looking for a Mate in India" indicated by the number in parentheses, find the word or phrase that best fits the meaning given. Your teacher may want to read these aloud as you quickly scan the paragraph to find the answer.

1. (7) What word means *put off to a later time; delay?*

2. (8) What word means *accepting varied points of view?*

3. (8) What word means *honest; direct; clear?*

4. (12) What phrase means *go ahead; take the next step; try for something valuable; commit oneself to?*

Selection 2C   **Magazine Article**

Before You Begin   Below is an article describing how people find marriage partners in Japan. Before you read, consider what you already know about Japanese marriage customs. In what ways do you expect them to be similar to the customs you have read about in India? In what ways might they be different?

As you read "Japanese Marriage," consider the ways it is similar to your predictions and those in which it is different. Your teacher may want you to do the Vocabulary from Context exercise on pages 234–35 before you begin.

Japanese Marriage

1   When Mitsuko Shimomura, Japan's most famous female journalist, was sent to report from New York City for two years (the first Japanese woman reporter sent to live abroad), she came without Koichiro, her husband of eighteen years. Her U.S. colleagues thought Mitsuko must be very Westernized. "But I'm very Japanese," she laughs. "People in the U.S. just don't understand the way Japanese men and women relate. The physical separation wasn't a problem for our marriage. For us, marriage is a serious lifetime project.

2   "Our wedding speeches don't mention happiness. We say, 'Don't expect too much. Things are difficult, and marriage is really a partnership in problem solving.' We work toward thoughtfulness, patience, and sacrifice, which are much deeper than romance."

3   The traditional belief is that romantic love weakens a man. Although Asian literature is rich in great love stories, they usually end tragically instead of happily ever after, so many Japanese men don't trust romantic love.

4   Kiyofumi is a handsome executive with a Tokyo company. At twenty-five he is ready for marriage, but he will not follow his heart. "Once in my life, when I was in college, I experienced a strong romantic feeling for a young woman. And once was enough. I don't trust romance. I could meet someone nice at a disco and start to see her, then think I'm in love. But I can pretend to be a great guy for three months, so how do I know that this person isn't doing that to me? I have no confidence in my judgment. That's what my parents are for. Marriage is too important a step to take on the basis of romance."

5   A wedding in Japan is viewed as an expected social step, which 98 percent of the population takes. Because marriage is seen as something of a family merger, many families still follow the ancient custom of consulting a matchmaker. Frequently, however, they use the most modern of marriage brokers: the computer. Many large corporations, such as Mitsubishi and Fuji Banks, put their computers to work for their employees. Just enter preferences for looks, job, salary, hobbies, the ever-important family background, and out come as many as 130 possibilities, which, with the help of a counselor, are reduced to 3 candidates—all for a small fee. A larger fee is charged if marriage results.

6   Parents who are more traditional ask a friend, work mate, or neighbor to be the matchmaker and help find a suitable spouse for their son or daughter. A photograph and a report on family background are given, and the process begins. If everything seems okay, an arranged meeting *(omiai)* takes place.

7   "I was very nervous for my *omiai*," remembers Mihoko, a twenty-nine year old. "A woman in my Chinese cooking class knew Kiyoshi. I took one look at his photograph and was sure things would never work out. But I'd never had an *omiai* before and my parents thought I should go. We met at a hotel restaurant—his family, mine, and the matchmaker. It was very uncomfortable. Everyone talked but us. Then, after coffee, he and I took a walk through the hotel gardens and had a really boring conversation. I didn't like him at all, and I could tell he thought I was only so-so.

Adapted from "Japanese Marriage," by Judy Markey, *Cosmopolitan*, August, 1984, 210–15.

8   "A second meeting would indicate serious interest, so I was going to call the matchmaker and refuse another *omiai,* but she called me first and said Kiyoshi wanted to see me again. I talked with my family for a long time. They liked him very much. My mother especially liked the way he treated his mother. Somehow, their opinion seemed more important to me than just mine. That surprised me because I'd been working at *Newsweek*'s Tokyo offices for several years and thought I was very Westernized. Clearly, I was much more traditional than I thought. I just didn't trust my own feelings. My parents could see more because they had more experience of life.

9   "Our second meeting was better," says Mihoko, "and as time passed I grew to care very much about him. We were married six months later, and now it's five years. I think I was lucky, because Kiyoshi is very kind." (Mihoko's use of the word *kind* is important; when a group of Japanese college women were asked what quality they most wanted in a man, nearly all of them answered, "Gentleness.")

10   Even so-called love marriages do not sound the same as Western romance. When Kazuko met her husband Tetsuya, she recalls, "I thought he'd be a good man to marry because he understood that I would want to work even after having children. Tetsuya just wrote my father directly for permission to marry. My father asked, 'Do you think this is the *right* man?'—much more typically Japanese than 'Is this the man you love?' We call ours a love marriage, but it wasn't like Cinderella. We Japanese don't believe in that."

Restatement and Inference

Below are paragraphs from the article "Japanese Marriage." Each paragraph is followed by several statements.* The statements are of four types:

1. Some of the statements are restatements of ideas in the original sentence. They give the same information in a different way.
2. Some of the statements are inferences (conclusions) that can be drawn from the information given in the sentence.
3. Some of the statements are not true based on the information given.
4. Some of the statements cannot be proved true or false based on the information given.

Put a check (✓) next to those that are restatements and inferences of ideas presented in the paragraph. Remember, do not check a statement that is true of itself but cannot be inferred from the paragraph. There is not always a single correct set of answers. Be prepared to discuss your choices with your classmates.

Paragraph 1   When Mitsuko Shimomura, Japan's most famous female journalist, was sent to report from New York City for two years (the first Japanese woman reporter sent to live abroad), she came without Koichiro, her husband of eighteen years. Her U.S. colleagues thought Mitsuko must be very Westernized. "But I'm very Japanese," she laughs. "People in the U.S. just don't understand the way Japanese men and women relate. The physical separation wasn't a problem for our marriage. For us, marriage is a serious lifetime project."

*For an introduction to restatement and inference, see Unit 3.

___ a. Mitsuko Shimomura is Japan's most well-known journalist.

___ b. When Shimomura came to the U.S., her husband was only 18 years old.

___ c. Mitsuko is very Japanese.

___ d. Physical separation was not a problem for Mitsuko and Koichiro's marriage.

___ e. In the U.S., marriage is not a serious lifetime undertaking.

Paragraph 2   "Our wedding speeches don't mention happiness. We say, 'Don't expect too much. Things are difficult, and marriage is really a partnership in problem solving.' We work toward thoughtfulness, patience, and sacrifice, which are much deeper than romance."

___ a. Weddings in Japan are not happy events.

___ b. Americans expect too much from marriage.

___ c. Mitsuko thinks life is difficult.

___ d. Mitsuko thinks marriage requires problem solving.

___ e. Mitsuko thinks romance is less important than thoughtfulness for a successful marriage.

Paragraph 3   The traditional belief is that romantic love weakens a man. Although Asian literature is rich in great love stories, they usually end tragically instead of happily ever after, so many Japanese men don't trust romantic love.

___ a. Japanese men believe romantic love makes a man weak.

___ b. Japanese readers know Asian love stories.

___ c. In Asian literature, many love stories end unhappily.

___ d. When choosing a marriage partner, Japanese men are very romantic.

___ e. Japanese women are not romantic.

Paragraph 4   Kiyofumi is a handsome executive with a Tokyo company. At twenty-five he is ready for marriage, but he will not follow his heart. "Once in my life, when I was in college, I experienced a strong romantic feeling for a young woman. And once was enough. I don't trust romance. I could meet someone nice at a disco and start to see her, then think I'm in love. But I can pretend to be a great guy for three months, so how do I know that this person isn't doing that to me? I have no confidence in my judgment. That's what my parents are for. Marriage is too important a step to take on the basis of romance."

___ a. Kiyofumi believes in romantic love.

___ b. Kiyofumi has never experienced romantic love.

___ c. Kiyofumi believes that people can pretend to be what they are not.

___ d. Kiyofumi has more confidence in his parents' judgment about a wife for him than he has in his own judgment.

___ e. Kiyofumi believes that marriage is too important a step to take.

Paragraph 5   A wedding in Japan is viewed as an expected social step, which 98 percent of the population takes. Because marriage is seen as something of a family merger, many families still follow the ancient custom of consulting a matchmaker. Frequently, however, they use the most modern of marriage brokers: the computer. Many large corporations, such as Mitsubishi and Fuji Banks, put their computers to work for their employees. Just enter preferences for looks, job, salary, hobbies, the ever-important family background, and out come as many as 130 possibilities, which, with the help of a counselor, are reduced to 3 candidates—all for a small fee. A larger fee is charged if marriage results.

___ a. Most people in Japan merge.

___ b. When individuals marry in Japan, in a sense the families also marry.

___ c. Some people use a computer as a matchmaker.

___ d. Employees must pay to use company computers to find marriage partners.

___ e. The company computer produces three possible partners.

___ f. One of the most important qualities for a marriage partner is family background.

Paragraph 6   Parents who are more traditional ask a friend, work mate, or neighbor to be the matchmaker and help find a suitable spouse for their son or daughter. A photograph and a report on family background are given, and the process begins. If everything seems okay, an arranged meeting *(omiai)* takes place.

— a. Only traditional families use matchmakers.

— b. Apparently, any trusted person can act as a matchmaker in Japan.

— c. A couple always agrees to meet once they have exchanged photographs.

— d. It is unusual for a detective to be used to check on a potential spouse's family.

— e. An arranged marriage includes an arranged meeting.

Paragraph 7   "I was very nervous for my *omiai*," remembers Mihoko, a twenty-nine year old. "A woman in my Chinese cooking class knew Kiyoshi. I took one look at his photograph and was sure things would never work out. But I'd never had an *omiai* before and my parents thought I should go. We met at a hotel restaurant—his family, mine, and the matchmaker. It was very uncomfortable. Everyone talked but us. Then, after coffee, he and I took a walk through the hotel gardens and had a really boring conversation. I didn't like him at all, and I could tell he thought I was only so-so."

— a. Apparently, a woman in Mihoko's Chinese cooking class acted as a matchmaker.

— b. Because Mihoko didn't like Kiyoshi's photograph, she didn't want to meet him.

— c. Mihoko's parents made her have the *omiai*.

— d. Several people went to the restaurant with Mihoko and Kiyoshi.

— e. Mihoko didn't like Kiyoshi at first.

Paragraph 8   "A second meeting would indicate serious interest, so I was going to call the matchmaker and refuse another *omiai*, but she called me first and said Kiyoshi wanted to see me again. I talked with my family for a long time. They liked him very much. My mother especially liked the way he treated his mother. Somehow, their opinion seemed more important to me than just mine. That surprised me because I'd been working at *Newsweek*'s Tokyo offices for several years and thought I was very Westernized. Clearly, I was much more traditional than I thought. I just didn't trust my own feelings. My parents could see more because they had more experience of life."

___ a. If Mihoko met Kiyoshi again, this would mean that she was interested in marriage.

___ b. Mihoko refused another *omiai*.

___ c. Mihoko's mother wanted her to meet Kiyoshi again because of the way he acted toward his mother.

___ d. Mihoko believes it is traditional to follow your parents' advice.

___ e. Mihoko trusts her parents' judgment more than she trusts her own.

Paragraph 9   "Our second meeting was better," says Mihoko, "and as time passed I grew to care very much about him. We were married six months later, and now it's five years. I think I was lucky, because Kiyoshi is very kind." (Mihoko's use of the word *kind* is important; when a group of Japanese college women were asked what quality they most wanted in a man, nearly all of them answered, "Gentleness.")

___ a. Mihoko and Kiyoshi's second meeting was romantic.

___ b. At the second meeting, Mihoko came to love Kiyoshi.

___ c. Kiyoshi and Mihoko have been married for five years.

___ d. Mihoko married Kiyoshi because he was kind.

___ e. Japanese women believe that kindness is an important quality in a man.

Paragraph 10   Even so-called love marriages do not sound the same as Western romance. When Kazuko met her husband Tetsuya, she recalls, "I thought he'd be a good man to marry because he understood that I would want to work even after having children. Tetsuya just wrote my father directly for permission to marry. My father asked, 'Do you think this is the *right* man?'—much more typically Japanese than 'Is this the man you love?' We call ours a love marriage, but it wasn't like Cinderella. We Japanese don't believe in that."

___ a. Japanese love marriages are similar to love marriages in North America.

___ b. Kazuko agreed to marry Tetsuya because he was a good man.

___ c. Apparently, most women work after having children in Japan.

___ d. The matchmaker asked Kazuko's father for permission for Tetsuya to marry her.

___ e. Apparently, the Japanese don't know about the Cinderella story.

Critical Reading

1. In what ways is this article what you expected? Was there anything in the article that you did not expect? Are there statements in the article that you do not believe either because you do not have enough information or because of your personal experience?

2. For what kind of a magazine do you think this article was written? Who is the audience? Find parts of the article to support your opinion.

Discussion/Composition

1. In what ways is the marriage situation described in this article similar to and different from what you are familiar with? Write a similar article describing customs you are familiar with.

2. Why do you think cultures have such well-developed customs for finding marriage partners? Do you think everyone should get married? What are reasons why some people choose never to marry? Write an essay arguing that it is or is not important that everyone marry.

Vocabulary from Context

Both the ideas and the vocabulary in the exercise below are taken from "Japanese Marriage." Use the context provided to decide on meanings for the italicized words. Write a definition, synonym, or description in the space provided.

1. _____

2. _____

3. _____

4. _____

For many Japanese, the appropriate way to find a marriage partner is through a *matchmaker.* The marriage broker arranges a meeting—and hopefully a marriage—between two people who are thought to be *suitable* mates. Suitability is determined by such characteristics as family background, job, and education. But these are not the only *qualities* that are important. Japanese college women say that kindness is the most important quality in a *potential* marriage partner, someone they would consider a possible spouse.

5. _____

6. _____

7. _____

8. _____

9. _____

If they are to be chosen, marriage *candidates* also have to be acceptable to the parents of young people. Some young people say that they don't have faith in their own *judgment* for such an important decision. They *trust* instead the opinion of their parents. They also *have confidence in* the judgment of *counselors* whose job it is to give advice and help people make these difficult decisions.

10. _____

In Japan, many men say that they don't trust *romance,* feelings based on love or emotional attraction. In fact, although there are many

11. _____   stories about romantic love, something quite terrible (usually death) occurs at the end. These *tragic* endings don't give people confidence in romance. Another reason people don't trust it is because romantic

12. _____   feelings aren't based on real information. Anyone can *pretend* to be a nice person for a few months, but they may really be quite awful.

13. _____   Instead, marriage is seen as a *merger* of families. People do not simply marry; their two families join together. Perhaps this helps create the

14. _____   feeling that matrimony is a great undertaking, a lifetime *project* that

15. _____   involves *sacrifice.* To be successful, it is thought, one must be able to give up what one very much wants for the benefit of the marriage project.

Selection 2D   **Magazine Article**

Before You Begin   The articles you have just read describe meeting partners through advertisements and matchmakers. What are other methods people use around the world to find partners? What do you know about the way single people meet partners in North America?

Skimming

The following article describes different ways that people find marriage partners in the U.S. Skim the article quickly to locate at least five different ways of meeting spouses.* Your teacher may want you to do this exercise in writing, orally, or by underlining parts of the text.

The New Mating Game

1   In the United States, men and women are using new ways to find marriage partners. Some single people used to rely on "singles bars" to meet people. But these are no longer as popular because of fears of AIDS and the experience of disappointing meetings. As the single population has grown older and more sophisticated, people are looking for spouses in "relationship" classes, expensive dating services, and singles nights at places like art museums. But while single people today admit that they want what their mothers always said they *should* want, they're having a difficult time finding it.

Adapted from "The New Mating Games," by Barbara Kantrowitz with Deborah Witherspoon, Elisa Williams, and Patricia King, *Newsweek,* June 2, 1986, 58.

*For an introduction to skimming, see Unit 1.

2   Hundreds of people are signing up for how-to classes with names like, "Fifty Ways to Meet Your Lover" or "Love Shopping: How to Be Married One Year From Today." Miami attorney Margaret Kent's course on "How to Marry the Man of Your Choice" costs $295 at the beginning and another $1,000 after the wedding. The first step is "Meet the man."

3   But a lot of women can't meet the man—and many men say they're having just as much trouble meeting women. As a result, we are beginning to see expensive dating services. The service Gentlepeople, with offices from San Francisco to London, costs $950 a year and includes lawyers and doctors in its files. No computers or videotapes are used. Gentlepeople's consultants look for potential spouses, matching people with people.

4   Video dating is still popular. Joan Hendrickson, owner of the Georgetown Connection in Washington, DC, says men and women judge potential partners differently. "Women look at the written information; men just look at the pictures."

5   The search can also be found in mainstream newspapers and magazines. Once the "personal" ads were used only by a few, but now they attract a wide range of people. And they're not shy. "Beautiful and looking" is how one 40-year-old divorcee described herself in the *New York* magazine recently.

6   Some singles prefer something more intellectual. Singles nights at museums have become popular in several cities. At Washington's Smithsonian Institution, 150 singles—carefully selected so that there is an equal number of men and women—listen to a lecture and then sip champagne while discussing such topics as high technology in Japan and U.S. art.

7   When all else fails, there's always that "nice boy Aunt Elsie knows." It's the oldest method of matchmaking, but, says New York writer Faith Popcorn, "we are seeing a return to traditional values and practices."

Discussion/Composition

How are the ways people meet each other in the United States similar to and different from customs you are familiar with from other parts of the world? Give examples from your readings and personal experience.

Reading Selections 3A–3D

Questionnaire, Newspaper Articles, Prose and Poetry

Following are reading selections about the choices people make in life.

Selection 3A   **Questionnaire**

Before You Begin   Answer the following questions in the space provided. Your teacher may want you to compare your answers with classmates.

1. Are you happy with your life?
2. Do you consider yourself successful? Are you on the road to success?
3. What is success?
4. Are happiness and success the same thing? Can you have one without the other?
5. Do you think your opinion about success and happiness is similar to the opinions of other people from your culture/community? Is it similar to what most people from the U.S. believe?

The Meaning of Success

The answers to these important questions will vary from person to person and from culture to culture. The following questionnaire has been designed to help you think about your understanding of success and to identify possible differences between what you want in life and the goals of others in your culture/ community and most people in the United States. Understanding these differences will help you to understand cultural differences and to work with others more effectively.

For each item, you will answer three times. First, circle the number that best represents your opinion. The numbers 1 to 5 represent the strength of your opinion: Circle 1 if you strongly disagree with the statement and 5 if you strongly agree. A 2 indicates that you disagree slightly and a 4 indicates you agree slightly. A 3 indicates that you have no opinion on the matter.

On the second line, circle the number that you think represents what others from your culture/ community would answer. This is just your opinion, but you should be prepared to defend your answer with examples of behavior or events.

On the third line, circle the number that you think represents what the U.S. public in general would answer. This is also your opinion; there are no "correct" answers. Your opinion might be based on personal experiences, or things you have read or seen on TV. Following is an example.

| **Example** | A new car is an important indicator of success. If you are successful, you will own a new car. |

	Disagree ↔ Agree	
a. Self	① 2 3 4 5	I ride my bike.
b. Others from my community/culture	1 2 3 ④ 5	Most want a car, but some ride the bus.
c. Most people in U.S.	1 2 3 4 ⑤	Everyone has a car, many have two.

The person who answered this item circled a 1 for "Self," indicating that s/he strongly disagrees with this statement. S/he circled a 4 for "Others from my community/culture," indicating that s/he thinks that the majority of people in his/ her community/culture would agree with this statement. And s/he circled a 5 for "Most people in U.S." to show that, in his/her opinion, this is very important for most people in the U.S. Remember, this is a matter of personal opinion. Circle the numbers to indicate your opinion and make notes in the margin to support your opinion.

1. An individual needs a college education to have a happy life.

	Disagree ↔ Agree
Self	1 2 3 4 5
Others from my community/culture	1 2 3 4 5
Most people in U.S.	1 2 3 4 5

2. It is important to keep up with the fashions; one should dress well, go to the popular restaurants, see current movies, etc.

	Disagree ↔ Agree
Self	1 2 3 4 5
Others from my community/culture	1 2 3 4 5
Most people in U.S.	1 2 3 4 5

3. It is important to have knowledge of literature and the arts, to read poetry, attend plays and concerts, etc.

	Disagree ↔ Agree
Self	1 2 3 4 5
Others from my community/culture	1 2 3 4 5
Most people in U.S.	1 2 3 4 5

4. To be successful one must be aware of current events and politics; one must be involved in political events.

	Disagree ↔ Agree
Self	1 2 3 4 5
Others from my community/culture	1 2 3 4 5
Most people in U.S.	1 2 3 4 5

5. A person should be active in sports and exercise regularly (jogging, bicycling, skiing, etc.).

	Disagree ↔ Agree
Self	1 2 3 4 5
Others from my community/culture	1 2 3 4 5
Most people in U.S.	1 2 3 4 5

6. A person should have many children. (Indicate number: _____)

	Disagree ↔ Agree
Self	1 2 3 4 5
Others from my community/culture	1 2 3 4 5
Most people in U.S.	1 2 3 4 5

7. One must be able to speak at least two languages.

	Disagree ↔ Agree
Self	1 2 3 4 5
Others from my community/culture	1 2 3 4 5
Most people in U.S.	1 2 3 4 5

8. Good looks are important; being physically attractive and taking care of oneself is important to one's happiness.

	Disagree ↔ Agree
Self	1 2 3 4 5
Others from my community/culture	1 2 3 4 5
Most people in U.S.	1 2 3 4 5

9. Belonging to the right class or group of people is essential for success.

	Disagree ↔ Agree
Self	1 2 3 4 5
Others from my community/culture	1 2 3 4 5
Most people in U.S.	1 2 3 4 5

10. Hard work makes success possible; if one works hard one will be successful.

	Disagree ↔ Agree
Self	1 2 3 4 5
Others from my community/culture	1 2 3 4 5
Most people in U.S.	1 2 3 4 5

11. Money is important.

	Disagree ↔ Agree
Self	1 2 3 4 5
Others from my community/culture	1 2 3 4 5
Most people in U.S.	1 2 3 4 5

12. Family is important; one should live close to and keep in close contact with one's parents, grandparents, brothers, sisters, etc.

	Disagree ↔ Agree
Self	1 2 3 4 5
Others from my community/culture	1 2 3 4 5
Most people in U.S.	1 2 3 4 5

13. Travel is important; one should see the world.

	Disagree ↔ Agree
Self	1 2 3 4 5
Others from my community/culture	1 2 3 4 5
Most people in U.S.	1 2 3 4 5

14. One must help others who are less fortunate—the poor, the homeless, the ill, etc.

	Disagree ↔ Agree
Self	1 2 3 4 5
Others from my community/culture	1 2 3 4 5
Most people in U.S.	1 2 3 4 5

15. A large, comfortable house is necessary for one to be happy; it is the natural result of success.

	Disagree ↔ Agree
Self	1 2 3 4 5
Others from my community/culture	1 2 3 4 5
Most people in U.S.	1 2 3 4 5

16. One must be a leader in the community, a respected member of society.

	Disagree ↔ Agree
Self	1 2 3 4 5
Others from my community/culture	1 2 3 4 5
Most people in U.S.	1 2 3 4 5

17. One sign of success is that a person is always able to get away for long holidays.

	Disagree ↔ Agree
Self	1 2 3 4 5
Others from my community/culture	1 2 3 4 5
Most people in U.S.	1 2 3 4 5

18. One sign of success is that one's career is so totally satisfying that one does not need holidays.

	Disagree ↔ Agree
Self	1 2 3 4 5
Others from my community/culture	1 2 3 4 5
Most people in U.S.	1 2 3 4 5

19. Success means not having to do things that one does not want to do.

	Disagree ↔ Agree
Self	1 2 3 4 5
Others from my community/culture	1 2 3 4 5
Most people in U.S.	1 2 3 4 5

20. It is important to take a shower every day.

	Disagree ↔ Agree
Self	1 2 3 4 5
Others from my community/culture	1 2 3 4 5
Most people in U.S.	1 2 3 4 5

Scoring Your Answers

1. Self-Knowledge Score

Go back to questions 1, 3, 4, 5, 8, 9, and 20. Count the number of times you circled each number and put the total in the appropriate column. Then put the row totals in the Total column. This indicates the amount of importance you give to self-improvement, knowledge, etc. It also indicates your opinion of the importance of these for people from your culture/community and for people in the U.S. in general.

| | Disagree ← → Agree | | | | | Total |
	1	2	3	4	5	
Self	___	___	___	___	___	___
Others from my community/culture	___	___	___	___	___	___
Most people in U.S.	___	___	___	___	___	___

2. Family and Community Responsibilities Score

Go back to questions 11, 12, 14, 16, 18, and 19. Count the number of times you circled each number and put the put the row totals in the appropriate column. Then put the row totals in the Total column. This indicates the amount of importance you give to responsibilities to others. It also indicates your opinion of the importance of these for others from your culture/community and for people in the U.S. in general.

	Disagree 1	2	3	4	Agree 5	Total
Self	____	____	____	____	____	____
Others from my community/culture	____	____	____	____	____	____
Most people in U.S.	____	____	____	____	____	____

3. Other People's Opinion Score

Go back to questions 2, 6, 7, 10, 13, 15, and 17. Count the number of times you circled each number and put the total in the appropriate column. Then put the row totals in the Total column. This indicates the amount of importance you give to what other people think about you. It also indicates your opinion of the importance of this for your culture/community and for people in the U.S. in general.

	Disagree 1	2	3	4	Agree 5	Total
Self	____	____	____	____	____	____
Others from my community/culture	____	____	____	____	____	____
Most people in U.S.	____	____	____	____	____	____

Discussion

Compare the scores in the three areas, Self-Knowledge, Family and Community Responsibilities, and Other People's Opinions. Discuss your scores with your classmates.

a. Which characteristic did you score the highest on? Do you think this accurately reflects what you think is important in life? Is this how you see yourself?

b. Compare the scores you gave yourself and people from your community/culture. Are there significant differences?

c. Compare the scores you gave people from your community/culture and people from the U.S. in general. Do you think these scores represent true differences?

d. Does this information help you understand yourself better? Will you try to change anything about yourself as a result of completing this questionnaire?

e. What about your relationships with others? Do these scores suggest how you might work better with people from your community/culture or people from the U.S. in general?

Discussion/Composition

1. Go back through the questionnaire and select a question that interests you.

   a. For each of the responses (Self, Community/Culture, U.S.) give an example of a behavior or an event or situation that supports your opinion on this item.
   b. Write a paragraph comparing yourself to others on this item, and explaining your opinion.

2. Compare your opinion of success and happiness to that of others. Give examples from the questionnaire results, your reading, and your personal experience.

Selection 3B   **Newspaper Article**

In the United States, the high school graduation ceremony is celebrated as an important event in young people's lives. Prizes and certificates are awarded and many people give speeches. Very often a community leader or well-known politician gives a speech. It is also common for the best students in the graduating class to give speeches to their classmates and families. These speeches usually focus on accomplishments of the past and hopes for the future. Everyone feels good, and the event is a celebration of the work that the students have completed during their four years of high school. Some students will go on to college. Others will begin working, or get married, or join the army. No one wants to think about problems they have had or may have in the future.

The following newspaper story reports on an unusual graduation speech delivered by the salutatorian (the student with the second best grade-point average in the graduating class) in a small town in Montana. Unlike most speakers at graduation ceremonies, Gary Lee Christensen did not say the pleasant things that people were expecting to hear.

Before You Begin   Following are a sampling of things that speakers at graduation ceremonies might say. Check (✓) the ones that you would expect to hear.

   ___ a. "And as you go off into the world remember that your best friends are your oldest friends, the ones you grew up with. You are always welcome here at home."

   ___ b. "This is a big day in your lives. You have done a lot, and you have a lot left to do. Make us proud of you."

   ___ c. "The world today is a complicated and dangerous place. The education you received here is a solid foundation for you to build on, but you cannot stop learning. You must always try to improve your understanding of the world."

   ___ d. "Today is an important day in your lives. You will leave the safety of your friends and family, and you will find that the world is a difficult place. You may have problems that you are not well prepared to meet."

___ e. "You have spent the past four years playing around, having a good time and avoiding work. Unfortunately, high school is not the real world, and you will soon pay for your laziness."

___ f. "I am pleased to be talking to you for the last time. You are not very intelligent or enjoyable people. My four years in this school have not been pleasant, and I am looking forward to going off to college."

Now read the following newspaper story about the graduation speech given by Gary Lee Christensen to see what he had to say to his classmates. Your teacher may want you to do the Vocabulary from Context exercise on page 246 before you begin.

Graduation Speech Protested
"Intolerance" Talk Angers Montana Town

WEST YELLOWSTONE, MONTANA (AP)

1 The West Yellowstone School Board may consider setting guidelines for future graduation speeches when it meets next week, but apparently it will not take any action against Gary Lee Christensen for his commencement address.

2 About 40 parents, students, and townspeople interrupted a special meeting of the board last week to complain about Christensen's comments during his speech at commencement. Some people said that his scholarships should be revoked.

3 Christensen, 17, told his 15 classmates and several hundred townspeople that he had "survived years of intolerance" from classmates at the school, which he attended from kindergarten, because he "dared to be different." "I was a good student when it was not popular to be a good student . . . an Eagle Scout when it was not popular to be a Scout,"

Christensen said. He added that he had "played the piano when everyone else was playing football."

4 He said his self-esteem was threatened by students who were intolerant, and he told the graduates, "West Yellowstone High School is not reality." His classmates now will have to compete with the best, he said. "You can no longer cling to your friends. Know that by not following the crowd you can succeed."

5 Parents, students and alumni complained that the remarks were criticism of Christensen's classmates, the football team and other boys who did not become Scouts. Some people, parents and teachers, said they did not want to violate Christensen's right of free speech, but they also objected to his making such comments because they spoiled the ceremony for his classmates.

6 Principal John Balber reviewed the speech and gave Christensen permis-

sion to deliver it. He said it was well written. "He attacked no particular person, but his classmates' behavior in general," the principal said. "Did I like what he said? It doesn't matter. Did he have the right to say it? Yes, I think he had that right."

7 Lois Klatt, a former school board member, said most scholarships are based on something besides grades: "I think we all see his behavior as not exactly scholarship material."

8 Christensen graduated with a 3.85 grade-point average (out of a possible 4.0), and received scholarships from four community organizations and Boise State University in Idaho, where he plans to attend. He was the only high school student from Montana chosen to attend a Department of Energy program on computers at the Lawrence Livermore National Laboratory at Livermore, California.

Adapted from "Graduation Speech Protested," *Denver Post,* June 5, 1990.

Comprehension

Answer the following questions according to your understanding of the story. Your teacher may want you to work individually, in small groups, or in pairs. True/False items are indicated by a T / F before a statement. Some questions may have more than one answer. Others require an opinion. Choose the answer you like best; be prepared to defend your choices.

1. T / F   West Yellowstone is a small town.

2. How many students were in the graduating class? _____

3. Who gave the speech that is being protested? _____

4. What did he say to make everyone so angry? _____

_____

5. How would you describe Christensen's speech? You may check (✓) more than one answer.

___ a. criticism of social problems in West Yellowstone
___ b. complaining about childhood problems
___ c. anger caused by intolerance
___ d. advice for friends and community

6. Christensen says that he "dared to be different." What are some of the things that he did that were

different? _____

_____

7. T / F   The principal liked Christensen's speech.

8. T / F   The people of West Yellowstone believe in "freedom of speech."

9. T / F   The parents, students, and townspeople who complained about Christensen's speech did not understand what he was trying to say.

10. What is Lois Klatt's opinion of Christensen? What does she think "scholarship material" is? _____

_____

11. T / F   The principal may lose his job because of this speech.

12. Would you like to live in West Yellowstone? _____ If you had been among the graduating

class would you have been more like Christensen or more like his classmates? _____

Vocabulary from Context

Both the ideas and the vocabulary in the exercise below are taken from "Graduation Speech Protested." Use the context provided to decide on meanings for the italicized words. Write a definition, synonym, or description in the space provided.

1. _____   At the end of four years, high schools hold a *commencement* ceremony. This is a celebration, a formal event which recognizes the work students have done and which marks the beginning of the rest of their lives. Some students will go on to college. Others will begin working, or get married, or join the army. Because the graduates will be beginning their lives as adults, the ceremony is called a commencement rather than a conclusion.

2. _____   An important part of the ceremony is the speech given by the best student in the class. This *address* is usually a hopeful message concerning the future of the graduates.

3. _____   Many students cannot afford to pay for college expenses, but if they have good grades they can sometimes get *scholarships* from universities or community organizations to help pay their expenses.

4. _____   Of course, if the students do not keep their grades up, or if they do something illegal, the scholarships can be *revoked*.

5. _____   One of the things that an education is supposed to produce is *tolerance* for others. We hope that the more people know about the world, the more understanding they will be of differences. We believe that this understanding will help us tolerate ideas and behaviors that are different from ours.

6. _____   Even when we should know better, we *cling* to ideas that are false. Sometimes holding tight to a familiar idea, even when it is false, is more comforting than trying to understand a new idea.

7. _____   In modern societies, we tend to respect people with an advanced education. And people with an advanced education tend to have more *self-esteem.*

8. _____   On the other hand, some people feel *threatened* by people who have an education. Apparently, some believe that they will be attacked or their ideas laughed at by those who have more formal education.

Composition/Discussion

1. a. What is the meaning of "freedom of speech"? Do you think that Gary Lee Christensen should have been allowed to say what he said? Do you think his scholarships should have been revoked?
   b. When does freedom of speech become dangerous or unhealthy? Give examples from this article or from your own experience to support your point of view.

2. Do you have similar commencement ceremonies in your community/country? What kind of advice do you think young people should be given when they graduate from high school? Do you agree with the kind of advice that Gary Lee Christensen gave?

3. Do you have opinions that are unpopular or that are not held by others? Do you ever think about telling people what you think? Write a paragraph that expresses an opinion you have that might not be popular. Give examples and details to support your point of view.

4. What is your opinion of Gary Lee Christensen? Do you think you would have been his friend if you lived in West Yellowstone? What are the qualities about him that you like/dislike? Write a paragraph beginning with a general statement of your opinion of Christensen, then follow it with examples to support your opinion.

Selection 3C   **Newspaper Article**

The following article reports on a study of 81 students who were at the top of their high school classes ten years ago. Read the article to discover what the researchers believe is important in life, and decide if you agree with them. Then answer the Comprehension questions on page 248.

High School Honors Not Always Key to Life Success

1 URBANA, ILL. (AP)—Mike dropped out of college to support his pregnant girlfriend and now works as a manager of a trucking company. Lynn graduated with honors from Harvard University and was hired as a lawyer with a top law firm in a major city. What do these two people have in common? Ten years ago they were both high school valedictorians.

2 A University of Illinois study follows the lives of 81 valedictorians and salutatorians who graduated a decade ago from public and private high schools in the state.

Tales of Success and Failure

3 The study found tales of success and failure. The research on 46 women and 35 men found that some were doctors and scientists, one was a drug addict, another was a waitress with emotional problems.

4 "There is a popular idea about people who do well in school doing well in life," said Terry Denny, professor of education. Denny conducted the study with Karen Arnold, a former graduate student of Denny's who is now a professor at Boston College. Denny and Arnold contacted the 81 students before graduation, and then followed up with interviews nearly every other year. They also sent them questionnaires in the mail.

Varied Careers

5 One third of the students are doctors, lawyers, or have earned a doctorate. Nineteen are in business and 15 are engineers or computer scientists. Others include a farmer, a stock broker, and an aerobics instructor.

6 Arnold says many of the students have only average positions in the work world and that "most are not headed for greatness in their careers." Denny, however, says that it is too early to make such predictions. "Who expects someone to be on the Supreme Court at the age of 28 or to be the discoverer of an important scientific invention right after college?" he said. "These students are just getting started in life. They are just beginning to find out what life is all about."

Adapted from "High School Honors Not Always Key to Life Success," *Denver Post,* June 19, 1991, 1E.

Comprehension

Answer the following questions according to your understanding of the article. Your teacher may want you to work individually, in small groups, or in pairs. True/False items are indicated by a T / F before a statement. Some questions may have more than one correct answer. Others require an opinion. Choose the answer you like best; in the space provided, give reasons for your answer.

1. T / F   This story was written by reporters from the Associated Press news service.

2. T / F   Mike and Lynn both graduated first in their high school class.

3. How many students did the professors study? _____

    a. What are given as some examples of the "successes" that the professors found? _____

    _____

    b. What are given as some examples of "failures"? _____

    _____

4. What definition of "success" are the professors using? _____

_____

5. T / F   In general, people believe that success in school will lead to success in life.

6. Who is the older professor, Denny or Arnold? _____

_____

7. Circle the jobs that you think a successful person might hold:

aerobics instructor	engineer	doctor	cook
business person	lawyer	farmer	professor

8. How many of the students believe that they are failures today? _____

9. T / F   Denny is more tolerant than Arnold.

10. T / F   This study proves that success in education does not predict success in later life.

Discussion/Composition

1. Do you think that high school success predicts success for people later in life? Express your opinion clearly and give reasons for your beliefs.

2. In the first paragraph of this article we are told that Mike works for a trucking company and Lynn works for a law firm. Based on this amount of information, can you say if either one of them is a success or failure? Explain your answer.

Selection 3D   **Prose and Poetry**

In the selections that follow, two people look back on their lives and wonder what might have happened if they had made different choices at points in their lives. The poem is a well-known selection from the work of Robert Frost, the Pulitzer Prize–winning poet. The prose selection is a paraphrase of the poem, written in a simple style, as if the author were speaking to a grandchild. John Bomer is just the name we have given to the fictitious author of the selection.

1. First, read through the prose selection, "Choices," without pausing.

2. Then, read through "The Road Not Taken" without pausing. Your teacher may want to read the poem aloud as you read along silently. Compare the ideas in both pieces.

Choices

John Bomer

1   Yes, I suppose things might have been different, but who knows? I have more time to think these days, of course, and it's funny what comes to mind. Like the year I left home for the first time. It was a beautiful fall morning. The woods were shades of gold and yellow, and the sun warmed my neck as I walked along. I came to a point where the road split in two, and I stood there, looking down those roads for the longest time, feeling sorry I couldn't take them both.

2   I remember peering down one lane as far as I could see, to where it turned and disappeared in the grass, then setting off down the other, thinking the one I had chosen was a little less worn. But to tell the truth, they were traveled just about the same. They were covered with leaves and I knew that I was the first one to come along that day, because there were no footprints in the road, no blackened steps where the leaves had been trodden into the mud. I told myself that someday I would return to that fork in the road and take the other way, just to see where it led, but even then I knew I probably would not come back.

3   Still, I think about that day and the road I chose, and I wonder what might have happened if I had gone the other way. I might not have met your grandmother, for example, and where would that leave you? I wouldn't be here answering your questions over and over again, that's for sure. Oh, I've had good times and bad times, and on the whole I can't complain. If I had chosen the other road, I'd probably be sitting on a different chair somewhere else, answering someone else's questions.

The Road Not Taken

Robert Frost

1 Two roads diverged in a yellow wood
2 And sorry I could not travel both
3 And be one traveler, long I stood
4 And looked down one as far as I could
5 To where it bent in the undergrowth;

6 Then took the other, as just as fair,
7 And having perhaps the better claim,
8 Because it was green and wanted wear;
9 Though as for that, the passing there
10 Had worn them really about the same,

11 And both that morning equally lay
12 In leaves no step had trodden black.
13 Oh, I kept the first for another day!
14 Yet knowing how way leads on to way,
15 I doubted if I would ever come back.

16 I shall be telling this with a sigh
17 Somewhere ages and ages hence:
18 Two roads diverged in a wood and I—
19 I took the one less traveled by,
20 And that has made all the difference.

From *The Poetry of Robert Frost,* edited by Edward Connery Lathem (New York: Holt, 1969), 105.

Comprehension

Answer the following questions according to your understanding of the selections. Your teacher may want you to work individually, in small groups, or in pairs. True/False items are indicated by a T / F before a statement. Some questions may have more than one answer. Others require an opinion. Choose the answer you like best; be prepared to defend your choices.

1. T / F   In both the poem and the prose piece it is spring.

2. T / F   Bomer and Frost wrote these as young men.

3. T / F   The roads run through pine forests.

4. T / F   Frost is traveling alone.

5. T / F   Many travelers had passed down the same roads before Frost and Bomer.

6. Both men had to choose between two roads at one point in their travels. Which road did they take, the first one, or the second?

   _____

7. T / F   The "road" symbolizes life.

8. The poet took the second road, rather than the first, and he comments that this "has made all the difference."

   a. What does he mean? _____

   _____

   b. How many choices did he have at the time? _____

   c. What might have happened if he had taken the other road? Would he feel the same if he had taken the other road?

   _____

   _____

   _____

9. As the men think about their choices, they compare the two roads. What are the differences between the two roads?

   _____

   _____

10. Frost says he will be telling this story, "with a sigh" (line 16). Read the dictionary definition of *sigh* below, then answer the question that follows it.

> **sigh** (sī), *v.i.* **1.** to let out one's breath audibly, as from sorrow, weariness, or relief. **2.** to yearn or long; pine. **3.** to make a sound suggesting a sigh: *sighing wind.* —*v.t.* **4.** to express or utter with a sigh. **5.** to lament with sighing. —*n.* **6.** the act or sound of sighing. [1250–1300; (v.) ME *sighen*, back formation from *sihte* sighed, past tense of ME *siken*, *sichen*, OE *sican* to sigh; (n.) ME, deriv. of the v.] —**sigh′er**, *n.*

T / F   Frost is sorry he did not take the other road.

Discussion/Composition

Your teacher may want you to do parts of this orally or in writing, individually, or in small groups.

1. List the similarities of these two texts.

2. List the differences.

3. Which selection do you prefer? Why?

4. What are major decisions you have made in your life? Which one do you consider the most important?

   a. List the things that have come from that decision (for example, the events that have followed it, or the people you have met, the opportunities you have had as a result).

   b. List the things that might have happened if you had chosen differently.

5. Robert Frost says that he tended to choose less traveled roads.

   a. What does he mean by that?

   b. How do you make important decisions? Do you follow rules taught to you by family members or teachers? Is "Take the road less traveled!" a rule you might follow?

6. Write a letter to a friend or family member expressing your opinion of the important decisions you have made in your life.

From *Random House Unabridged Dictionary* (New York: Random House, 1967), 1325.

Vocabulary from Context

This exercise should be done after you have finished reading "The Road Not Taken." The exercise will give you practice deciding on the meaning of unfamiliar words. Give a definition, synonym, or description of each of the words below. The number in parentheses indicates the line of poetry in which the word can be found. Your teacher may want you to do these orally or in writing.

1. (1) diverged: _____

2. (5) bent: _____

3. (5) undergrowth: _____

4. (12) trodden: _____

5. (17) hence: _____

Appendix

Below is a list of the stems and affixes that appear in *Choice Readings*. The number in parentheses indicates the unit in which the item appears.

Prefixes

(7) **a-, an-** without, not

(7) **ante-** before

(5) **anti-** against

(1) **bi-** two

(7) **com-, con-, col-, cor-, co-** together, with

(3) **de-** away, down, reverse the action of

(3) **e-, ex-** out, away

(7) **extra-, extro-** outside, beyond

(3) **in-, im-** in, into, on

(5) **in-, im-, il-, ir-** not

(7) **inter-** between

(7) **intro-, intra-** within, into

(5) **micro-** small

(1) **mono-** one

(1) **multi-** many

(5) **peri-** around

(1) **poly-** many

(7) **post-** after

(3) **pre-** before

(3) **re-, retro-** again, back

(1) **semi-** half

(5) **sub-** under

(5) **super-** above, greater,

(5) **syn-, sym-, syl-** with, together, same, alike

(3) **tele-** far, distant

(3) **trans-** across

(1) **tri-** three

(1) **uni-** one

Stems

(5) **-anthropo-** human

(5) **-aqua-** water

(3) **-audi-, -audit-** hear

(5) **-bio-** life

(7) **-ced-** go, move, yield

(5) **-chron-** time

(7) **-cred-** believe

(3) **-dic-, -dict-** say, speak

(7) **-duc-** lead

(3) **-fact-, -fect-, -fic-** make, do

(5) **-geo-** earth

(3) **-graph-, -gram-** write, writing

(5) **-hydr-, -hydro-** water, liquid

(5) **-log-, -logy-** speech, word, study

(3) **-mit-, -miss-** send

(7) **-mort-** death

(5) **-path-, -pathy-** feeling, disease

(5) **-phon-** sound

(7) **-polis-** city, state

(3) **-pon-, -pos-** put, place

(3) **-port-** carry

(5) **-psych-** mind

(3) **-scrib-, -script-** write

(5) **-son-** sound

(3) **-spect-** look

(7) **-spir-** breathe

(7) **-terra-** earth

(7) **-theo-** god

(5) **-therm-, -thermo-** heat

(7) **-vac-** empty

(7) **-ven-, -vene-** come

(7) **-ver-** truth

(3) **-vid-, -vis-** see

(7) **-vita-, -viv-** life

(3) **-voc-, -vok-** call

Suffixes

(3) **-able, -ible, -ble** (adj.) capable of, fit for

(5) **-ate** (verb) to make

(3) **-er, -or** (noun) one who

(7) **-fy** (verb) to make

(5) **-ic, -al** (adj.) relating to, having the characteristics of

(3) **-ion, -tion** (noun) state, condition, the act of

(7) **-ism** (noun) action or practice, theory or set of beliefs

(5) **-ist** (noun) one who

(7) **-ity** (noun) condition, quality, state of being

(3) **-ize** (verb) to make, to become

(5) **-meter** (noun) measuring instrument, measure

(7) **-ous, -ious, -ose** (adj.) full of, having the qualities of

(5) **-scope** (noun) instrument for looking

Answer Key

The processes involved in arriving at an answer are often more important than the answer itself. It is expected that students will not use the Answer Key until they have completed the exercises and are prepared to defend their answers. If a student's answer does not agree with the Key, it is important for the student to return to the exercise to discover the reason why. In some cases, no answer is provided. This is because the students have been asked to express their own opinion. In other cases, the answer provided by the authors invites more discussion and thought by students. Teachers should look upon the Answer Key as another opportunity to engage students in meaningful interaction.

Unit 1

Discourse Focus: Reading for Different Goals

Skimming (pages 1–2)
1. This page provides information about entertainment possibilities for the weekend; it is organized by day.
2. It lists times, places, and descriptions of events. Your reaction to this page will depend on your interests.
3. No. Information on renting an apartment will be found in the classified advertisements.
4. It depends on when your friends have dinner, but you could go to the auto exhibit (9 A.M.–4 P.M.) or you could do some origami at 3 P.M. or you could listen to the Colorado Honor Band at 2:30 P.M.

Scanning (page 2)
1. Jazz: Friday and Saturday Eddie Daniels will be playing with the Colorado Symphony Orchestra, Boettcher Concert Hall at 8 P.M.; tickets cost from $8.00 to $26.00. Saturday the Ron Miles Trio Plus will perform at the New Dance Theatre of Cleo Parker Robinson at 8:30 P.M.; tickets are $10.00, $8.00 for students.
2. Auto exhibit: True; Sunday, 9 A.M. to 4 P.M. at University Hills Mall, $5.00.
3. Friday night; Red Rocks Amphitheatre; 7:30 P.M.; $19.50.

Thorough Comprehension (page 3)
1. At the Denver Auditorium Theatre
2. F   3. T   4. F

Critical Reading (pages 3–5)
1. Jazz seems to be popular, as are outdoor events and informal gatherings. What do you think?
2. F (Bluegrass is a type of music.)
3. F
4. a. a variety of classical and popular songs
   b. T (But if you want to give some money, it won't be refused.)
   c. T or F, depending on you and your new friends. What do you think?
5. Origami is the age-old art of Japanese paper folding. In a workshop, you learn by doing.
6. Answers will vary according to your interests.

Nonprose Reading: Airline Terminal Maps

Part 1: Getting Oriented (page 6)
1. This depends on you. Possible answers include: Use the rest room, change a ticket, find flight information, get your luggage, go shopping.
2. No rest rooms are shown on the map.
3. At JFK, Customs and Immigration is located in terminal 4A, in the center of gates 21–32. At Atlanta, Immigration is located in the North Terminal, near the International Concourse.
4. In JFK, there are two baggage claim areas; in terminal 4B, the baggage claim area is located in the lower level, and in terminal 4A, the baggage claim area is located near the street, next to the Ambassadors Club.

Part 2: JFK International Airport (pages 6–7)
5. Flights within the U.S. (domestic flights) usually leave from terminal 4B. To get there from terminal 4A, you can take the shuttle bus from gate 21 to gate 17, or you could leave terminal 4A, turn right and walk to terminal 4B.
6. The map does not say exactly where to catch the bus or taxi. You could ask a TWA employee, or you could just walk outside to find the taxi stands or bus stops.

Part 3: Atlanta International Airport (pages 7–8)
7. According to the map, the terminal does not appear to be too far from the gates, but you might want to ask someone who knows the airport.
8. The closest place would be the "Ticketing Station" located just between the terminal and the concourses, or you could go to "Ticketing," in the North Terminal.
9. F. Baggage claim for TWA is located in the North Terminal.
10. F. All "public ground transportation" (e.g., taxis and buses) is available just outside the terminal on the west end.
11. This item is intended for discussion; the answer depends on your opinion. (But we like Atlanta better than JFK.)

Word Study: Context Clues

Exercise 1 (pages 11–12)

1. perched: sat upon
2. adopt: to take someone into a family, especially used when children become legal members of a family that is not their biological family
3. tusks: long teeth that stick out of the elephant's mouth
4. railing: shouting and complaining and arguing
5. slithered: to move like a snake
6. poking: to push with a pointed object
7. periodontist: a kind of dentist, a dentist who specializes in gums
8. taciturn: quiet; serious
9. ravenous: extremely hungry
10. curb: reduce; control

Word Study: Stems and Affixes

Exercise 1 (pages 13–16)

1. bilingual, trilingual or multilingual
2. c, a, b
3. a.

   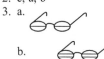

   b.

4. polygamy: having two or more marriage partners at one time (What is bigamy?)
5. automobile, television, sister, computer, woman, syllable
6. a
7. Here is one kind of triangle: △ . Triangles have three angles.
8. b
9. Semiskilled workers use the simpler machines.
10. semiprivate rooms: rooms with two or three patients
11. multicultural: concerning many cultures
12. multiracial: concerning many races
13. triplets: three children born to the same mother at one time
14. uniform: one form; having the same clothing
15. Multimillionaires have more than one million dollars (but that doesn't mean *you* would be happy with all that money).
16. 1976
17. multicolored: having many colors
18. tripod: a stand with three legs (feet) used by photographers to hold their cameras still
19. b

Exercise 2 (pages 16–17)

1. semiannually: twice a year (at the halfway points in the year)
2. multipurpose: having many purposes
3. monocle: an eyeglass for one eye
4. triple: increase by three times
5. unification: bringing together; making one
6. monotone: a sound with only one tone
7. semifinal: in a competition, the event that determines who will play for the championship; the game before the final game
8. bilateral: agreed to by two sides
9. multistory: having many floors
10. semidarkness: partial darkness; the theatre is almost completely dark

Sentence Study: Comprehension (pages 21–23)

1. c   3. d   5. d   7. a   9. b
2. a   4. a   6. b   8. a   10. c

Paragraph Reading: Main Idea (pages 25–29)

1. c   4. d   7. d
2. d   5. c   8. a
3. b   6. b   9. c

Unit 2

Reading Selection 1: Newspaper Article "Is McDonald's Fair?"

Comprehension (page 31)

1. a fast-food restaurant
2. T
3. T
4. 13%
5. $5.00
6. T
7. F
8. Slaves were not paid for their work, and Edward believed that he was not paid enough for his work.
9. T

Vocabulary from Context

Exercise 1 (page 32)

1. exploited: treated unfairly; in a position that you have no choice
2. slave labor: work without pay and done against one's will; slaves are people who are sold to work for others. They earn nothing except food and a place to sleep.
3. fired: forced to leave your job; told by the boss to leave
4. quit: decide to leave your job
5. intense: very great; extreme; too strong
6. praise: good things said about someone or something; compliments

Exercise 2 (page 33)

1. counter: the long table where you place your order at McDonald's
2. hire: give a job to someone
3. critics: people who have negative opinions about something or someone

Reading Selection 2: Technical Prose "Language Mirrors Immigration, Provides Key to Nation's Past, Present"

Comprehension (pages 36–37)

1. F
2. T
3. F
4. F
5. T
6. F
7. Mon-Khmer
8. French Creole
9. F
10. F
11. T
12. European immigrants who came to the U.S. in the early 1900s are dying, and fewer European immigrants are entering the United States now.

13. California, New York, Florida
14. F
15. F
16. T
17. T
18. T
19. Indonesian is not one of the 25 languages (other than English) most commonly spoken in the United States.
20. Answers will vary.

Selection 3A: Trade Book
"Introduction"

Vocabulary from Context (pages 39–41)
1. spouses: marriage partners; husbands or wives
2. mother-in-law: the mother of one's spouse; colloquially, this term is sometimes used to describe the mother of one's partner whether or not one is married
3. stepchildren: spouse's children from a previous marriage
4. impression: feeling; sense; uncertain belief
5. adopt: to take someone into a family, especially used when children become legal members of a family that is not their biological family
6. guardian: a person who has legal responsibility for someone who cannot take care of him/herself, for example, an adult for a child
7. gay: homosexual; referring to people whose love/sexual relationships are with members of the same sex (Note, people often use the term *lesbians* to refer to homosexual women.)
8. commitment: promise
9. diversity: variety
10. acknowledgment: section of a book in which the author thanks those who have been of help; recognition or showing of a fact

Reading Selection 4: Technical Prose
"Marriage Taking a Back Seat"

Overview (page 52)
1. T
2. T
3. F
4. F

Comprehension (page 53)
1. F
2. F
3. F
4. T
5. F
6. T
7. F
8. T

Critical Reading (page 53)
Because most of the unmarried couples were younger, the assumption is that older people do marry. However, by referring to single people as people who have "not yet married," the article also might be seen as assuming that everyone will/should marry. People who are single by choice or who never marry might feel that this is an unfortunate choice of words because it can assume that being single is only a step on the way to marriage, not an adult way of life on its own. On the other hand, one might feel this is a statistically accurate description of the situation.

Discussion/Composition (pages 53–54)
1. For reasons why people choose not to marry, you might have thought of such things as wanting more time to oneself, wanting to pursue a career, being homosexual, not wanting children. The rest of this question calls for personal opinion.
2. This question calls for personal opinion.
3. As reasons for the decline in marriage age, you might have thought about the effects of industrialization—the fact that people were moving from farms into cities where they had more money and greater opportunity to meet partners. The marriage age probably rose in part because of the availability of higher education, especially to women. As advanced education has become more available, the average marriage age has increased.

Vocabulary from Context (page 54)
1. separation: when a married couple lives apart without legally ending the marriage
2. divorce: legal ending of a marriage
3. nuclear family: two biological parents and their children
4. arrangements: structure; organization; the way things are arranged
5. out of wedlock: her biological parents were not married to each other
6. widowed: to have had one's spouse die
7. delay: put off until later; postpone
8. decline: decrease; go down; lower
9. status: legal position
10. proportion: fraction

Reading Selection 5: Literature
Silas Marner

Comprehension (pages 56–57)
1. F
2. It was his only source of money; also, it filled up his days.
3. Silas was in his late thirties, but he looked like an old man.
4. 15 years
5. a, b, d (You might also have checked *f* because "love was not quite dead in his heart.")
6. F
7. a, b (This item is open to discussion. If you did not choose *a,* you might believe that Marner did not miss people.)
8. He moved his hands through the coins as if they were water.
9. a.  b.

Discussion (page 57)
2. Marner becomes part of the community because he adopts a child.

Vocabulary from Context (pages 57–59)
1. pounds and shillings: amounts of money
2. loom: a machine used to make cloth from thread or yarn
3. weaving: the act of making cloth on the loom
4. possession: something that belongs to someone
5. pleasures: things or events that please you, make you happy
6. satisfaction: a feeling of happiness or pleasure
7. memorial: an object that is intended to remind us of something or someone

8. boring: without interest, always the same
9. click: a sharp snapping sound, such as made when two hard objects are struck together
10. threads: thin strings made from wool or cotton, used to make cloth
11. celebration: a time of happiness and joy, usually in honor of someone or something
12. shutter: to pull closed wood that fits over windows, blocking out light and making the house safe
13. columns: vertical, round objects; cylinders
14. fond of: happy with, pleased with

Unit 3

Nonprose Reading: Campus Map

Part 1 (page 60)
1. 12
2. More Literate
3. More Sociable
4. This item is intended for discussion; the section you choose depends on your opinion.

Part 2 (pages 60–61)
5. The library is located in D3, on the East Mall. The bookstore is located in E3, on the East Mall.
6. The tennis courts are located in H2.
7. a. The East Mall leads directly from the library to the tennis courts.
   b. Probably not. There are no bus stops directly in front of the library or the tennis courts; however, you might use the bus stops at the Bus Loop (near the library) and the bus stops in front of either the University Hospital or Chris Spencer Pitch. However, this would not save you much walking.
   c. If you get hurt at the Tennis Bubble, you could go to the University Hospital, located in F2.
8. It appears that the restaurant closest to the hospital is the Old Barn Coffee Shop, just south of the hospital in F3. You might call Directory Assistance at 822-2211 or the Community Relations Office at 822-3131.
9. Yes.
10. F3. No. It appears that the road connecting the Main Library and the Old Barn Coffee shop is for pedestrians only.
11. Directory Assistance at 822-2211 or the Community Relations Office at 822-3131
12. a. 822-2211.
    b. On Saturday, directory assistance at UBC is not answered; you might try using a phone book or calling directory assistance for the city of Vancouver.

Word Study: Stems and Affixes

Exercise 1 (page 66)
1. a
2. television: an instrument that produces a picture of something that is far away (*tele:* far; *vis:* see) telegram: a written message sent far away (*tele:* far; *gram:* writing) transportation: the act of moving or carrying something from one place to another (*trans:* across; *port:* carry; *tion:* the act of)
3. For example, prepay, preread, preheat
4. presage: something that gives one knowledge of something before it happens; a warning

5. Immigration is the movement of people into a country; Emigration is the movement of people out of a country.
6. repaint, reuse, remake, reform, reborn, reread

Exercise 2 (pages 67–68)
1. vocal: singing; of or pertaining to the voice
2. portable: capable of being carried; easily carried or moved
3. transmit: to send from one place to another
4. videotape: to use a camera to make a tape of moving pictures that can be shown on television
5. porters: people whose job it is to carry suitcases for travelers
6. dictated: said or read material aloud for the purpose of having it recorded by a machine or written by a person
7. telephoto: of or related to a lens used to produce a large picture of something that is far away
8. imports: brings into the country
9. audiovisual: of or related to materials or equipment that present information so that it can be heard and seen
10. imposed: forced upon
11. inscribing: writing in the surface of something
12. manufactured: made; built
13. visualizing: seeing in his mind; imagining
14. autograph: a person's name written by that person; a signature
15. predictions: guesses about what will happen
16. prepay: pay ahead of time; pay before
17. remit: send back
18. emissions: what comes (is sent) out
19. spectators: people who were looking
20. edict: an official law or command of a ruler, often read out loud
21. dictator: a ruler who has total control of a country; people must do whatever the dictator says to do
22. deposed: removed from power; taken out of a position of power
23. evokes: calls forth; calls up; awakens
24. deforestation: the act of cutting down trees or forests
25. factory: a building in which products are made
26. inspectors: people who look at or examine something carefully, often looking for problems
27. televized: shown on television; made into a television program
28. remarried: married again
29. reapply: apply again; ask for admission again
30. de-ice: take the ice off of; remove the ice from
31. vista: view; scene

Word Study: Dictionary Use

Exercise 1 (pages 70–72)
1. It's always safe to use the first entry. However, in many dictionaries, unless indicated, all entries are acceptable.
2. two: dis-count; this dictionary uses a dot (·). When you reach the end of a line, you will want to hyphenate long words at the syllable divisions.
3. a. The first pronunciation has the stress on the first syllable.
4. Verb: 9; noun: 7
5. F (*discount* comes from French via Old French and Middle Latin.)
6. Derived words: words with related meaning that have been produced from the key word, as "discountable."
7. At the bottom of the page
   a. out
   b. at the beginning or the end of the dictionary

8. Answers will vary.
9. Usage labels help us know how, where, or if a word is used.
10. a. 16
    b. 2
    c. 5

Exercise 2 (pages 72–73)

1. a. T
   b. F
   c. F
2. four: cro/cid/o/lite
3. the first: *cro*nyism
4. a. F (A crocus is a flower.)
   b. over
   c. the *a,* as in *a*lone
5. kro' sha
6. a. cropped
   b. crookedly
   c. cronies
7. F (He was English; he died in 1827.)
8. a. croissant: French
   b. cronk: Yiddish
   c. crochet: French
   d. crony: Greek
9. crop
10. a. 12 synonyms
    b. 0 antonyms

Sentence Study: Comprehension (pages 74–76)

1. a   4. d   7. c   10. b
2. d   5. a   8. c   11. a
3. b   6. b   9. a   12. a

Paragraph Reading: Restatement and Inference (pages 78–81)

1. b, c
2. a, d
3. c, d (Note: you may have checked *a*. This is reasonable if you believe that anyone who worries about how a napkin is folded is always neat and clean.)
4. b
5. b, d
6. b, c
7. a
8. b, c
9. d
10. c (Note, you may have also checked *a*. This is a reasonable guess. In fact, Helen Keller was a pacifist who did not believe in war; but one doesn't necessarily know this from the sentence.)

Discourse Focus: Careful Reading / Drawing Inferences (Mysteries) (pages 82–85)

1. "The Case of the Big Deal": Vance claimed he had a barber shave off "seven months of beard" the day before he met Haledjian. Yet his cheeks and chin were "tanned." If he had really been in the sun seven months without shaving, his chin would not have been suntanned.
2. "The Case of the Lying Gardener": A legal will could not be dated November 31. There are only 30 days in November.
3. "The Case of the Fake Robbery": The candles "dripped down the side facing the windows." If the window really had been left open as long as Mrs. Sidney said, some wax would have dripped on the other side, away from the direction of the wind.

4. "The Case of the Buried Treasure": If the pure silver candlestick had been lying in a bag from 1956 until "immediately" before Bertie took it to Haledjian, it would not have been "shining."
5. "The Case of the Dentist's Patient": Burton said he had never heard of Dr. Williams. If this were true, he would not have known the doctor was a dentist and a woman.

Unit 4

Reading Selection 1: Newspaper Article *"Farmer Calls Hole His Home"*

Comprehension (page 88)

1. F
2. F
3. F
4. F
5. T
6. F
7. F
8. F

Critical Reading (pages 88–89)

These questions call for your opinions.

Vocabulary from Context (pages 89–90)

1. bachelor: an unmarried man
2. trailer: mobile home; a vehicle used as a home; a home on wheels
3. shovels: tools used to dig earth or snow
4. ceiling: top of a room
5. skylight: a window in a roof that lets in light
6. concrete: a hard material used to build roads and buildings; it's made by mixing water, sand, and small rocks with a powder called cement. When these harden, the concrete becomes like stone.
7. storage: a place to keep things not currently being used
8. unconcerned: not concerned; free from worry; not caring about
9. affectionately: warmly; lovingly; showing that she likes them
10. favor: kind or helpful act
11. hermit: person who lives away from other people
12. mean: hateful; unkind

Reading Selection 2: Popular Social Science *"Lies Are So Commonplace, They Almost Seem Like the Truth"*

Comprehension

Exercise 1 (pages 92–93)
2, 3, 4, 5, 7, 8, 9

Exercise 2 (pages 93–94)
1. c (perhaps a)
2. d (perhaps c)
3. d, h
4. a, b
5. h
6. g

Exercise 3 (page 94)
1. a. A
   b. A
   c. A

d. A
e. E
f. E
g. E
h. A

2. Probably not. This is not a scholarly or academic discussion of the subject.

Vocabulary from Context

Exercise 1 (page 95)
1. lies: untruths
2. fudge: tell small lies
3. claim: say; state
4. newborn: infant; baby who has just been born
5. do (lunch): have a meal together
6. leap: jump

Exercise 2 (page 96)
1. behaviors: actions
2. purposes: functions; ends; goals
3. avoid: keep from doing; keep away from
4. memory: what we remember; a remembrance
5. destroy: get rid of; kill; ruin
6. trust: belief in truthfulness; confidence

**Selection 3A: Popular Social Science
"Who's Doing the Work around the House?"**

Comprehension

Exercise 1 (pages 100–101)

TABLE 1. Sharing Tasks: Reports of Who Does Household Chores (%)

Who Does Chores	Family Arrangement	
	All Families (Women's reports)	Families in Which Both Spouses Work (Men's reports)
Women do nearly all	41	24
Women do most; husbands help	41	42
Task evenly divided	15	28
Husbands do more	2	5

TABLE 2. Sharing Money: Men's and Women's Reports When Both Work (%)

Salaries combined for all things	79
Some money kept separately	15

TABLE 3. Exchanging Roles: Respect for Stay-At-Home Husbands (%)

Respect for the husband	Year		
	1970	1980	Now
Would respect a man less	63	41	25
Would respect him more	8	6	12
Would respect him the same	15	42	50

TABLE 4. Teenagers Sharing Chores (%)

Who Does Chore	Chore					
	Vacuum	Mop	Cook	Wash Dishes	Wash Car	Mow Lawn
Women's work	40	50	39	59	2	✕
Shared work	38		46		39	✕
Man's work		50	2	46	40	64
Doesn't matter who does it	20		13		19	✕

Exercise 2 (page 101)
1. T
2. T
3. F
4. F
5. T

Vocabulary from Context

Exercise 1 (pages 102–3)
1. chores: tasks; regular household jobs
2. gap: difference; separation
3. salaries: money paid for working; earnings
4. expenses: costs; bills; money owed
5. roles: jobs; functions; responsibilities
6. attitudes: feelings; point of view
7. generation: period of time between the birth of parents and the birth of their children; people born at the same time
8. have less respect for: think less of; have a lower opinion of; have less regard for; have less esteem for
9. child-rearing: taking care of children; raising children; bringing up children; child care
10. responsibility: duty; job
11. disciplining: correcting; training; punishing

Exercise 2 (page 103)
1. savings
2. the norm
3. breadwinners
4. likely

5. duty
6. primarily
7. are determined
8. significance
9. newfound

Selection 3B: Cartoons
"Sally Forth" (pages 104–6)

Monday
1. Sally wants them both to know how much work the other does ("how big a load the other is carrying") so they will recognize the importance of what one another does ("won't take each other for granted").
2. Ted will wash the dishes; Sally will read about sports in the newspaper.

Tuesday
1. Ted is doing the laundry.
2. He doesn't want to have to clean it up (which Sally usually does).

Wednesday
1. Ted is cleaning the house.
2. Ted is complaining ("nagging") about Sally's not cleaning up after herself; Sally seems to be giving a speech she has heard from Ted about not being able to change.

Thursday
1. Ted is loading the dishwasher.
2. Ted is starting to become angry because others are doing the things that he usually does (like not putting his dirty dishes in the dishwasher). His annoyance (or the fact that he sounds just like Sally usually does in the same situation) tells their daughter that Sally and Ted really have changed roles and, perhaps, he has learned something.

Friday
1. Yes and no. Ted says that switching roles has "opened [his] eyes." At the same time, he still expects Sally to make him breakfast while he reads the newspaper.
2. Ted still expects to be able to read the newspaper while Sally makes breakfast.

Selection 3C: Magazine Article
"The 'New Father': No Real Role Reversal"

Comprehension (page 108)
1. F
2. T
3. F
4. F
5. The author seems to feel that parents need to find an arrangement that meets both of their individual needs.

Vocabulary from Context

Exercise 1 (page 110)
1. involvement: participation; taking part in
2. child-rearing: taking care of children; raising children; bringing up children; child care
3. responsibility: duties; involvement
4. roles: jobs; functions; responsibilities
5. status: position; rank; place in society; standing
6. privilege: special right or power

7. penalty: punishment; disadvantage; loss; hardship
8. arrangements: structures; organizations; the way things are arranged

Exercise 2 (page 111)
1. satisfied
2. participation
3. overlooked
4. child-caring
5. suits

Reading Selection 4: Magazine Graphic
"Summit to Save the Earth: The World's Next Trouble Spots"

Getting Oriented (page 113)
1. Air Pollution; Population Growth; Safe Drinking Water; Protected Lands
2. By location: North America; Latin America; Europe; Africa; Asia and Oceania

Grading the World (pages 114–16)
1. a. This calls for your opinion.
   b. F (number of births compared with size of population = % increase in population)
   c. In general, the earth must be protected from humans.
   d. This calls for your opinion.
2. F
3. This calls for your opinion.
4. F
5. T
6. F
7. Ecuador and Argentina
8. This calls for your opinion.
9. This calls for your opinion.
10. Protected Lands received 7 F's, followed by Safe Drinking Water, with 5.
11. U.S., Canada, Australia
12. F
13. This calls for your opinion.

Reporting on the World (page 116)
1. T
2. T
3. a. This calls for your opinion. The government is cleaning 23 miles of river, but critics say this is for the diamond industry, not for drinking water.
   b. T (Clearing the forests creates farmland today, but the land may not be usable in the future.)
   c. We do not know what will happen. If cutting down of the forests continues, this will be true.
4. Mining, logging, tourism, and overgrazing of cattle and sheep.
5. F, but they are working on it.
6. This calls for your opinion.

Vocabulary from Context

Exercise 1 (pages 120–21)
1. population: number of people
2. environmental: having to do with the environment; concerning the land, water, and air surrounding the earth.
3. summits: high-level meetings
4. industrialization: the growth of industry, of factories and machinery

5. economies: the system of business, farm, and labor that produces money for a country
6. polluted: filled with dangerous chemicals or gases
7. toxic: dangerous; poisonous
8. chemical waste: unused or unusable liquids from factories
9. dammed: stopped rivers or streams for human use
10. lumber: wood taken from trees and used in building houses
11. timber: wood; lumber
12. clear-cut: to cut all of the trees down
13. erosion: the washing or wearing away of soil by water
14. rate: speed
15. threatened: in danger (of being hurt or damaged)
16. displaced: forced to move
17. damage: hurt; injury
18. trash: garbage; paper, metal, plastic, etc., that people do not use up.
19. disposing: putting away; putting in a safe place
20. balance: equal weight on two sides
21. hunters: people who kill animals
22. wild: living in forests or deserts, away from people
23. tropical: warm, wet parts of the world
24. rare: uncommon; not easily found
25. extinct: no longer on earth; killed out completely
26. protect: to save from harm
27. preserves: safe places for animals
28. quality of life: amount of comfort and health in living

Exercise 2 (page 122)
1. marine sanctuary
2. fragile
3. scarred
4. overgrazing

Unit 5

Nonprose Reading: College Application and Tuition Chart

Part 1: College Application

Getting Oriented (page 123)
1. Address; Military experience; Previous education; Income; Educational goals; Marital status
2. This item requires your opinion.

Comprehension (pages 123–27)
1. a. $15.00
   b. No.
3. b. This item is intended for discussion. Possible answers include: Schools know that students move a lot and they want to make sure they know how to contact you (and where to send your bills).
4. a. This item is intended for discussion. Perhaps residents of the county get special benefits or perhaps WCC gets money from the county for residents who are enrolled in classes. Perhaps the school just wants to keep statistics on student enrollment.
   b. Proof of residency might include driver's license, rental contract, address labels from magazine subscriptions, a letter from your landlord.
5. a. This item is intended for discussion.
   b. If something should happen to you, the school wants to have a way to contact your family or friends.

6. b. F. It says that your answers will *not* affect your admission status.
   d. Possible answers are 1 and 2.
7. T
8. T
9. Discussion item. WCC probably wants to know where its students are coming from and what factors influenced their decisions. This knowledge will help the school plan better.
10. T
11. This item requires your opinion.
12. F

Part 2: Tuition Chart (page 127)
1. $133.20
2. $159.15
3. A South East Asia veteran
4. Possible reasons include: It might be a government regulation to give special tuition to veterans. The community might have a large number of veterans, and this is the way the college helps them.
5. To answer this question, you need to decide which type of student you are and then read the tuition amount for a three credit class.
6. Your answer depends on whether you want to save money or time. If you take all three courses in one term, the cost would be less.

Word Study: Context Clues

Passage 1: "Fixing Broken Bones with Sound" (page 129)
1. heal: become healthy again; repair; fix; mend
2. technique: way; method
3. fractured: broken
4. vibrate: move
5. mend: heal
6. reduce: shorten; make less

Passage 2: "World Population Continues to Rise" (page 130)
1. decade: a period of ten years
2. pace: speed; rate
3. roughly: approximately; about
4. equivalent: equal; the same as
5. global: world
6. peak: highest point
7. racing: running very fast; running against time to get something done

Word Study: Stems and Affixes

Exercise 1 (pages 132–33)
1. speedometer: the speed something travels
   chronometer: time
   thermometer: heat; temperature
   micrometer: very small things
   telemeter: distance to objects that are far away
   hydrometer: liquids (the specific gravity of liquids)
2. telescope: to see things far away
   microscope: to see things that are very small
   periscope: to see around (above the water, from under the water)
3. phonology: d
   anthropology: a
   pathology: g

psychology: b
hydrology: i
biology: e
microbiology: h
psychobiology: f
geology: c
4. synonym: a
antonym: b
homonym (or homophone): c
5. water
6. energy in or from hot water
7. a liquid
8. superscript: a
subscript: b
9. for example, incomplete, impossible, illogical, illegal,
irresponsible, irrational
10. c

Exercise 2 (pages 133–34)

1. perimeter: distance around
2. submarines: ships that can travel under water
3. sonar: machine that sends out sound waves through water
and records their reflection off of underwater objects
4. supersonic: greater than the speed of sound
5. psychopath: a person with a serious mental disorder; a
crazy (often violent) person
6. dehydrated: very dry from the loss of too much water
from the body
7. biochemistry: the study of the chemistry of living things
and life processes
8. psychologist: a person who studies the mind and mental
processes and behaviors
9. antibiotic: a chemical substance that kills harmful bacte-
ria and other microorganisms
10. aquatic: growing in or living in water
11. invisible: not able to be seen
12. subvocalizing: moving one's lips as if one is talking, but
making no sound (talking "under" one's voice)
13. insignificant: not meaningful; not important
14. inexpensive: not costly; not expensive; cheap
15. subway: underground railway
16. anthropomorphize: make animals have human
characteristics
17. sympathize: share the same feelings; pity
18. thermostat: a device for controlling temperature
19. vocalist: singer
20. antipathy: bad feelings; dislike
21. antiwar: against the war; opposed to the war
22. chronic: lasting a long time; continuous; constant
23. synchronize: make them show the same time; set them to
the same time

Sentence Study: Restatement and Inference (pages 136–37)

1. b, c, d
2. a, e
3. e
4. a, e
5. b, c, e
6. a, b, e
7. a, c
8. a, b, c, d
9. b, c
10. d, e

Paragraph Reading: Main Idea (Fables) (pages 138–42)

Before You Begin Fable moral: Tell the truth.
Fable 1 moral: People should work together. In unity there is
strength. Hang together. United we stand,
divided we fall.
Fable 2 moral: Be happy with what you have. Don't be
greedy. Don't lose what you have by trying to
get something more.
Fable 3 moral: Force is not always the answer.
Fable 4 moral: Plan ahead. Don't trust anyone.
Fable 5 moral: Work hard. Speed is not everything; hard
work can lead to success.
Fable 6 moral: Don't lose what you have by dreaming about
something you want. Don't assume you have
something until you have it. Also, don't be
self-centered.
Fable 7 moral: Small friends can be great friends. Help
people who need help; someday you may
need their help. People who seem unimportant
may one day be very important after all.
Fable 8 moral: If everyone does a little, no one will have to
do too much.
Fable 9 moral: It is easy to suggest impossible solutions to
problems. Talk is cheap.

Vocabulary Study: Idiomatic Expressions (page 142):

1. 5
2. Before You Begin
3. 6
4. 2
5. 4
6. 9

Discourse Focus: Careful Reading / Drawing Inferences (Mysteries) (pages 143–46)

1. "The Case of the Telltale Clock": Nick talked about hearing the ticking of the clock, whose electric cord had been
used to kill Buffalo Fenn. Sadly for Nick, electric clocks
don't tick.
2. "The Case of the Murdered Brother": If John Page had
been innocent, he would not have known that his brother
had been "beaten" to death. When he saw the "gun that
was used to murder him," he would have thought Mark
had been shot.
3. "The Case of the Suicide Room": Sir Cecil and Haledjian
found the door to the "suicide room" closed. As the room
had no floor, it would have been impossible for Ritchie to
have closed the heavy door from the inside and then
turned and jumped.
4. "The Case of Willie the Wisp": Willie the Wisp was a
known criminal. He knew that when he crossed the
border, the guards would think he was smuggling something. Therefore, he decided to confuse them about what
he was taking into the country illegally. Haledjian realized that the bottles and their contents were in Willie's
suitcases only to confuse the guards. Willie was smuggling expensive black sports cars!
5. "The Case of the Locked Room": No one could have
heard ice melting. Marty had brought frozen cubes of
soda with him when he came to visit the blind musician.
After Skeat agreed to the bet, Marty put the soda cubes
into the glass. They melted while sitting in the glass.

Unit 6

Reading Selection 1: Advice Column
"Adamant Smoker Says Stop Nagging" and "Ann Landers's Response"

Comprehension (pages 148–49)

1. F
2. 29 years old
3. We do not know.
4. We do not know, but s/he mentions that s/he has not been living in a cave for the past ten years, so perhaps s/he started smoking ten years ago.
5. a. bullying and begging
   b. leaving notes
   c. offering money to others
6. The deal s/he proposes is to not say anything to members of the family when they do something foolish, if they will not say anything to him/her when s/he lights up. Eating fatty foods such as butter and ice cream is a health risk for some people because it contributes to heart disease, but it does not hurt anyone else, while smoking harms both the smoker and others in the same room. On the other hand, you could argue that if a parent dies of a heart attack s/he deprives the children of his/her love and support, so that there are dangers to others in poor eating habits.
7. Ann Landers prints the letter, as Friend asked, but her answer is really addressed to everyone who is trying to change someone else's behavior. She tells us to stop bothering others and to just let them know you care and are willing to help when they decide to stop their risky behavior.
8. F. She calls it a type of self-destructive behavior.
9. smoking, drinking, eating too much, taking drugs

Vocabulary from Context

Exercise 1 (page 151)
1. adamant: unchanging, determined
2. hazards: risks, dangers
3. irritated: unhappy, slightly angry; bothered
4. defensiveness: quickness to argue; being too sensitive; acting as if you are being attacked and defending yourself.

Exercise 2 (page 152)
1. keep it to yourself
2. bullying
3. a. a quantity of food
   b. *Chunk* is used with solid food, such as butter or cheese. *Dollop* usually indicates a spoonful. A *scoop* is rounded by the instrument that is used.
4. nagging
5. popping pills

Reading Selection 2: Newspaper Article
"Bugs Make Skin Crawl in Midwest"

Comprehension (pages 153–56)

1. an insect
2. Chicago, Illinois. Los Angeles and New York will not be having the problem because cicadas are coming only to Illinois, Iowa, Indiana, and Wisconsin.
3. F (every 17 years)

4. F (They arrive from the ground.)
5. a couple of months (May to July); to mate
6. a, c
7. F
8. a. shriek: make a high-pitched sound; scream
   b. silent: mute
   c. nuisance: bother, irritation
   d. hot line: a special telephone number set up to get or give information about a specific topic
9. a, b, c, d, e
10. That's up to you!
11. a, b, c

Selection 3A: Survey
"What We Don't Know"

Comprehension (pages 158–59)

1. F
2. T
3. T
4. N
5. N
6. question 4
7. a

Selection 3B: Popular Science Article
"Tornado in the Drain"

Comprehension (pages 162–63)

1. T
2. T
3. D
4. F
5. F
6. T
7. F
8. T
9. T
10. T
11. T
12. T
13. a, b, c, d, e, g

Vocabulary from Context (page 163)

1. tornados: violent wind storms (with circular winds) that form over land
2. hurricanes: violent wind storms (with circular winds) that form over water
3. rotate: circle; spin
4. sucked: pulled
5. drain: the hole at the bottom of the bathtub down which water goes
6. hemisphere: half of the Earth
7. swirl: circle; rotate
8. counterclockwise: in a circular motion to the left
9. spin: circle; rotate; swirl
10. clockwise: in a circular motion to the right
11. fronts: patterns; large masses of air
12. deflected: turned; pushed

Selection 3C: Popular Science Article
"Making Water Wetter"

Comprehension (pages 166–67)

1. T

2. T
3. F
4. T
5. F
6. T
7. F
8. a. Hard water is water containing large amounts of calcium.
   b. Soft water does not contain large amounts of calcium.
   c. It is difficult to get clothes clean in hard water because the calcium in hard water attracts soap before the soap can start to clean.
9. Phosphates caused too much algae to grow in lakes, killing fish; and, rivers became full of suds from detergents.
10. F
11. F
12. F
13. T
14. F

Vocabulary from Context

Exercise 1 (page 168)
1. soil: dirt
2. grease: an oily substance
3. dissolve: break up
4. droplets: small drops; small, round pieces
5. beads: small, round drops of a liquid
6. incompatible: not able to mix with each other; not able to form a chemical bond between them
7. overcome: solve
8. laundry: clothing to be washed
9. additives: substances added to something else in order to strengthen it, improve it, or change it in some way
10. suds: bubbles
11. foam: soap bubbles
12. algae: plants that live in the water

Exercise 2 (pages 168–69)
1. stick to
2. distributed
3. molecule
4. to bond with
5. surrounding
6. the drain
7. a model
8. a dye
9. absorbs

Dictionary Study (pages 169–70)
1. noun 2 (in the first entry for compound)
2. 2b

Vocabulary Review (page 170)
1. models
2. laundry
3. molecule
4. dissolve
5. drains

Reading Selection 4: Children's Literature "The Meeting"

Before You Begin (page 171)
1. This question calls for your personal opinion. You might have thought of reasons such as the fact that mice spend time with prisoners, are not often noticed by humans, or can easily get into and out of enclosed places.

Comprehension (pages 174–75)
1. T
2. F
3. F
4. It was very difficult to get to and the Head Jailer's cat was very large and dangerous.
5. F
6. F
7. T
8. She will have to get in touch with a Norwegian mouse.
9. T
10. He was wearing the Tybalt Star, a medal for bravery in the face of cats.
11. F

Restatement and Inference (pages 175–77)
1. a, b
2. a, c, d
3. a, b
4. c
5. a, c
6. b, c, d
7. a, b, c
8. d
9. a, d
10. c, d

Vocabulary from Context

Exercise 1 (pages 178–79)
1. rescued: freed (from danger); saved; released
2. aid: help
3. prisoners: people in jail; those without freedom; people held against their will
4. crumbs: small bits of baked food, for example, bread
5. cheer: to make glad or happy; to give hope, courage, comfort
6. assemblies: large meetings; groups of people gathered to make decisions
7. Secretary: an important position in an organization
8. eloquence: ability to speak beautifully, effectively, or persuasively
9. interrupts: begins talking while someone else is speaking; stops the speech of another by breaking in
10. anxious: worried; uneasy or troubled of mind
11. trembles: shakes with fear; shivers; shudders
12. shudders: shakes with fear; shivers; trembles
13. dungeons: dark, underground prisons
14. medal: a piece of metal, often shaped like a coin, that is given to a person for an act of excellence or bravery
15. deserve: have earned; are worthy
16. defeatist: believing that they will be unsuccessful or defeated
17. gaping: opening mouths wide in surprise
18. gasped: made a sound as they caught their breaths with surprise
19. mumbling: speaking so softly that the words can't be heard
20. wits: cleverness; intelligence
21. transferred: moved (The ambassador is being made the ambassador of a different country.)
22. diplomatic bag: a bag that carries government papers and therefore cannot be opened or searched

23. capital: the seat of government
24. rumors: talk or opinions that have no obvious source; thus, there is no way to check whether they are true

Exercise 2 (page 179)
1. branch: part; section; division
2. Head: chief; most important; lead; the person in charge
3. astounding: amazing; surprising
4. case: situation; circumstance
5. free verse: poetry whose rhythm is not regular in some way; nonrhyming poetry
6. tongue: language
7. get in touch with: communicate with; contact
8. gleam: (reflected) light

Unit 7

Nonprose Reading: Maps

Getting Oriented (page 180)
1. Russia is the largest. Moldova appears to be the smallest.
2. Minsk is the capital; population 1.5 million. (Capital cities are indicated on the map on page 182 and with the pie charts. Populations of major cities are given on the population map.)
3. 10.2 million (according to the pie chart)

Comprehension (pages 180–81)
1. a. The Commonwealth of Independent States and the Baltic Republics.
   b. They are independent groups, politically and economically. The Commonwealth of Independent States includes Russia and all of the smaller countries that became independent on December 26, 1991. They continue to have economic connections with each other. The Baltic Republics became independent from the USSR in 1990, and they have close economic and political connections with each other.
2. Cold! −50 degrees Fahrenheit!
3. a. Most people live in the large cities in the west.
   b. Moscow. It has a population of 8.5 million.
   c. Tashkent has a population of 2.1 million.
4. Vladivostok is not among the most populous cities in Russia (or it would have been included in the Population map). However, it must be one of the largest cities in the country because it is indicated on the map with a large dot.
5. a. According to the Population map, more than 200 ethnic groups live in the former USSR.
   b. Latvia has the highest percentage of Russians, with 33%.
   c. Lithuania has 9%.
6. Kazakhstan, with 41%.
7. Georgia, with 9%
8. Armenia
9. Russia
10. Russia
11. and 12. Your opinion is all that matters here. However, you might consider such things as climate, natural resources, size of cities, etc.

Word Study: Context Clues

Passage 1: "Think Positive!" (page 186)
1. optimist: a person who sees things in a positive way and expects things to go well

2. sightseeing: seeing the places of interest in a location
3. digs: negative comments
4. pessimists: people with a negative view of things, who expect that things will go badly
5. portrayed: described; represented
6. maintain: say; claim; state
7. proclaims: says; states; insists; says proudly and publicly
8. links: connects; shows a connection between

Passage 2: "Dumping Health Risks on Developing Nations" (page 187)
1. adopt: to make; to accept formally and put into effect
2. promotion: attempts to sell; publicity (in order to sell); encouragement; pushing
3. ban: an official rule that stops, forbids, or prohibits something
4. fund/funded: a supply of money for a particular purpose/paid for
5. tax: a payment to the government, in this case, based on the price of each item sold
6. declined: gone down; decreased
7. prematurely: young; too early; before being old; before their time
8. thrust: most important purpose; principal concern; goal
9. strive: work; make great efforts
10. emerging: developing
11. dumping ground: a place to which unwanted things are sent
12. marketable: able to be sold

Word Study: Stems and Affixes

Exercise 1 (page 189)
1. *Vacation* comes from *vac,* meaning empty. A vacation is a time "empty" of work.
2. *Introduction* comes from *intro* (into), *duct* (lead), and *tion* (the act of). The introduction to a book is a section that leads readers into the main part of the book.
3. *Political* comes from *polis* (city or state) and *al* (relating to). *Political* means related to government or to the state.
4. ball
5. *Anterior* means in, on, or toward the front; *posterior* means in, on, or toward the back.
6. Introverts prefer to be alone; extroverts like to talk to others.

Exercise 2 (pages 189–91)
1. post–Cold War: after the Cold War
2. collaborating: working (laboring) together
3. aqueducts: large, bridgelike structures for carrying water long distances
4. mortality: death
5. subterranean: below the ground
6. vivacious: full of life; lively
7. reconvene: come together again; meet again
8. theology: the study of God; the study of religion
9. incredulous: not able to believe; unbelieving; doubting
10. immortal: going to live forever; not going to die
11. metropolitan: related to a large, central city and the smaller communities around it
12. monotheistic: relating to the belief that there is only one God
13. polytheism: belief in more than one god
14. postmortem: after death
15. cooperated: worked together

16. evacuated: emptied of people
17. receded: went back; moved back
18. intervene: come between in order to have an effect on or to influence what happens; get involved
19. atheist: a person who believes there is no god
20. interaction: activity between
21. postponed: put off until a later time; delayed
22. veracity: truth
23. extraterrestrial: from outside the Earth
24. co-workers: people who work together
25. verified: proved to be true
26. respiration: breathing
27. vital: related to life
28. introspection: looking into one's own mind; observation and analysis of oneself
29. convention: meeting of members of an organization
30. vacated: all left
31. terrain: the area of land; the ground
32. vivid: lifelike; clear

Sentence Study: Restatement and Inference (pages 192–94)

1. c, d
2. a, b, d, e
3. a, c, d
4. a, b, c (Note: you may also have checked *e*. This is a good guess; the passage does, in fact, go on to say this, but we cannot yet be sure that the author does not like the book.)
5. b, c
6. a, d, e
7. d
8. a, b, c
9. c, d, e
10. b, e

Paragraph Reading: Main Idea (pages 196–98)

Here are possible ways to state the main ideas.
Paragraph 1: Oceanographers classify all things that live in the oceans as plankton, nekton, or benthos.
Paragraph 2: Messages travel through the nervous system by electricity and by chemical reactions.
Paragraph 3: The dolphin is a species with high intelligence.
Paragraph 4: The nervous system of insects is different from ours because insect behavior does not require thought. (Insects work on instinct.)
Paragraph 5: Although most people don't see the changes, the night sky is always changing.

Paragraph Reading: Reading for Full Understanding

Passage 1 (pages 201–2)

1. b   5. c
2. d   6. a
3. a   7. c
4. a   8. b

Passage 2 (pages 203–4)

1. d   4. a
2. b   5. c
3. b

Passage 3 (pages 204–5)

1. b   3. b
2. d   4. a

Passage 4 (pages 205–6)

1. a   4. F
2. b   5. T
3. c

Discourse Focus: Prediction (pages 208–9)

5. You might expect to read something about the new reports or what was previously thought. The paragraph talks about "two new reports" and the disappearance of rain forests being "faster than scientists thought."
6. If you expected the next part to discuss the current reports, this would also have been reasonable.
9. Because the last part we read referred to "two possible reasons," the next section will probably discuss these reasons.
11. The content of the rest of the article is summarized by the following choices for question 12: a, c, d, f, g. The article goes on to discuss a second reason for underestimating deforestation. It then explains why deforestation is a problem and surveys the problem worldwide. It next discusses how to carry out better studies and finally describes efforts to save the rain forests.

Unit 8

Selection 1B: Magazine Articles "Procrastination"

Comprehension (pages 216–17)

1. F
2. F
3. T
4. T
5. F
6. People who try to be perfect have expectations for themselves that are not possible to achieve—they are "unrealistic."
7. If you procrastinate, you can never be judged on your real ability because you have never really shown what you can do. For some people, procrastination assures that they can never fail, because their ability can never be tested.
8. T
9. F
10. We don't know, but if he always eats as much as he did when writing his dissertation (paragraph 28), he may well have a problem.

Vocabulary from Context

Exercise 1 (pages 217–18)

1. pressure: a situation that causes great worry; feeling as if one is carrying a great weight
2. stress: pressure
3. deadline: time limit; time by which something must be done
4. anxiety: worry; uneasiness; fearful concern
5. irrational: not rational; not reasonable or logical
6. delays: events that make things late, put things off, slow things down, cause them to be postponed; setbacks
7. embarrassed: self-conscious; awkward; ashamed
8. guilt: being responsible for a bad situation or crime
9. conflict: arguing; disagreement; fight
10. depressed: deeply unhappy; feeling hopeless; downhearted

11. unbearable: too painful; not bearable; insupportable; not able to be stood; can't be put up with
12. interview: meeting; formal meeting to evaluate a person for a job
13. executives: people in charge of, who make the decisions for, a business; administrators; managers
14. canceled: discontinued; removed; called off; withdrawn
15. distinguish: to see a difference; to mentally separate; to differentiate
16. relevant: related; having an important connection
17. benefit: value; helpfulness; usefulness; advantage
18. commitment: promise

Exercise 2 (page 219)
1. chronic
2. chart
3. subordinate
4. trivial
5. mindless

Dictionary Study (page 219)
1. *v2*
2. *n2*
3. *v4*

Selection 2B: Newspaper Article
"Looking for a Mate in India"

Comprehension (page 225)
1. F
2. b
3. F
4. F
5. F
6. F
7. Punit probably gave a false name so that people who knew her would not recognize her. Perhaps she would be embarrassed or would embarrass her family.
8. F
9. F
10. He will probably send a picture to Punit (in return for hers) and perhaps to others if he and Punit do not like each other.
11. This question calls for your personal opinion.

Vocabulary from Context

Exercise 1 (pages 226–27)
1. matrimonial: marriage
2. marriage broker: a person who arranges marriages
3. mate: marriage partner; spouse
4. ad/advertisements: notice(s) published in the newspaper
5. mature: not childish; adult
6. hypocrisy: insincerity; pretending to be what you are not
7. unfaithfulness: not keeping one's marriage/partnership promise; having a physical relationship with someone when you are promised to someone else; infidelity
8. enthusiastically: with excitement; eagerly; with great interest

Exercise 2 (page 227)
1. postpone
2. broad-minded
3. straightforward
4. go for it

Selection 2C: Magazine Article
"Japanese Marriage"

Restatement and Inference (pages 229–33)
1. c, d
2. c, d, e
3. a, b, c
4. c, d
5. b, c, d, f
6. b, e
7. a, b, d, e (Note: you might also have checked c if you believe that Mihoko did not have a real choice in agreeing to meet Kiyoshi.)
8. a, c, d, e
9. c, e
10. none

Critical Reading (page 234)
These questions call for your opinion.

Vocabulary from Context (pages 234–35)
1. matchmaker: person who arranges marriages; marriage broker
2. suitable: right for the purpose; appropriate; acceptable; qualified
3. qualities: characteristics; things that are special in a person
4. potential: possible; describing something that could happen
5. candidates: possibilities; potential choices
6. judgment: opinion; evaluation
7. trust: have faith in; believe in
8. have confidence in: trust; have faith in; believe in
9. counselors: experienced or professional persons who give advice; advisors
10. romance: feelings based on love or emotional attraction
11. tragic: causing great sadness; terrible; horrible
12. pretend: give a false appearance
13. merger: combining; uniting; joining together
14. project: undertaking; task
15. sacrifice: giving up something valued for the sake of something more important

Selection 2D: Magazine Article
"The New Mating Game"

Skimming (page 235)
Six ways are mentioned: singles bars, expensive dating services, video dating, personal ads, intellectual singles nights, and matchmaking.

Selection 3B: Newspaper Article
"Graduation Speech Protested"

Comprehension (page 245)
1. T
2. 16
3. Gary Lee Christensen
4. He criticized them for their treatment of him. He said that they did not value him because he was different.
5. All of the answers are possible, depending on your point of view. Which one of the answers do you think Gary would have picked? Lois Klatt? The star football player?
6. He was a good student, an Eagle Scout, a pianist.
7. We don't know; he avoided giving his opinion. Do you think he liked it?

8. They say they do. What do you think?
9. F. The reason they were angry was because they understood him.
10. Lois Klatt did not like the speech. She thinks Gary Lee is not "scholarship material," but she does not say what this means.
11. F. We have no reason to believe this, and by not expressing his opinion of the speech, he probably hopes to avoid making people angrier than they already are.
12. This calls for your opinion.

Vocabulary from Context (page 246)

1. commencement: a ceremony/celebration that marks the end of school and the beginning of the rest of one's life
2. address: speech
3. scholarships: financial assistance to students who show academic promise
4. revoked: taken away
5. tolerance: an attitude of acceptance or forgiveness
6. cling: to hold tightly to something or someone
7. self-esteem: self-respect
8. threatened: afraid of someone or something

Selection 3C: Newspaper Article
"High School Honors Not Always Key to Life Success"

Comprehension (page 248)

1. T
2. T
3. 81 students were studied
   a. successes: doctors, scientists
   b. failures: drug addict, waitress with emotional problems
4. We do not know how Denny or Arnold define success.
5. T (according to Denny)
6. Denny is probably older than Arnold, because he was her professor, but we do not know their ages.
7. We circled them all.
8. We do not know what the individuals think about their lives.
9. T. In the final paragraph we read quotes from Arnold and Denny that indicate that Arnold has made up her mind about the successes and failures of the students, while

Denny seems to think that success is still possible for the students.
10. This calls for your opinion. It depends on how much proof you want. The study provides some evidence that success in school does not guarantee success in life.

Selection 3D: Prose and Poetry
"Choices" and "The Road Not Taken"

Comprehension (pages 251–52)

1. F
2. F
3. F
4. T
5. T, but no one had been along the road that day.
6. They took the second road.
7. T
8. a. He seems to think that if he had taken another road he would have had different experiences in his life. What do you think he meant?
   b. He had at least three choices, if he wanted to stay on the road—to go forward on one of the two roads or to return the way he had come. Of course, he could have also chosen to leave the road and go through the woods.
   c. He might believe that his life has been different because he chose to take roads less commonly chosen by other travelers. Being a poet, Frost was probably used to making choices that were different from choices made by other people.
9. One road looks like it is more traveled, that is, more people have taken it.
10. Either T or F can be defended, using the dictionary definition.

Vocabulary from Context (page 253)

1. diverged: split; divided; forked
2. bent: turned; curved
3. undergrowth: grass, weeds, bushes—anything growing low to the ground
4. trodden: stepped upon (from *to tread,* to step)
5. hence: from now—ten years hence = ten years from now

Grateful acknowledgment is made to the following for permission to reprint previously published material.

Ann Arbor Observer for material from "The Adventures of Robin Hood," *Ann Arbor Observer,* July 1991. Reprinted with permission.

Associated Press for "Bugs Make Skin Crawl in Midwest," in *Denver Post,* May 30, 1990; "Graduation Speech Protested," in *Denver Post,* June 5, 1990; "High School Honors Not Always Key to Life Success," in *Denver Post,* June 19, 1991, and "Farmer Calls Hole His Home," in the *Seattle Times/Seattle Post-Intelligencer,* Sunday March 7, 1993. Reprinted with permission.

Bellevue Community College, Tuition Chart, Fall-Winter-Spring, 1994–1995. Reprinted with permission.

Boston Globe for "Basic Science, Technology Leave Americans in Dark," by Richard Saltus, in *Boston Globe,* February 26, 1989. Reprinted by permission.

Diane Cole for "Stop Procrastinating," by Diane Cole, in *Working Mother,* December 1990. Reprinted with permission of the author.

Denver Post for "Where To Go, What To Do," weekend section in *Denver Post,* May 17, 1991. Copyright © 1991 the Denver Post. Reprinted with permission.

Joseph Di Bona for "Brides and Grooms Wanted: Looking for a Wife in India—Not for the Faint of Heart," by Joseph Di Bona in *Christian Science Monitor,* July 19, 1981. Reprinted with permission of the author.

Fort Worth Star-Telegram for Lies Are So Commonplace, "They Almost Seem Like the Truth," by Terry Lee (Goodrich) Jones, in *Seattle Post-Intelligencer,* October 29, 1990. Reprint Courtesy of the Fort Worth Star-Telegram.

HarperCollins for excerpts from *Sleep and Dreams,* by Alvin and Virginia B. Silverstein. Copyright © 1974 by Alvin and Virginia B. Silverstein. Reprinted by permission of HarperCollins Publishers.

Henry Holt and Company, Inc., for "The Road Not Taken," by Robert Frost, in *The Poetry of Robert Frost,* edited by Edward Connery Lathem. Copyright © 1969 Henry Holt and Company, Inc. Reprinted with permission.

Houghton Mifflin Co. for excerpts from *Families.* Copyright © 1990 Aylette Jenness. Reprinted by permission of Houghton Mifflin Co. All rights reserved. And for material from *Technical Writing,* by Frances B. Emerson. Copyright © 1987 by Houghton Mifflin Company. Reprinted with permission.

King Features Syndicate for six "Sally Forth" cartoons by Greg Howard. Copyright © 1990. Reprinted with special permission of King Features Syndicate.

Ann Landers and Creators Syndicate for "Adamant Smoker Says Stop Nagging," in *Denver Post,* June 18, 1990. Copyright © 1990. Permission granted by Ann Landers and Creators Syndicate.

Little, Brown and Company for excerpts from *The Rescuers* by Margery Sharp. Copyright © 1959 by Margery Sharp; © renewed 1987 by Margery Sharp. By permission of Little, Brown and Company.

Judy Markey for "Japanese Marriage," by Judy Markey, in *Cosmopolitan,* August 1984. Reprinted with permission of the author.

McIntosh and Otis, Inc., for "The Case of the Buried Treasure," "The Case of the Dentist's Patient," "The Case of the Bogus Robbery," "The Case of the Blackmailer," "The Case of the Big Deal," "The Case of the Telltale Clock," "The Case of the Suicide Room," "The Case of the Locked Room," "The Case of the Murdered Wife," and "The Case of Willie the Wisp." Copyright © 1967 by Donald J. Sobol. Adapted from a story by Donald J. Sobol, from the book, *Two-Minute Mysteries* published by Scholastic Book Services. Reprinted by permission of McIntosh and Otis, Inc.

Michigan Alumnus for "Think Positive!" *Michigan Alumnus,* March/April 1992, and "After All, Tomorrow Is Another Day," *Michigan Alumnus,* May/June, 1990. Reprinted with permission.

News for You for "Is McDonald's Fair," *News for You,* May 16, 1990. Copyright © 1990. Reprinted with permission.

Newsweek, Inc., for "The New Mating Games," by Barbara Kantrowitz, from *Newsweek,* June 2, 1986. Copyright ©1986, Newsweek, Inc. All rights reserved. Reprinted by permission.

Oxford University Press for entries from *Oxford American Dictionary.* Copyright © 1980 by Oxford University Press, Inc. Reprinted with permission.

Parents for "What's the Attraction?" by Ingrid Groller, in *Parents,* February 1990. Copyright © 1990 Gruner + Jahr USA Publishing. Reprinted from *Parents* magazine by permission.

Penguin Books USA, Inc., for excerpts from "A Laden Ass and a Horse" and "The Hare and the Tortoise," in *Aesop's Fables,* by Heide Holder, illustrator. Copyright © 1981 by Viking Penguin, Inc., text. Used by permission of Viking Penguin, a division of Penguin Books USA, Inc.

Penton Publishing Inc., for "Procrastination," by James Braham, in *IndustryWeek,* March 3, 1986. Reprinted with permission from *IndustryWeek,* March 3, 1986. Copyright © Penton Publishing, Inc., Cleveland, Ohio.

Prentice Hall for material from *Psychology,* by Robert E. Silverman. Copyright © 1971. Reprinted by permission of Prentice Hall, Englewood Cliffs, New Jersey.

Prentice Hall Higher Education Division for material from *A World View,* by Arlene C. Rengert, Robert N. Saveland, Kenneth S. Cooper, and Patricia T. Caro. Copyright © 1988 Patton, Silver, Burdett, and Ginn, Prentice Hall Higher Education Division. Reprinted with permission.

Putnam Berkeley Group, Inc., for "The Rabbit and the Turtle," in *Twelve*

Tales from Aesop, retold by Eric Carle. Copyright © 1980 Eric Carle.

Random House for entries from *The Random House Unabridged Dictionary, Second Edition.* Copyright © 1987, 1993, by Random House, Inc. Reprinted with permission.

Research News for material from "Anxiety and Smoking," *Research News,* Sept.-Oct. 1990, 22. Copyright ©1990 the University of Michigan. Reprinted with permission.

Science Services, Inc., for "The Fall of the Forest," by Richard Monastersky, in *Science News,* July 21, 1990. Reprinted with permission from *Science News,* the weekly newsmagazine of science. Copyright © 1990 by Science Service, Inc.

Seattle Times for "The New Order," edited by John Gomes and Roger Ainsley, in *Seattle Times,* January 5, 1992. Reprinted with permission.

Simon and Schuster, Inc., for entries for "compound" and "uniform" in *Webster's New World Dictionary, Second College Edition.* Copyright ©1984. And for material from the Macmillan College text *The Macmillan Guide to Writing Research Papers,* by William Coyle. Copyright ©1990 by the Macmillan College Publishing Company, Inc. Reprinted with the permission of Simon and Schuster, Inc.

Simon and Schuster for excerpts from "The Four Oxen and the Lion," "The Milkmaid and Her Pail," and "Belling the Cat," in *The Fables of Aesop,* retold by Joseph Jacobs, illustrated by David Levine. Copyright © 1964 Macmillan Publishing Company. Reprinted with the permission of Macmillan Books for Young Readers, an imprint of Simon and Schuster Children's Publishing Division.

Sussex Publishers, Inc., for material from "The Eye of the Beholder," adaptation by T. F. Cash and L. H. Janda, in *Psychology Today,* December, 1984. Reprinted with permission from *Psychology Today Magazine,* Copyright ©1984 (Sussex Publishers, Inc.).

Time Picture Syndication for "The World's Next Trouble Spots," *Time,* June 1, 1992. Copyright © 1992 Time Inc. Reprinted by permission.

TWA Ambassador for the maps "TWA-Atlanta International Airport, Atlanta" and "TWA-JFK International Airport, New York," *TWA Ambassador,* April, 1994. Reprinted with permission.

United Press International for "Marriage Taking a Back Seat," in *Seattle Post-Intelligencer,* July 12, 1990. Copyright © 1990 United Press International. Reprinted with permission.

Universal Press Syndicate for the cartoon "Duffy" by Bruce Hammond. Copyright © Universal Press Syndicate. Reprinted with permission. All rights reserved.

University of British Columbia Community Relations Office for campus map and accompanying text, "The University of British Columbia: You'll Go Home a Different Person." Reprinted with the permission of the Community Relations Office, University of British Columbia.

University of Michigan English Language Institute for questions adapted from the "Examination for the Certificate in English, 1994," by the English Language Institute, University of Michigan. Reprinted with permission.

USA Today for "Language Mirrors Immigration, Provides Key to Nation's Past, Present," by Margaret L. Usdansky, in *USA Today,* April 28, 1993, and "Census: Languages Not Foreign at Home," by Margaret L. Usdansky, in *USA Today,* April 28, 1993. Copyright © 1993, *USA Today.* Reprinted with permission.

USA Today Magazine for "The 'New Father': No Real Role Reversal," *USA Today,* July, 1989, and "Dumping Health Risks on Developing Nations," *USA Today,* April, 1993. Reprinted with permission.

Vintage Books for "How Nice to Have a Man Around the House—If He Shares the Chores," from *Inside America,* by Louis Harris. Copyright ©1987 by Louis Harris. Reprinted by permission of Vintage Books, a Division of Random House, Inc.

Wadsworth Publishing Company for material from *The Research Paper: Process, Form, and Content,* 6th ed., by Audrey J. Roth. Copyright ©1989 Wadsworth Publishing Company. Reprinted with permission.

Washtenaw Community College, Application for Admission. Reprinted with permission.

Franklin Watts for excerpts from "The Boy Who Cried Wolf," "Much Wants More," "The North Wind and the Sun," "Look Before You Leap," and "The Dove and the Ant," in *Tales from Aesop,* written and illustrated by Harold Jones. Copyright © 1981 Julia MacRae Books, a division of Franklin Watts.

William Morrow and Company, Inc., for material from "A Real Soap Opera: Making Water Wetter" and "Tornado in the Drain" from *Rainbows, Curve Balls, and Other Wonders of the Natural World Explained,* by Ira Flatow. Copyright © 1988 by Ira Flatow. Reprinted by permission of William Morrow and Company, Inc. And for material from *World of the Brain,* by Alvin and Virginia B. Silverstein. Copyright © 1986 by Alvin and Virginia B. Silverstein. Reprinted by permission of Morrow Junior Books, a division of William Morrow and Company, Inc.

World Future Society for "Aromacology: The Psychic Effects of Fragrances," *Futurist* 24, no. 5 (Sept.-Oct. 1990): 49; "World Population Continues to Rise," by Nafis Sadik, *Futurist,* March-April 1991, 9; and "Levitating Trains: Hope for Gridlocked Transportation," by Richard Uher, *Futurist* 24, no. 5 (Sept.-Oct. 1990): 28. Reproduced with permission from the *Futurist,* published by the World Future Society, 7910 Woodmont Avenue, Suite 450, Bethesda, Maryland 20814.

Z Magazine, Cartoon by Kirk, July/August 1994.

Every effort has been made to trace the ownership of all copyrighted material in this book and to obtain permission for its use.